In the LANGUAGE OF MY Country

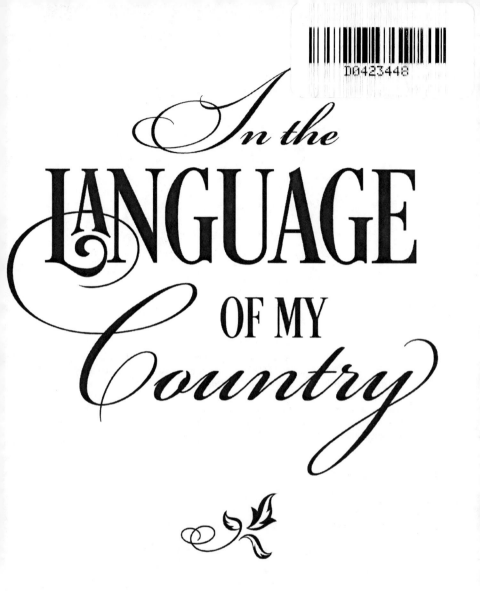

LOIS SPENCER

outskirts
press

"What a writer is, really, is someone who tells the truth in the language of the country they're in, and sustains that language, and invigorates that language ... and keeps lighting up what isn't known."
—*Grace Paley*

Contents

Author's Note

Writing is a lot like life—you can never predict where it will take you. That's especially true of this project, which began with the desire to preserve family history, including events from my earlier years, and pass it on to my children and grandchildren. When it comes to family history, I am fortunate to have had a direct window into the past through parents who were great storytellers. Like bright threads against a darker field, the tales they told sparked my imagination and gave me a sense of lineage during a childhood beset by uncertainty and turmoil.

Before I handed their stories off as truth, however, I had to check names and dates and historical events, so I became a regular at Washington County Public Library's Local History and Genealogy Department in Marietta, Ohio, scouring through family history tomes and searching genealogy websites. Emerging from the warm enclosure on Washington Street into the early winter dusk, I felt again, as I had when I heard the stories as a child, a profound connection to those people whose mingled bloodlines had created mine.

The most immediate of my forbears, Raymond Rippey and Leona Hosom, entered into marriage singularly unprepared. Both had reached their mid-thirties, survived some regrettable choices, and escaped with a fair amount of baggage. Not long into the marriage, they found that living with someone you just don't like is no fun at all, but neither was willing to call it quits. At least they agreed on one issue. The last thing they needed was a child. But I arrived anyway, insinuating myself into their affections and bearing a truth neither would ever deny: The child they had brought into the world together was the single bright spot in their union. Even from a child's perspective, our home life seemed off-kilter. My father's quirkiness and lack of direction combined with my mother's low self-esteem and regular bouts with depression made for a dysfunctional soup. Their undeniable love for me, regardless of how they felt about each other, kept me afloat, and my own resilience kept me paddling, even later when I found that I, like my parents, had emotional and psychological gaps to fill.

Thus began a life-long search for security, self-confidence, and personal achievement. Born in the mid-forties, I settled into the traditional role of wife and mother in the sixties. During the eighties, I joined the silent, unrelenting force which was redefining the place of the ordinary woman in American society. At thirty-eight, I began a teaching career, reclaiming the dream I had once discarded.

The title of this narrative comes from something I read in *Listen to Their Voices: 20 Interviews with Women Who Write* by Mickey Pearlman. In her introduction, Pearlman refers to Grace Paley's comments about the newer writers, who see the world from unique perspectives. In truth, Paley's words apply to any writer and confirm what I learned from years of teaching. Students' individual truths, spoken in the language and context of a small farming community, exposed the crippling restrictions that dysfunctional homes and societal divisions place on a child. In those poignant voices, I recognized my own childhood, and I knew that I, too, had a story to share.

Chapter 1

MY MOTHER STOOD shivering in front of the fireplace in our home in Duncan Falls, Ohio, wearing only her slip, the cigarette in her hand burning down to gray ash. A sharp rap on the door prompted Grandma Rippey to help her into a dress, the way I was helped at bedtime, lifting passive arms and guiding them through the sleeves. She carefully unrolled each gartered stocking over a bluish foot and past the ankle, ending just above the knee. Next were the shoes, which required buckling just as mine did.

Through all of this, my mother remained voiceless, her eyes never leaving my father's face, a silent supplication he ignored. The second rap on wood was even sharper. And when Grandma brought out the green wool coat, my mother's pleading became audible and shrill. "Please, Raymond! Please let me stay!"

Daddy strode across the linoleum floor, pulled the door open, and admitted the sheriff's deputy, who tipped his black hat toward Grandma and nodded toward Grandpa Rippey, dozing in a rocker beside the fireplace. "Morning, Rip," he addressed my father, averting his eyes as Daddy led Mommy, resisting, toward the door, his hand grasping her elbow.

Hot, stinging tears tracked down my cheeks, and Grandma drew me in against her fresh morning apron. Before the door closed, I got a glimpse of the long, black car with its plumes of exhaust and my parents in the back seat. Grandma explained that Mommy was going away so she could get well. At three years old, I was vaguely aware that Mommy had been quieter, less engaged than usual, but her presence alone was enough to keep me safe. Words the adults had whispered about a court order to commit my mother to Columbus State Hospital had no point of reference in my world. The abandonment I felt that morning was equally un-namable.

I was also too young to realize that more may have been afoot in sending my mother away than her welfare. The second of my father's siblings, Florence, had remained dependent until her death in March of 1946, a couple of months before I was born. A Down syndrome child, she had served as Grandma Rippey's closest companion, and the old farmhouse was empty without her. One mother's need to fill a void coincided handily with the other's illness, opening the door for Grandma as Mother's surrogate. *His* mother, Daddy had informed my mother as the dark moods overtook her, was the one he wanted to raise *his* child.

⟫⟪⟫⟪

The farmhouse on Olivet Ridge in East Windsor Township, near Stockport, Ohio, seemed dark that winter, darker than when we visited my grandparents there in better days. Then, I had loved the warm barn smelling of hay where Grandpa's wood working tools hung from hooks and nails along one wall. I loved the coalhouse too, in which a modest heap of blue-black coal awaited shovel and bucket. In the second part of the building, kindling and lengths of firewood were stored, along with walnuts, their black outer shells leaving stains on my hands that even homemade soap couldn't wash off. Over time, their oils had infused the walls with walnut scent.

The house was a mix of fragrances too, with the smell of Grandma's soap ever present. Kettles of brown beans seasoned with jowl bacon rinds bubbled on the kitchen range. And on the warming shelf a crock of pungent sour milk thickened. Separated from the whey and seasoned with salt and cream, the curds became cottage cheese, tangy and cool on the tongue. My favorite smell of all, though, was fresh baked bread. Grandma always let us eat the first loaf straight from the oven, pulled apart in tender chunks and dripping with homemade butter.

On those visits, when it was time to return to Duncan Falls, Grandma had a kiss for me and a hug for Mommy. It took several hugs and kisses for her to say good-bye to Daddy, though. If Grandpa was awake, he would make an effort at good-byes. Even if he was asleep, I kissed the whiskery cheek with its tiny blue veins running beneath the skin. On the way home, conversation was never pleasant. Young as I was, I realized that if Daddy had his way we would live on Olivet Ridge, and I knew with equal certainty that Mommy was dead set against it. Every time, though, the rhythm of the wheels on the road and the swaying of the vehicle lulled me to sleep, so I never knew how the argument ended. It was years before I realized that the rift between them would never be resolved by so simple a thing as an argument.

———⚬———

The winter days on Olivet Ridge were long and gloomy. The single bulb in Grandpa's reading lamp cast eerie shadows on papered walls, and the burning coal visible through the glass in the living room stove offered only a small warming glow. The wonderful smells were still there, no doubt, but they didn't penetrate my wall of sadness. I missed the soft grilled cheese sandwiches Mommy made me and the spoon of chocolate syrup she put in my milk. By contrast, Grandma served tasteless soups in shallow dishes and fatty meat wrapped in flour and fried to hardness. But no one wasted food in Grandma's house, so I learned to eat whatever was put before me. As for comfort, Grandma's lap was always open, but it wasn't Mommy's.

Besides seeing to all of my personal needs, Grandma showed me how to paste pictures in a scrapbook. She read aloud from *McGuffey's Reader*, moralistic tales far over the head of a three-year-old. Some afternoons, she turned on the radio to *The Guiding Light* or *Our Gal Sunday*. She took offense if one of the characters said something inappropriate, but she tuned in again the next day anyway. Grandpa took naps beside the stove while I trailed Grandma about the house, but when he went to the barn I went too, bundled up in leggings and boots. Grandma and I gathered eggs from the grumpy hens and fetched water from way down over the hill. On rare, sunny days, she and I might walk up the gravel road to visit a neighbor.

Aside from foot travel, our transportation was an ancient black hearse that Grandpa had managed to acquire. Between the driver's seat and a backless chair where Grandma rode, sat a wooden box for me. On trips into Stockport, we purchased bags of grain at the feed store, which Grandpa slid into the empty space behind the seats among tools and miscellany. Then we purchased the commodities that Grandma's cupboards didn't provide: coffee, flour, sugar, salt meat. These joined the supplies in the back. We always had to stop at least once and let Grandpa take a nap; otherwise, he would nod off behind the wheel and Grandma would have to shake his arm to wake him.

Daddy showed up one time with a shiny new red tricycle which I peddled through living room, dining room, and kitchen. Another little girl, Ada, listened as I told her I was on my way to Duncan Falls. Back home, my imaginary playmate had been tolerated as the harmless invention of a solitary child in the company of adults. Here, Grandma Rippey believed that addressing empty doorways and vacant chairs was unnatural.

Even in Grandma's highly regulated universe, things sometimes went wrong. One chilly morning in early spring, I followed her onto the cement stoop beside the kitchen door while she threw out the dishwater. Silent, I watched a lone cardinal pecking at a spot of green bared from a snowmelt, and Grandma had no idea I was so close. When the pan swung back, it caught me in the temple. For the first seconds, I was too shocked to feel the pain. Grandma gathered me into her arms and rushed inside. By then I was crying for all I was worth. Grandma applied a cold compress to the rising bump and sat down in the wooden rocker beside the kitchen range, holding me close, murmuring. Long after the pain had subsided, I continued to sob. The short-lived assault had opened the floodgates, and pent-up emotions came screaming out like banshees. My no-nonsense grandmother was flummoxed by the displaced little person spilling out her misery in hysterical howls. Soon Grandma was in tears too, and we had a good long bawl together, sharing her apron to mop our faces.

Winter gave way to stiff winds that dried the mud and dogwood blossoms popped up white and pink throughout the woods and lilacs and forsythia bloomed in Grandma's yard. When May first, my fourth birthday, arrived, Grandma said we were going to visit my parents. She did her best to impress upon me that I would not be staying in Duncan Falls because Mommy wasn't well yet. Another memory, as vivid as Mommy's begging Daddy to let her stay home, is of the promise I made to myself that morning as I stood at Grandma's knees while she braided my pigtails. The decision I made in that moment was as intentional as any I've made since: When I get home, I am *not* leaving Mommy.

The ride to Duncan Falls in Grandpa's hearse is lost to memory. The hissy fit I reportedly pitched when my grandmother announced the visit was over is also forgotten. As I grew older, I realized that a tantrum would not have convinced Grandma to renege on her role as surrogate mother.

The sharpness of Florence's absence had begun to fade, and the full-time care of an energetic child wasn't easy for a woman of Grandma's age. Even more fundamental, she, of all people, understood the bond between mother and child.

The greatest lesson from that winter came much later when I recognized the glitch in my father's agenda. Having seen my mother at her lowest, he mistook her misery for weakness. The shock treatments did their job and lifted the pall that clouded her perceptions. She withstood the cheerless environs of the hospital, the ghost-like company who wandered there, and eventually her banishment. Her motivation? She had to return to her child.

And what was Daddy thinking as the old hearse pulled onto the street that bright May afternoon, Grandpa stripping gears, Grandma sitting Sphinx-like in her passenger chair, the box between them empty? I'd like to think he was happy to have his child back home, but when it came to my father and what he was thinking, I learned early on to avoid assumptions.

Chapter 2

WHAT FRUSTRATED MY mother the most about my father was what she considered an unnatural attachment to his mother. No woman alive would ever live up to Nora Belle Jenkins Rippey. And the feeling was mutual; Belle's firstborn, Raymond Jenkins Rippey, retained golden boy status throughout her lifetime. The seeds of this alliance can be traced back to Watertown, Ohio, and the turn of the twentieth century where Belle, the eldest of her mother's second round of offspring, was coming of age and weighing her limited options. Widowed and with four young children, Belle's mother, Florence Amelia Hagerman Ramsey, had married eighteen year old William Jenkins III if for no other reason than this: In the 1880s, a woman whose husband had inconveniently died on her couldn't be choosy.

By Belle's time, Watertown was a flourishing village surrounded by farms carved from forests and fertile meadowlands. Saturday mornings brought country folk into town to trade and gossip, including William and Florence Jenkins and their expanding clan. Among the shops and businesses, houses with lacy white curtains and porticoes were far removed from the homestead where the Jenkins family resided.

Belle never tired of telling the story of the first William Jenkins, a skilled tradesman, who crossed the Atlantic Ocean in 1806 to help construct a grist mill in Watertown. He arrived with full intention of returning to Scotland when the mill was finished. Falling prey to the allure of Wolf Creek as it gushed over rocks and settled into eddies, William had a change of heart. Instead of returning to Scotland, where only the gentry owned forested lands, he applied for a grant of one hundred sixty acres through the Ohio Company, and before long his fiancée, Elizabeth, joined him. Considered a British alien at the start of the War of 1812, William made his loyalties clear by enlisting in the Third Regiment of Ohio Volunteers and Militia and adding his muzzle-loader to the larger purpose of sending the British back across the water, this time for good.

His son, William Jenkins II, continued farming the original tract and married a local girl, Joanna Waterman. Joanna's father, Sherman, had the unlucky distinction of being the only Watertown resident to die during the Indian Wars, a widespread conflict between Native Americans and white settlers. Sherman was caught off-guard collecting bark to repair his bed. The gunshot wound near his liver claimed his life the following day.

At this point in the narrative, Belle liked to skip over the stories that circulated in Watertown. William Jenkins III, Belle's father, was less inclined to farming and more inclined to the whiskey manufactured in the hills, and this cost him all but the least productive forty acres of his grandfather's tract. The Jenkins' place where she grew up bore testament to this in its disintegrating outbuildings and frame houses where floors warped and chimneys remained upright by the grace of God. Mornings, Belle's mother, Florence, might find her husband sleeping off an all-nighter on the kitchen floor.

Speculation about Florence's morals is also woven into family lore. Ethel, one of Belle's sisters, bore the strong features of the Native settlers in the Ohio Valley, believed to be offshoots of the Delaware Nation. These renegades inhabited ancestral hunting grounds close to the Muskingum River, *Mooskingum i* in the Delaware tongue. Having lost favor among others of their nation, they associated with the poor white settlers. Native American features existed in the Hagerman family long before Florence's time; nevertheless, she was suspected of sharing her table with descendants of the renegades and may have shared other hospitalities too. No one knew for sure, but indiscretion, proven or otherwise, always makes a hot topic.

However unlikely it seems, Florence Jenkins' ancestry traces back to two notables found in accounts of the *Mayflower* and Plymouth Colony, Miles Standish and John Alden. Alexander Standish, Miles' son, married Sarah Alden, John's daughter. From this union came a line of descendants bearing the names Standish, Delano, Chandler, Bingham, and Hagerman, Florence's maiden name. My father loved to quote lines from the poem, "The Courtship of Miles Standish" by Henry Wadsworth Longfellow, feeling an affinity for the principals, no doubt. He also repeated the gossip his mother kept to herself.

In those days the eldest daughter customarily dropped

out of school to help at home as babies came along, but Belle was determined to become a schoolmarm and stuck it out all the way through eighth grade. She sat for the Normal Test but failed to pass, even on the second try. Giving up her dream of becoming a teacher, she took a job in the Watertown Post Office. Marriage didn't look promising for Belle. Watertown families of substance moved in a separate sphere, and the poor farm boys got a cold shoulder. She had made up her mind to have a life as far removed from Wolf Creek as possible. The old maid in the family at twenty, she continued to stash her money and wait. And then, sometime in 1904, a stranger showed up in Watertown. By Wolf Creek standards he was polished and suave. He had money in his pocket and an eye for the young postmistress.

━━━━•《◉》•━━━━

Lew Allan Rippey's family was well-established in Sturgis, Michigan. Lew's eldest brother was a lawyer; another was a successful farmer whose farm and family showed up in a series of paintings by Norman Rockwell and later a feature story in *The Saturday Evening Post*. A third son was a draftsman and the youngest, Postmaster of Sturgis. A sister, who owned an upholstery shop with her husband, became the family historian. What she recorded about the family has never fallen into my hands, but my father was quite adamant about our Rippey origins being French.

Researching, I found that the ancester my father spoke of was indeed a Frenchman named William Ripy--born, educated, and practicing medicine during the mid-sixteenth century in Paris. A Huguenot, William gained passage to Ireland just in time to escape the Massacre of St. Bartholomew's Eve, August 24, 1572, which decimated the Protestant population. His known descendants began with a grandson, also named William, and from there proceeds a direct line to the well-dressed man from Michigan who discovered the enticing young woman in the Watertown Post Office.

Lew's father, yet another William Rippey, had sent his least productive offspring to purchase building stock for his buggy construction and carpentry business. Even the sting of being singled out as dispensable couldn't dampen Lew's enthusiasm for a reprieve from the aura of disapproval that surrounded him in Sturgis. Arriving in Watertown, Lew walked the dusty street to the general store. In the same building he found the post office where a slender, dark-haired woman with keen gray eyes caught his attention and sent him head-over-heels in the same glance. Securing and shipping lumber back to Michigan took a back seat as Lew set out to win this woman. When a letter from his father demanded quick results, Lew wrapped up his business and proposed to the postmistress. In this smooth-talking stranger, who clipped his r's and narrowed his vowels, was the chance Belle had been waiting for, and if she had misgivings, her desire to escape overrode them.

The Rippey family home, well-known to my father during his earliest years, was every bit as substantial as the largest houses in Watertown, but Belle soon learned that she had married a far different Rippey from the others. Lew started building jobs with elaborate designs only to lose interest and move on to a new project. And he took an alarming number of naps. Regardless of the family's opinion of Lew, everyone welcomed Belle. The black sheep had brought home a winner, and anyone could see that he worshiped her. For reasons long forgotten, Lew nick-named his bride Susie, and Susie she remained to him until the end of his days.

Around the time Henry Ford began mass producing the Model T, Lew put every cent he could scratch up into a flailing buggy business. Predictably, the business crashed, and he lost their home. Awake and on task, Lew was a skilled carpenter, but he couldn't depend on staying awake. In those days, Lew's unplanned naps were blamed on laziness. Years later, his eldest son, Raymond, developed the same condition, and found a remedy in medication. But for Lew, narcolepsy was just one more aberration which separated him from his otherwise successful family. Fewer and fewer jobs came his way, and nothing was left but to start over, the farther away from Sturgis the better. Watertown, Ohio, might be just the place.

By the time they left Sturgis, Belle had two little boys, Raymond and Carl, and a baby girl, Florence. Despite her eagerness to escape Wolf Creek, Belle was only too glad to see her mother and sisters again. For a time, Belle and Lew lived in the second house on Wolf Creek. Later, they rented a dismal log cabin perched on a hillside near Stockport along the Muskingum River. Access to the cabin from the roadway was a steep, overgrown lane. Two small rooms and a lean-to kitchen made up the living space. Heavily wooded and rocky, the spot provided a plentitude of springs as well as narrow openings between rocks, ideal for copperheads and of supreme interest to small boys. Adding to Belle's anxieties was the fact that Florence, her grandmother's namesake, wasn't progressing the way the boys had. Belle had heard of children with Down syndrome, known then as Mongoloid babies, but realizing her sweet baby girl was afflicted added one more assault to her shaky universe. While she blamed Lew for their losses in Sturgis, she blamed herself for Florence's plight. Even in later years, she expressed regret over the troubled pregnancy.

Chastened by his most recent fall from grace, Lew found building jobs that enabled them to save the down payment on a house and twenty-five acres on Olivet Ridge in East Windsor Township, a few miles from the hillside dwelling. Belle claimed half-interest in the property, signing her name right beside Lew's on the deed. Never again would Lew Rippey fool away a home from under his wife's firmly planted feet. The house on Olivet Ridge was a considerable step-up from what Belle had known as a girl. While it was not as grand as the Rippey home in Michigan, the floors were sturdy, and the wide baseboards and woodwork revealed craftsmanship that Lew, the carpenter, could appreciate. There was a separate dining room and just beyond the east door lay the perfect spot for a garden. Lilacs and honeysuckle perfumed the front yard. Peach trees and an orchard of pie apples lay to the west.

Lew was no farmer, and the twenty-five acres remained unproductive. As the years passed, he completed fewer and fewer building jobs in Morgan County and his reputation as a carpenter soured there as in Michigan. His greatest success came in selling and installing lightning rods, a job which took him away from home for weeks at a time. Staying on the move and discovering new audiences for his tired stories and jokes was about as good as it could get for Lew Rippey.

Raymond was aware that Belle dreaded Lew's return following an absence, and he surmised that she was uncomfortable with the physical aspects of marriage. The warmth that she might have shown a less disappointing husband she lavished upon her firstborn, forging a strong bond between mother and son. Besides Raymond, Carl, and Florence, Belle gave birth to Donald and Joyce. Even with Lew working, the family barely got by. The boys worked for neighboring farmers. Belle and Joyce picked berries and gathered peaches and apples, preserving fruits and jellies along with vegetables from the garden. Nothing went to waste.

In 1926, Raymond was the first of the Jenkins line to graduate high school, having traveled by horseback to Stockport all four years. When the newly created Stanford-Benet Intelligence Test was administered that year, he scored highest at Windsor School, making him the talk of Olivet Ridge. But how he managed to attend nursing school in Massachusetts remains a mystery. It is doubtful Lew made a windfall profit selling lightning rods, so my best guess is Belle had squirreled away a secret stash for just such a purpose.

Raymond's ultimate goal, which he kept to himself until years later, was to use nursing school as a first step toward a degree in medicine. After all, the Frenchman, his distant ancestor, had been a doctor. Unfortunately, during his early teens, Raymond had suffered from mumps and taken a tumble from the hay mow. Following that, he developed narcolepsy, the condition that had beleaguered Lew his entire life. During nursing school, Raymond felt its full impact, falling asleep during lectures and struggling with his duties as an orderly at McClain Hospital, an asylum for mental patients, required work for male students of nursing.

Despite these drawbacks, Raymond's instructors saw him as a bright young man with a correctable problem and presented him with conditions for continuing: Take a newly developed medication. Raymond deplored any connection to deficiency. Added to that, the cultural and financial differences between Raymond and the young men pursuing medical studies at Massachusetts General Hospital were glaringly obvious. The definition of smart and sophisticated in Morgan County wasn't quite the same as in a prestigious East Coast medical facility. So Raymond packed his bag and returned to Olivet Ridge, if not in disgrace, certainly in disappointment. After sufficient time to lick his wounds and bask in his mother's reassurances, he apprenticed to a barber in Stockport, learned the trade, and began a career that he always felt was beneath him.

Chapter 3

DURING MY FATHER'S teenage years, my mother, Leona May Hosom, was growing up on and around Olivet Ridge also. Like Raymond, Leona was an eldest child, but that position didn't garner her any favors. Instead, she endured the carping of a mother who always expected the worst, usually managed to find it, and never seemed happy even when calamity was averted. Leona's father, Willis Claredon Hosom, had learned the value of keeping his mouth shut a year or so before Leona's birth, when he married Misha May McVey, the daughter of a circuit riding preacher. For as long as I knew Grandpa Hosom, his complaints were uttered *sotto voce* to avoid Grandma's wrath.

Unlike the Rippeys, who had landed on Olivet Ridge more or less by chance, the Hosoms had been there for at least two generations. Over time, the name Hosom, like Rippey, had undergone variations from the original Horsham. Emigration from England for those later known as Hosom occurred during the early 1600s, and the line includes a Revolutionary War soldier, Jacob Hossom, who lived in Maine. From Jacob, the line goes straight to the Hosoms of

East Windsor. As a side note, a Rippey ancestor also fought in the Revolutionary War and is referenced in family lore as Captain John Rippey.

Willis Claredon's father, James Perry Hosom, was responsible for the final spelling change when he received an early discharge from the Army of the Republic in 1864 because of a heart irregularity. One "s" had been left out in his discharge papers. Rather than risk losing his medical and service pensions, he went with the present spelling. James Perry had enlisted in the infantry at sixteen, without parental consent. Having second thoughts, he wrote his mother begging her to notify the Army that he was underage. Since his mother refused to rescue him and he had no desire to meet the firing squad for desertion, the scared country boy in Company C, 97th Regiment out of Zanesville, Ohio, turned himself into a soldier and brought home a hat with a bullet hole through the crown.

When asked to talk about the War, though, he omitted the brutal fighting that the 97th is known for at Mission Ridge and Chickamauga; instead, he told about eating kernels of corn which had fallen around the horses' feet when rations ran short. Despite an early end to his military career, James Perry enjoyed ninety-two healthy years and preferred foot travel over buggy or wagon. Easily riled, he once took a roundhouse swing at another man. Observers swore that if the blow had connected, it would have been fatal. His reputation as a hot head remained with him to the end.

James Perry married a local girl, Prudence Emmaline Hindman. Two of their offspring were somewhat notable. The only daughter, Olive Belle, escaped a tragic house fire that killed her husband and daughter and then lived to the age of 102 in California. The youngest was Otis, a commercial artist, who designed the Pure Oil Company logo, a blue circle with the word "Pure" inside. He was the first Hosom to make enough money to pay income tax. One of the middle sons, Willis Claredon, known only as Claredon, left less of a mark on the world. Part of the time, he carried mail horseback and picked up farm work when it presented itself. Claredon wasn't lazy, just unmotivated and worn down by his complaining wife Misha May McVey Hosom, known to her family and acquaintances as Mishie and to those who knew her best as a certifiable crepe hanger.

Having grown up believing the name McVey was of Irish origin, I was surprised to find that my first traceable McVey ancestor's headstone is in Scotland, bearing the inscription, "Mcvey, 1700." His son Benjamin left Scotland for America, and four generations later, Albert Maywood McVey, Mishie's father, was born in Stafford, Ohio. Albert was married twice, the first time to Sarah Hostetter, who gave birth to my grandmother, Mishie, in Deep Valley, West Virginia, and John Earl five years later. Sarah died from a urinary tract blockage when Mishie was around twelve, old enough to contemplate the horror of her mother's ruptured bladder.

Mishie and John were placed with church families so Albert could continue his evangelistic duties, and Mishie learned first-hand about the difference between professed and practiced Christianity. One of the foster families had two older daughters, ideal mentors, Albert was told, for a girl Mishie's age. With the preacher gone, pretense disappeared. When Mishie began menstruating, ignorance drove her to the creek early morning and late evening to wash her undergarments and put them on again wet. For all she knew, she was dying of the same disease that had killed her mother. Enjoying her naiveté, the older girls threatened to expose her secret journeys to the creek. By the time Mishie returned to Albert's home, she knew better than to expect a hand or a kindness from those who voiced "amen" the loudest.

Within a year of his first wife's death, Albert McVey brought home a new wife, Olive Hosom. Olive was soon pregnant and bore three children in quick succession, and it fell to Mishie to aid in their care. When Mishie reached a marriageable age, she caught the attention of Olive's brother Claredon and began a family of her own. My mother, Leona May, was born in a log cabin on a rocky hillside, the same dwelling which would later serve the Rippey family following the Sturgis debacle.

Tragedy was to strike the McVey family again. One chilly night, the kerosene furnace which heated Albert and Olive's home touched off a fire. Olive and the boys, Ira and Oral, escaped unharmed. But dry timbers and laths were fast consumed, and Albert and twelve year old Icy Honor were not so fortunate. Later, in a neighboring house, Albert lay dying, Icy in the home of another. Just before her death, Icy whispered, "Hush, I hear Papa praying." Albert *had* been praying as he died and, according to those in attendance, while his daughter spoke her final words.

The early loss of her mother, maltreatment in foster homes, and the deaths of Albert and Icy left a pall of irreparable sadness on Mishie's personality. As the years passed, my mother's siblings arrived—Homer, Edith, James—but Mishie's outlook never brightened. Having listened to tales from my mother's childhood, I believe it's fair to say that her low self-esteem and sense of dread were first learned from Mishie. Underneath it all, though, Grandma Hosom had a good and courageous heart, and I am alive today because of her quick intervention. Her early experiences with make-believe Christians might well have left her with distaste for religion, but she remained a staunch believer to the end of her days.

Throughout Leona's growing-up years, Claredon and Mishie rented first one house and then another in East Windsor and for a time were next door neighbors to the Rippeys on Olivet Ridge. Then, when my mother was fourteen, the Hosom family relocated in Parkersburg, West Virginia, a rapidly growing city of approximately 25,000. Visco, a new rayon producing plant in South Side, had opened, and Claredon hoped to get a job there. The house they rented on Lynn Street was a stacked affair with kitchen on the ground floor, living room and bedrooms on the second and third. Accustomed to clean, country spaces, the Hosoms found their city dwelling dirty and cramped.

Neighborhood gossips told Mishie that girls who went to Parkersburg High School became pregnant in startling numbers, so Mishie enrolled her elder daughter in Parkersburg Business School. Before she could finish the course of study, the school burned to the ground. At sixteen, Leona became a grocery clerk, riding the street car uptown and back. Later, Edith graduated from PHS. Either the incidence of pregnancy had diminished or Mishie had lost confidence in her neighbors. Claredon never landed a job at Visco. Instead, he threaded bristles into the power-driven brooms used on street sweepers.

For Mishie, Leona posed the greatest concern, out there in the city on her own. "Make your friends in the church," Mishie insisted, but Leona's natural shyness, compounded by the snobbery she encountered, made it impossible. When she was seventeen, she fell in love with a young man. The trouble was Henry was Catholic. To Mishie, Catholicism was worse than no religion at all, and Henry wasn't budging, so the relationship stalled out. Three years later, Leona and Henry dated again, raising Mishie's ire when Henry flatly stated, "I was born a Catholic, and I'll die a Catholic." There was no arguing with him, and certainly not with Mishie, so the couple split.

As the decade dwindled, city life gave Mishie the opportunity to admonish her once compliant elder daughter against a number of pitfalls. Mishie forbade Leona to bob her hair; Leona got a haircut. Skirts were too short; Leona shortened hers to knee length. Modern music was raucous, and dancing—always an abomination because Salome's gyrations had cost John the Baptist his head—had become downright vulgar. Mishie blamed the movies and forbade those too. Not surprisingly, Leona developed a passion for films, especially musicals, which were rife with dancing. According to Mishie, transgressors would rue their part in the Roaring Twenties.

Then the stock market crashed and the Great Depression set in and Mishie had proof of God's retribution. Claredon's job with the city ended. Observing the breadlines and Business Closed signs all over town, Mishie declared it was time to flee Sodom.

Back in Ohio, a few miles from Beverly on Hackney Ridge, the Hosoms found a farm for sale. After Mishie's sojourn in the sooty, triple-decker on Lynn Street, the roomy farmhouse on Hackney Ridge seemed like paradise. They purchased the place in summer, when the fruit trees were laden and the wide, sloping yard lush and green. Unfortunately, Mishie's enthusiasm was short-lived. Winter revealed weak chimneys and loose windows which let in the icy wind. The one time Mishie had failed to predict disaster, it had landed with a vengeance. She wasn't going to make that mistake again.

During the years when most young women were finding husbands, Leona worked in grocery and retail stores, sometimes in Beverly a few miles south of Hackney, sometimes back in Parkersburg, where she lived at the YWCA. Other than Henry, boyfriends proved inconsequential; that is, until the spring of 1935 when Leona turned twenty-seven and met the man who would become my sister's father. All I know of him is he had tuberculosis, he was from a prominent Beverly family, and he was married. Mishie had preached long and hard against all the small taboos that her daughter was breaking; perhaps Leona decided to smash the dickens out of a really big one. Or maybe she was just lonely. During the first months of her pregnancy, Leona disregarded missed periods and morning sickness, but when she finally began to show, she took to her bed. By the time her labor pains began, six weeks early, she was emotionally shut down.

The doctor arrived a few minutes after the baby's birth. My sister had no admitted father, no birth certificate, and small odds of survival. Her abdominal wall had not grown together, so after cutting the umbilical cord, the doctor pushed the protruding organs back into the baby's open abdomen, wrapped her in a towel, and laid her on a nearby sewing machine. The expectation was that the newborn would die, and better so, given not only her premature birth but the fact that she was the illegitimate product of a married man from a good family and a traumatized farm girl.

After the doctor left, Mishie heard a tiny mewling coming from the bundle. Even though the child's presence would serve as a life-long complication, Mishie took her up, bathed her, and bandaged the open abdomen. As weeks passed, the fragile preemie named Barbara Ann began to thrive. No one ever doubted that Mishie Hosom deplored sin, but in this case, she truly loved the sinner and the sinner's child. In stiff February winds, my gutsy grandmother hung the baby's diapers where the entire neighborhood could observe the flapping white evidence. She was outside the day Barbara's father drove by. If he was suffering from a guilty conscience, no one ever knew. No contact was made, and within a year or so, he died from tuberculosis.

Chapter 4

THERE'S JUST NO figuring what drives people to do things. When Raymond and Leona met again, years after their Olivet Ridge days, World War II was raging and the future looked grim. Even though neither felt an undying passion for the other, they decided to have a go at marriage. They set up housekeeping in Philo, Ohio, across the Muskingum River from the barber shop where my father worked in Duncan Falls. When they went apartment hunting, they found two possibilities. One was an attractive little space with a private bath and a matching living room suite. In the other, nothing matched, and tenants had to share a bathroom with the landlord and his wife. Since my father had just given my mother a set of rings originally purchased for another woman, his choice of apartment came as no surprise. For the time being, seven year old Barbara Ann would continue to live with her grandparents on Hackney Ridge.

In 1945, World War II ended, and the mood of the country shifted from tension and dread to optimism. Instead of producing fighter jets and Army jeeps, automotive plants resumed their original purpose. Returning soldiers started families and purchased everything from homes through the GI Bill to bassinets and Frigidaires. Even tiny hamlets like Philo and Duncan Falls felt the change. Housing additions went up, and hardware stores, appliance stores, and grocery markets saw an upshot in sales. During this period of resurgence, my parents decided to trade their cramped space in Philo for a fixer-upper across the river.

They got the boxy, two-story dwelling facing Main Street cheap from an old man who had turned it into a dump. Between a cinder path and the highway, a triad of maple trees saved the frontage from even grimmer aspect. The once-white siding was cracked and streaked with soot from the smokestacks of two industrial plants on the Philo side. Slate from the roof lay on the ground, and the lot was overgrown with weeds. At the rear of the lot stood a small barn, an outhouse, and a chicken coop. A few feet from the house and also facing the street, a newer, two-room building served as the major selling point for my father. Unlike the house, the shop had running water. All he had to do was scavenge a barber chair and miscellaneous furnishings, paint a barber's pole in red and white stripes, and letter "Rippey's Barber Shop" on the windows. Once he passed the state inspection, he was open for business.

The house was a different story. Walls had to be stripped and repapered, and woodwork, baseboards, and ceilings painted. Since my father was intent on getting his business up and running, work in the house fell primarily to my mother, who knew there was no possibility of updating with a bathroom or central heat. Still, she was glad to be out of the dismal little apartment where the landlord could hear all of their personal business and they could hear his.

Ironically, the move to Duncan Falls triggered an event neither of them had planned on. My mother's method of birth control had worked well in the apartment, but since my father saw indoor plumbing as a luxury, she did the best she could and crossed her fingers every month. Once summer ended, fatigue and a missed period or two made my mother think she had developed tuberculosis. It was November before she checked things out, and the doctor assured her that in about six months her TB would be cured. Even though she had agreed not to have children, she shared the news with a sense of relief. As she may have expected, my father harkened back to his fall from a hayloft at fourteen and having mumps "go down" on him, a poorly veiled suggestion that the child's paternity might be in question. Whatever she thought of his comment, she, like most pregnant women, had plenty to keep her occupied: morning sickness, heartburn, and hormones gone psycho. And, as the projected date of my birth drew nearer, she was presented with another complication.

Early morning, May 1, 1946, my father got into his pickup and headed for the Jenkins home place near Watertown, Ohio. His routine on days off was to spend time on Wolf Creek or Olivet Ridge. As she watched him leave, my mother noticed a few intestinal twinges, but since I wasn't expected for another three weeks, she dismissed them as indigestion. Grandma Hosom happened to be visiting, having left the farm on Hackney Ridge for an extended stay with her pregnant daughter. When Mother's twinges became full-on labor pains, Grandma hurried to the neighbor's house to call Dr. Daw. Given the transportation issues, he opted to drive to Duncan Falls for the delivery rather than try to get my mother to the hospital in Zanesville.

By the time Grandma returned to the house, Mother was in the final stages of labor. Within moments, I was out, slippery with blood and eerily still, the umbilical cord wrapped twice around my neck. Grandma's last baby had been stillborn because the cord, wrapped three times around her neck, had deprived her of oxygen. Remembering little Dorothy, Grandma wasted no time flipping the cord from my neck. Since the doctor was on his way, Grandma left us as we were, separate, yet attached. Once he had performed the necessary procedures, the doctor, a no-nonsense kind of man, handed me off to my grandmother with an abrupt, "Clean her up, Grandma." My grandmother took offence and never had a good word to say for Dr. Daw.

If there *was* to be a baby, my father had informed my mother once her pregnancy was confirmed, he expected it to be a son. But when he received the tiny figure wrapped in blankets and staring up at him with huge blue eyes, he forgot his mandate. In the crook of his arm lay the spit and image of the face he shaved every morning, remade in miniature and remarkably feminine. An overwhelming sense of recognition, he insisted later, passed between the two of us in that first look. He carried me to Huff's Grocery just up the street and laid me, blankets and all, in the meat scales. Then he returned with the blankets, weighed those, and calculated my weight at four pounds, ten ounces. In a spirit of compromise, each parent contributed a name, and I became Lois Rachel. Everyone who saw me commented on my striking resemblance to my father. "You can't deny that one, Rip" was the general consensus around town. I wonder if he ever thought to apologize to my mother.

———◦《◉》◦———

My first memories are bits and pieces—sitting in a high chair and staring at a huge lima bean in a sectioned plate and standing in my playpen at the screen door where I could watch passers-by through a film of soot stuck to the screen. Daddy worked consistently in his barber shop and spent his evenings lettering signs in the back room or reading and falling asleep in one of the over-stuffed rockers in the living room. In good weather, he and Mother might walk up the street to the bus stop restaurant for ice cream. At first, he carried me on his shoulders. When I could toddle on my own, they each held one of my hands and swung me into the air to hear my squeals.

In springtime, they cultivated the vegetable garden and planted rows of seeds and tiny plants. Daddy cut and drove tomato stakes, and later, as he suckered the young plants, I was at his heels, sun-warmed loam beneath my bare feet, watching as he dropped ugly green tomato worms into a can of kerosene. Evenings, the squeak of the porch swing and the snug spot between my parents' bodies provided the ultimate in comfort. I often snuggled into my father's lap as bedtime drew near. Without fail, he would read aloud from *The Saturday Evening Post* or the funny papers, and the rumble of his voice soothed me to sleep. The next morning I would wake up in my high-railed bed with sunlight invading the room and no memory of being laid there.

Many early experiences include my Hosom grandparents. I remember the sloping grassy yard on Hackney Ridge and trailing my grandfather around the farm. The huge setting sun was a ball and almost within my reach, if Grandpa just had a ladder tall enough. Grandpa's favorite part of Campbell's chicken noodle soup was the broth and mine was the noodles, so we made perfect soup-eating buddies. Then there's the story of my mother's attempt to remove me from my bottle, which I'm not sure I remember at all. I probably just heard it repeated so many times it feels like a memory. Tired of my insistent demands for my "ba-ba," Grandpa Hosom announced as a car passed, "That man's got your bottle." I took Grandpa at his word, and the next time the car went by, I ran to the edge of the porch and yelled, "Man! Bring my ba-ba back!"

I was still pretty young when my grandparents moved to a house in McConnelsville which they co-owned with Edith, my mother's sister, and her husband Hank, an ex-Navy man with a metal plate in his skull due to damage suffered during a torpedo strike. Edith had met Hank in nursing school, and they worked at Rocky Glen Tuberculosis Sanatorium, she as an RN and Hank as an orderly. In their house, I had my first experience in a bathtub, not a galvanized washtub filled with water heated in a teakettle, but a white porcelain rectangle complete with metal faucets and piped-in hot water. At first I wasn't sure I wanted any part of the strange contraption, but with coaxing and my sister Barbara willing to demonstrate the bathing experience, I finally agreed to give it a try. What a luxury I had discovered!

I barely remember Barbara back then. Pictures reveal that she hadn't outgrown her scrawniness, and she had a pixie smile and luxurious auburn hair which she wore in thick braids or a bouncy ponytail. If she harbored resentment toward the little sister who marshaled full-time attention from the woman who had seemed content with only part-time motherhood before, I never felt it. By then, Mother had a house large enough to include both daughters, yet Barbara remained with Grandma and Aunt Edie. What a life: a crepe hanging grandmother on one hand and a know-it-all aunt on the other. Then, when she was twelve, Barbara contracted rheumatic fever and developed a heart murmur; eventually the damaged valve would demand surgery.

Looking back, I realize that my mother's discontent with her marriage and feelings of guilt over abandoning Barbara fueled our frequent visits with the Hosoms. By the winter I was three and the sheriff's car pulled up in front of the Duncan Falls house, Mother had simply reached her limit. Leaving another daughter in someone else's hands was never her choice.

Chapter 5

DURING THE SUMMER of 1950, not long after I returned to Duncan Falls from Olivet Ridge, my sister Barbara, fourteen by that time, moved in with us. Aunt Edie had talked Grandma and Grandpa Hosom into selling the house in McConnelsville and buying a pair of house trailers, and there wasn't room for a teenage girl with either couple. Her coming to us meant sleeping arrangements had to change. The one downstairs bedroom had served all three of us until then; I slept in one end and my parents in the other. As soon as Barbara arrived, she was given the single bed and Mother and I shared the double. Daddy seemed only too happy to take the room upstairs, despite the meager warmth in winter and the suffocating heat in summer.

The antipathy between Barbara and my father did not aid the transition. In a surge of generosity when the marriage was new, he had mentioned adopting Barbara, and although she remained with our grandparents, she began calling him Daddy. When nothing further developed, Barbara dropped all overtures and nouns of address regarding him, except when he was out of earshot, and then he became His Majesty or His Royal Highness.

About that time, I became abnormally clingy. I had not forgotten losing my mother, and now another daughter was laying claim to her. And, in the early fifties, radio newscasts and conversations I overheard seemed focused on matters left unsettled by World War II. I sensed these as threats also, however vague. My panic when a plane flew over or a siren sounded seems a logical reaction for a four-year-old whose tender psyche mirrored the larger, American psyche of the times. At least I could feel safe with Mommy in easy reach. Adults didn't have that luxury.

During the following summer, an incomprehensible lump in my throat refused to allow the passage of food, and I stopped eating things that required chewing. Mother said it was nerves and pumped me full of chocolate milk and puddings, hoping to forestall weight loss. Grandma Hosom said it could be a goiter like Aunt Edie had had, which required surgery. Looking back, I can see why Mother hesitated having it checked. Any aberration in my condition rang alarm bells in Daddy's head and put Mother at risk of being blamed for either hysteria, if overly concerned, or neglect, if not concerned enough. Even so, she had adult reasoning at her disposal. Her daughter was engaged in a conflict every bit as frustrating, and at five years old, I had no idea whether I was tilting at dragons or windmills. In addition to clinginess and avoiding foods I didn't trust, I threw raging fits, the frightened child's fallback.

And just what was I so afraid of besides Russian bombers flying over Duncan Falls? By then, my mother had convinced me that my imagined bombers were harmless passenger planes. And, outwardly, things in the Rippey house did not appear so bad. No dishes smashed into walls, and nobody got punched or pushed around. But when a discussion started between my parents, I knew it would not end well. Daddy would stomp out mad, and Mother would cry and light a cigarette, her hands shaking. The Russians might not drop a bomb on our house, but there *was* a war going on in there, and I was collateral damage.

I soon learned that our family wasn't the only one with troubles. Aunt Edie and Uncle Hank decided to move to Canton, Ohio, where she had found a better-paying job, so my Hosom grandparents had their little green trailer towed to Duncan Falls. Something no one talked about except in whispers was Uncle Hank's drinking binges. Sober, he was as harmless as a puppy. Drunk, he roughed up his wife. Remorse always followed, along with purple bruises that Aunt Edie hid beneath make-up and long sleeves, excusing Hank because of his head injuries. Grandpa Hosom wasn't so lenient: A mean drunk was a mean drunk, steel plate in his head or no. Having her parents in Duncan Falls gave Mother an outlet for her frustrations besides Barbara and me. The tiny trailer became a safe haven for discussing, not only my father's utter failure as a husband, but also what Mother called his hair-brained schemes.

Daddy still believed barbering was beneath him and saw his clever ideas as potentials for profit. Impressed by the abundance of night-crawlers which surfaced in our garden every spring, he decided to mass produce and sell them to local fishermen. He filled a sizable square box with rich black loam. When this breeding ground didn't produce the desired number of worms, he buried a possum carcass in the box one evening and proceded upstairs where his dreams were likely filled with multitudes of money-making nightcrawlers. The next morning he found zero night-crawlers amidst the loam. Instead, the soil and the remainder of the unfortunate possum were overflowing with ugly white maggots. Word of the project got around Duncan Falls, thanks to my father's penchant for braggadocio. But once the worms were history, Barbara no longer had to endure the snide remarks among her classmates about her step-father's worms.

My father's oddities showed up in other undertakings over the course of several years. One involved a small blue paperbacked volume of melancholy poems titled *Heartache*, which he had self-published. Circulation, as far as I know, was limited to books he gave away. He still believed his words could sell and invented a cartoon character, a worm wearing monocle and top hat and voicing truisms my father thought were priceless coming from a dressed up worm. The market was to be the editorial page of *The Times Recorder*. None were ever published, and eventually this worm went the way of the others.

Later on, Daddy's attention shifted to inventing a new gadget. The first was a near-miss, a toothpaste container with a flip-top instead of a regular lid. He sent detailed plans to the Office of Patents in Washington, D.C. and waited hopefully until the rejection notice came. Later, when flip-tops appeared everywhere, I wondered if my father's idea had been over-looked or stolen, or if some enterprising soul had beaten him to the draw.

His most involved attempt he named "Cornstalk

Cut-Outs," necessitating crops of popcorn to be grown on Olivet Ridge. Again, he drew elaborate diagrams, showing each step of turning corn stalks into playthings or knick-knacks. From this grew a kit for potential customers, including lengths of corn stalk for non-farmers. Why popcorn, and not table or field corn? Popcorn stalks were easier to whittle, he said, and whittling was pretty much the concept behind the whole thing. Again, the Office of Patents failed to appreciate the genius behind the idea. A practical advantage that time was an abundance of popcorn.

Daddy's attempts to gain fame and fortune continued throughout my childhood, revisited as he imagined improvements in engineering or marketing. Without a doubt, he was an inventive soul, but understanding how others perceived the world was never his strong suit.

———◦((◦))◦———

Bored and needing someone to complain to, Grandma Hosom dropped by the house sometimes, in her cotton housedress and apron and black lace-up shoes with two inch heels from Sears and Roebuck. Besides lamenting all that had led to their current housing, Grandma criticized Homer's wife Gladys, who didn't have babies, and Jim's wife Betty, who had them too frequently. If Grandma was in an exceptional mood, she would sit down at the old player piano and sing, chording out melody and harmony on the keys. She had a clear alto voice and had sung at funerals and revivals back in the day. The McVeys had been a musical bunch, and

Great-Grandpa McVey and his son John led congregational singing. Mother had taken piano lessons as a girl and still played infrequently. She joined in when Grandma was at the piano, although years of heavy smoking had deepened her soprano to contralto. Those were good times, sitting next to Grandma on the piano bench, aware of passers-by just beyond the front screen pausing briefly to listen.

Grandma Hosom would never darken the door of a Presbyterian, Methodist, or Baptist church, the choices available in Duncan Falls. So every Sunday a Plymouth of pre-War vintage stopped at the green trailer, and my grandparents climbed into the backseat. Across the hills, in Chandlersville, was a narrow brick Church of Christ where the only instrument was a tuning fork. The children's Bible class met behind a thin curtain separating it from the adult class. All children listened to the same stories and colored the same mimeographed pictures of Bible characters.

During the service, I entertained myself with a hymnal, matching the number of beats in a measure to the number of syllables in the lyrics. Grape juice in tiny glass cups passed in front of me, along with a homemade wafer from which adults took pinches. The sermon lasted an eternity. Even though I understood little of what I heard, the basic concepts of Christianity bled through. Along with Grandma Hosom's influence and Mother's informal but consistent teachings, church attendance gave me a fair knowledge of the fundamentals by the time I started school.

The worst part of church was the drive to and from Chandlersville. My grandparents' personal hygiene was the primary reason I opted for the front seat rather than the back. I hated that woozy, half-dizzy feeling I got on Sunday mornings and the threat that whatever I had managed to swallow as breakfast would come splashing out into my lap. What my mother blamed on carsickness was my stomach's reaction to being trapped in that smelly car. Grandma did her laundry sparingly, and frequency of bathing had dwindled with advancing years. For church, they spruced up to look presentable, but those same clothes reappeared week after week without ever visiting a washtub or a drycleaner. The odor of neglectful old age permeated our car on Sunday.

Most Sundays Daddy was on Olivet Ridge or Wolf Creek. If he *was* home, we dined in a state of détente, and afternoon was like walking on eggshells, even when he snored in his chair. Tensions eased if he removed himself to the back room of his barber shop and worked on a sign or dabbled in another of his creative attempts, landscape painting. In those, the theme rarely varied and was often expressed in sharp peaked mountains and black timbers reflected in rocky streams. Daddy insisted that I had artistic talent too. Giving me the brush, he would guide my hand in long, even strokes that I could never duplicate on my own. One time, I talked him into lighting a candle. He fell asleep in his barber chair, and I managed to catch my hair on fire. My screaming woke him in time, but the smell of singed hair sent my mother into a tizzy when I returned to the house.

By the time I turned six, ladders of ribs showed through my tee shirts and my face was gaunt. My diet had dwindled to liquids or anything that would melt. If Daddy hadn't been gone so much and distracted by his own concerns when he was home, he would surely have noticed. With first grade approaching, Mother made an appointment with Dr. Thompson in Philo. If my father found out, so be it.

My only other doctor's visit had been the summer I was four, when I picked up a fishing line on the street and caught the hook in my finger. The jagged prongs refused to budge, so my parents took me to the antiseptic office across the river where strange instruments lay on sterile towels and a white cot held center stage. I was silent as Daddy lifted me onto the table, but when the nurse placed a smelly gauze mask over my mouth and nose, I fought frantically until the ether knocked me out. The rest of the afternoon I lay drowsily in the modified buggy seat swing on the back porch and listened to traffic on the street and the buzzing of insects in the hollyhocks climbing the porch post. My parents sat at the kitchen table just beyond the screen door, smoking cigarettes, differences set aside for the moment.

⟚⟚⟚⟨⦿⟩⟚⟚⟚

My second doctor's visit was less traumatic. The solemn-faced Dr. Thompson boosted me onto the white cot while my mother explained my symptoms. He placed smooth, cool fingers here and there on my neck and throat. A wide flat spatula secured my tongue while I obediently said, "A-ah." Satisfied, Dr. Thompson patted my knee and turned to Mother. "What's going on at home?" The stress we lived under was not to be discussed with outsiders, even those with MD after their names. Mother remained silent.

"This girl needs to hear that her father's a great guy." Dr.

Thompson said this as if imparting a common sense notion that everybody, except maybe my mother, understood.

Understanding crept into Mother's expression, and her eyes narrowed, but she had come for a medical diagnosis and intended to get one. "She can't swallow solid food. I need to know why."

He shrugged. "Her throat is not the problem. She needs reassurance."

Hearing that nothing was physically wrong with me, Mother visibly relaxed. The tall, thin doctor with the enigmatic expression and graying hair lifted me off the table in one easy motion. "When she hears from you that her father's a great guy, she will swallow just fine." He placed a finger under my chin, tilted my head upward, and gave me a wink. "She might even smile."

My mother's face flushed. "It won't matter what I tell her. She knows her father."

We exited the office, crossing a small strip of grass to the Plymouth parked on the street. My mother's hand shook as she lit her cigarette. All the way home she fumed. I said nothing, just stared out the open window, feeling the humid wind whipping into the car as we crossed the bridge back into Duncan Falls and turned up Main Street. Once home, my mother repeated the doctor's words to Barbara, who lay on her narrow bed with a *Photoplay* across her chest. Barbara hooted her derision and mouthed, "B.S."

Later that afternoon, we three walked up the hot paved sidewalk to my grandparents' lot. They were sitting in their green metal lawn chairs under twin maples whose mingled branches created a leafy canopy in an otherwise sun-drenched space of grass and gravel. When Mother told them about our eventful day, Grandpa mumbled profanities, and Grandma was so flabbergasted that it took her a few seconds before she could chide Grandpa for his language and then rip into Dr. Thompson.

As for my eating disorder, I had gained enough from the doctor's comments to know there was nothing wrong with me except nerves, just as Mother had said. She had been right about something else that day too: No one had to tell me anything about my father. I knew he said mean things to her and made her cry; on the other hand, she said way too much in my presence. Even though I was just a kid, I knew the adults in charge were not handling things well, and they were not above feeding each other and their kids a line. And now, thanks to Barbara, I knew what to call it.

Chapter 6

ON TUESDAY FOLLOWING Labor Day, 1952, my mother took me to Duncan Falls Elementary School. There I met a room full of other initiates and Mrs. Simms, my first grade teacher. Despite my attachment issues, I remained calm when Mother left, confident that I could reel off the alphabet, count forever, and clearly print my entire name. The only thing I couldn't do was read because Mother refused to teach me. Not to worry, I was reading like a pro in no time, and school was great except for two issues. First, *nobody* spoke in choppy, two-word sentences like "Run, Spot," so why did Dick and Jane? Second, why couldn't I talk to the little girl behind me? The teacher ignored my complaint, but socializing earned me a stint in the cloak room.

The nasty business at home receded to a place of lesser importance during the school day. And my parents' conflict lost its edge in the final weeks of the 1952 Presidential Campaign. Both Republicans, they found a common enemy in the Democratic nominee, Adlai Stevenson, and eased up on each other. I remember the crisp November evening when we walked to the brightly lit fire station and they cast their votes for Dwight D. Eisenhower.

To cap off the evening, we went for ice cream. At the restaurant, the warm smell of fried food and coffee welcomed us. My parents ordered sundaes in metal dishes on little pedestals. Daddy always went for hot fudge and Mother for vanilla with marshmallow crème. I was addicted to cones, any flavor. We sat at a table, but most of the other customers lined the bar with their coffee or Coca Cola and talked election business. Afterward, I shivered contentedly as we headed home, wishing the congenial mood could last. For that short while, it felt almost like old times, trotting between the two of them, their hands encircling mine.

My reprieve came to an end a few days after the election. It was early morning when I heard Daddy's heavy footsteps as he carried miscellaneous boxes down the stairs and through the back door. I stayed hunkered in the bed I shared with Mother, but I could hear their voices in the kitchen. "What are we supposed to live on?" The timbre of Mother's voice was higher than normal.

Daddy's comeback was harsh: "All you do is sit on your ass and holler for somebody to keep you." The kitchen door slammed, jarring the window panes. Mother reopened the door and followed him outside. I didn't witness the scene, but I could predict how it would end. His truck would roar away, and she would return to the kitchen crying and cursing in the same breath.

At first I tried to kid myself. This time would be like the others, when he retreated to Grandma's farm or Wolf Creek only to reappear a few days later and pick up his life where he'd left off. Waiting for his return, Mother would smoke endless cigarettes and keep her ears peeled for the sound of his truck. Then I would wake up one morning to find him at the kitchen table, ready for a day at the barber shop, just as if nothing had happened, his black hair wet and shiny, his white shirt crisply starched. And Mother, still in her housecoat, would join him at the table, the smoke from her cigarette rising with the steam from their cups, the silence between them thick.

This time, however, my father had loaded his pick-up with his barbering case and his painting supplies. For a week or two after his departure, customers knocked on our door, asking, "When's Rip coming back?" Eventually the men stopped coming by. Even if they did like the way Rip cut hair, they had to find a replacement. And the closed sign on the shop remained.

At school, I gave non-committal answers to the kids' questions about his absence. I came home every afternoon to the sound of Mother's radio, the warmth of a fire blazing in the grate, and the smell of food in the kitchen. But I wasn't entirely naive. I'd heard plenty of conversations about money. When the electric bill arrived every month, Daddy paid it grudgingly, harkening back to the good old days of oil lamps. The coal in the grate came from a pile in the barn, and anyone could see it was almost gone. Food appeared not only from the glass jars that mother put up, but also from Huff's Market up the street. Huffy expected cold hard cash, and I doubted there was enough money in my mother's purse to cover our needs much longer.

I knew finances had bottomed out when on a bitterly cold Saturday in late November my mother informed

Barbara and me that we were going to Wolf Creek. My sister objected at first, but we could see the pleading in Mother's eyes. I realized with the clarity of an observant six-year-old that, rational or not, the thought of being alone with my father in the backwoods frightened her.

—————««)»————

The heater in the car did a poor job of competing with the raw weather, and random flakes gusted against the windshield. We left the paved highway and turned up a bumpy gravel road leading to a passage gate marking the beginning of the Jenkins property. I had a flashback from the winter I lived with my grandparents and our visit here in the hearse. Grandma believed her cousin, Lizzie Curry, who had inherited neighboring land, had encroached upon Grandma's forty acres when she rebuilt line fences. The adults stood outside the vehicles in the cold and argued about property lines. Grandma was passionate about retaining every inch belonging to her. Once Armageddon was a triumphant memory and New Earth her dwelling, Grandma intended to enjoy unencumbered acreage for eternity.

Barbara got out and swung the gate open so Mother could drive through. As we bounced over the rutted ground toward a run-down house built on stilts, we could see a thin trail of gray smoke drifting from the stone chimney and disappearing into a sky the same color. Two inquisitive goats, tall and limber-legged, emerged from under the house and trotted toward us. Their whiskers twitched, and their ears perked with interest. Fearing their wicked horns, I stayed behind Mother as we approached, but the goats seemed content to stand and watch. Caked mud darkened their bristly winter coats; their mouths were busy on some invisible cud.

Stone steps led to a sagging door. Warmth from the coal and wood range and the whistling of a tea kettle told us my father wasn't far away. Mother's hands shook as she lit a cigarette, using a wooden kitchen match, and moved the teakettle aside to silence it. Boxes were stacked against the walls, along with tools and detritus. The adjoining room smelled of mothballs; a sagging bed was heaped with dark woolen comforters. Garments hung from nails in the wall.

Outside again, we heard Daddy's ax striking a metal wedge. As we eased down the uneven path beyond the barn, he came into view amidst a stand of scrub oaks and maples along the creek. The air was damp and still, the creek flowing freely from fall rains. The woods stretched on and on, dark and thick, even with the branches bare. My father had stripped down to his undershirt; his sweaty back was toward us, and if it hadn't been for the goats, tripping past, we might have touched him before he sensed we were there.

But the goats got his attention, and he turned and took in the three of us, and we must have made a fine parade. Barbara was scowling, in part from fear of the hovering goats. She had purchased a navy pea coat and saddle shoes that fall, thanks to Aid to Dependent Children. Bright auburn hair fluffed around her face, and her cheeks were red. By contrast, all of the color had drained out of Mother. Her hair was graying, and the cut Barbara had attempted showed up ragged in the brutal light. I was every bit as shabby. My coat was last year's, worn at the cuffs and tight in the shoulders. The only pair of shoes I owned left red creases where the straps bit in. "Hello, Raymond," Mother said, and I was amazed at her civility.

"Hello, Leona," he returned, equally neutral. The dark hair fell limp across his forehead. "Hi, Punkin," he said to me. Barbara received a slight nod. He picked up a flannel shirt. The goats put their noses against his chest like dogs.

"You know why we're here," Mother said. Her hand, wrapped around mine, was icy, and I could smell the cigarettes on her coat.

Instead of answering, he picked up his ax, wedge, and sharpening stone and started up the path, taking the slope with long strides. He and the prancing goats reached the house first, and he had already put wood on the fire and moved the kettle to the front of the range by the time we arrived. He took a coffee can from the old kitchen cupboard, fished out a roll of bills, peeled off several, and handed them to Mother. "Get her a coat, for God's sake," he said before turning back to the stove and adjusting the damper.

I could hear the new wood crackle as the draft opened. He dipped water from a bucket on the little table into a wash pan and submerged his hands, his back to us. Mother had the bills in one hand, but she still held mine with the other. I could sense her frustration. She never could tell Daddy what was really on her mind, and that wasn't likely to change.

Secure and territorial, the goats watched as we got back into the car and pulled slowly away. Wishing to avoid their rude stares, I crunched down in the seat and unbuckled the too-small shoes. Then, straightening, I tucked my cold legs under my skirt. Once we were through the gate and Barbara had climbed back into the car, Mother handed her the bills and nervously lit another cigarette. She eased the Plymouth down the tracks past the Curry house. Face pressed against the side window, I watched the goats frisking behind the gate and the house with its curling gray smoke until all receded out of sight.

As it turned out, my mother didn't have to use the money to buy me a coat. The Stark family across the street had a daughter who had outgrown some clothes. Mrs. Stark brought over a couple of grocery bags full and said she would like to give them to me, if my mother wouldn't be offended. As soon as our neighbor left, we emptied the bags. A winter coat with matching snow pants, a couple of dresses, a sweater or two, and corduroy overalls covered the worn living room sofa like manna from heaven. With money Daddy had given her, Mother bought me a pair of saddle shoes just like Barbara's with room to wiggle my toes.

The rest of our needs were not so easily met, once the money disappeared into coal and electricity and food. One Saturday morning, Mother, Grandpa Hosom, and I drove to a saw mill near Zanesville and picked up wood scraps to use as kindling. By the time we filled the trunk, the rear suspension hung low. Back home, Barbara had made potato soup which we ate with oyster crackers and gusto.

Christmas arrived unheralded, save by the Yuletide trumpet on a card from Uncle Donald in California. We had a scrub tree, purchased on Christmas Eve. It sat on the sewing machine cabinet in the living room and we decorated it with one string of lights, a few bulbs, and strands of tinsel which sold for ten cents a box. As for the meager gifts under the tree, Barbara had used most of her December ADC check, and my Hosom grandparents had contributed what they could from their Social Security allotments.

In January, Mother faced another decision. She could journey to Wolf Creek on icy roads, trusting the fumes left in the gas tank to get us there. Or she could abandon her last remnant of pride and ask Mr. Huff to let us have groceries on time. I was with her the day she walked up the slushy sidewalk to the market. By contrast to the chill outside, the store felt oven-warm, and the pungent odor of freshly sliced ham mingled with the scents of spices and oranges. Mother stood at the corner of the meat counter where Mr. Huff was working and explained our situation. Huffy listened with a thoughtful expression, rubbed his chin, and called to the woman restocking cans near the grocery counter. When she came over, he said. "Elsie, start an account for Mrs. Rippey."

Chapter 7

WHEN WINTER BROKE, Aunt Edie and Uncle Hank visited from Canton. Assessing our situation, my aunt told Mother to file for divorce on grounds of desertion and mental cruelty. That brought to boiling the simmering beast in Grandma Hosom's breast. Divorce was a direct violation of the vow Mother had made before God, and if she rued the day she had married my father, it was her cross to bear. There had been a day when Aunt Edie would have agreed, being nearly as hidebound as Grandma. But her job as charge nurse on hospital wards had taught her a thing or two about life. Given Hank's abuse, one might argue that she ought to take her own advice. But Hank's health was failing, making it easier to keep him away from the bottle. And as sole wage earner, Edith held the purse strings.

Mother ignored Grandma's predictions about her immortal soul. On a chilly March morning in 1953, Mother and I took the Greyhound commuter bus to Zanesville to visit the attorney who would serve as her advocate in the divorce action. Why did she take me along? Maybe if the attorney, Mr. Hollingsworth, saw in tangible form the child for whom Raymond was responsible, it would make her case for desertion stronger. Or maybe, given the fact that any situation outside her limited comfort zone compounded my mother's timidity, another presence, even a child's, bolstered her courage.

The lawyer's waiting room was similar to a doctor's, minus the antiseptic smell. As we waited in the outer office, I watched the secretary typing and taking calls, her long red nails hard and sharp. A portly man wearing a solemn dark suit and a shirt even whiter and stiffer than my father's ushered us through a doorway. When he took my mother's hand, gold cufflinks flashed at his wrist. Seated, Mother explained her situation and Mr. Hollingsworth nodded sympathetically. My father, he cautioned, once he had heard her out, would likely contest her action. Only part of their conversation made sense to me, so I examined the wall filled with pictures of men in suits, all smiling and shaking hands with Attorney Hollingsworth, and numerous framed documents with fancy script impossible for me to decipher.

Eventually, we were back outside where a gusty March wind made dirt devils from the street debris. We had a couple of hours before the return bus ride to Duncan Falls, and since something else had been troubling Mother, there was no time like the present to take care of it. We walked the few blocks to what had once been an opulent residence, now serving as office space for three obstetricians, one of them Dr. Daw, the man who had delivered me. The issue that had troubled Mother, even before my birth, was narcolepsy. She had always worried that I was at risk. I knew this, not because she had said so, but as I knew most things, picking up a word here and a word there and piecing them together. It would have been more convenient to take me to Philo, but something told me we had made our last visit to Dr. Thompson.

Standing with me in front of Dr. Daw's desk, Mother quickly explained the reason for our impromptu visit. Had she observed any symptoms? Dr. Daw asked from his desk chair. Her answer was negative. He motioned for me to stand beside him, and he looked directly and searchingly into a pair of clear blue eyes that returned his scrutiny with equal intensity. After a second or two, he placed his hand on my head and said, "Nothing's wrong with this girl."

"What about later, when she's older?" My mother had waited a long time for answers. Narcolepsy had shown up in at least two successive generations. And Daddy had seemed fine until he tumbled from the hayloft at fourteen. As a barber, he took medicine so he wouldn't slash someone's neck with a straight razor, but away from the shop, he ignored the pills. My mother had watched him drive away in his pickup numerous times, shaking her head at his disregard for human life. She had to know whether I was in danger of a similar fate.

Turning to her, Dr. Daw was emphatic. "She's fine and she'll stay fine. Don't worry, Mother."

Dr. Daw had made no examination beyond staring into my eyes, but Mother's belief in his knowledge and integrity gave her assurance. She was buoyant as we left his office and emerged onto a street where the wind had calmed and an early gloom had turned the buildings which crowded against each other into canyon walls. Traffic moving between them had become a river of headlights. When Mother decided to use the change remaining in her purse for a treat at the bus station, I could hardly believe it, but she tripped along the sidewalk, swinging my hand, as if she hadn't a care in the world. Later, of course, I would understand. Mother was soon to face a courtroom battle she had little chance of winning, real security was but a pipedream, and the specter of depression hung over her always. But on that somber March evening, she had at least one thing to celebrate. And celebrate she would.

The next several months blur together in my memory. There were trips to Zanesville to see Mr. Hollingsworth, but I don't know where the money came from to pay him. Aunt Edie may have contributed, and Mother's two brothers. Homer and Jim both had good jobs and had replaced the engine in the Plymouth when it went bad, refusing payment and covering the cost of the engine. Without exception, the entire Hosom family considered marrying Raymond Rippey Leona's most grievous error.

After Daddy received notice of the divorce action, he returned to Duncan Falls from time to time, more as a visitor than a resident. He hired another Zanesville attorney and set about refuting the charges. Grudgingly, he paid the outstanding bill at Huff's Market and made irregular hand-outs to Mother for household expenses. Even one with limited understanding would surely have pondered the obvious: Wouldn't accepting money put Mother in a vulnerable spot?

How could she say he wasn't supporting us? Did her attorney know he was paying the bills again? I couldn't ask these questions because I was just a kid and oblivious to how the law worked, but someone should have. And what about proving mental cruelty? To a judge, the testimony of combatants would come across as the classic he said, she said.

Even if my seven year old mind couldn't comprehend all that was going on, I knew in my bones that Mother was headed for a tough fight. The trial was scheduled for September, and as the summer passed, she appeared increasingly apprehensive, as if she felt what I did. The best case scenario, of course, would be my father supporting us in Duncan Falls while he lived elsewhere. And while Mother yearned for a rosy outcome, I knew she feared the worst. She would be stuck under Raymond's thumb for a lifetime.

For me, the summer of 1953 was a paradox of great drama and unrelenting sameness. Duncan Falls, always stained with coal dust and smoke and littered with ashes and cinders, added humidity to the mix in summer. Only a hint of breeze penetrated the house many days. Except for the absence of the burning sun, nights were equally oppressive. On the worst nights, Barbara, Mother, and I slept in the back yard on a pallet of heavy comforters to keep the damp away. Snuggling under the quilt, protected from crawling intruders by the presence of my mother on one side and my sister on the other, I stared at the starry sky. I usually fell asleep listening to radio dramas such as *The Great Gildersleeve*, *The Green Hornet*, or *Amos'n Andy*.

There wasn't much money for extras, but the variety store across from Huff's Market had bottles of soda, wet and icy from their metal tank; along with a five-cent bag of chips, one of those made a rare treat. And summer demanded the occasional Dream Sickle, Fudge Bar, or Ice Cream Drumstick. As I approached the start of my second grade year, I had new dresses, ordered from Alden's catalogue, new shoes, and a fat yellow tablet that smelled like school. All summer I had enjoyed a steady stream of books via the library bookmobile and anticipated that the second grade reading series would be an improvement over first grade's.

⟫⟨●⟩⟪

The actual day of the divorce hearing finally arrived. For the time being, Daddy was back on the Ridge and working in a barber shop in McConnelsville, probably on the advice of counsel, as he and his attorney worked to disarm Mother's divorce action. Since I didn't see him on D-Day, I can't speak to his demeanor, but my mother was a nervous wreck. Dressed in church clothes, feet squeezed into dress pumps, she looked fine on the outside, except for the steady stream of cigarettes burning down to her fingers. Until that day, I had worried that Barbara or I might have to go to court. Instead, Barbara took the bus across the river to the high school, and I walked to the elementary on my own once Mother saw me across the busy thoroughfare that passed our house.

Early fall is a lovely time in Ohio, past the miserable heat of summer and before the serious chill of autumn proper. The maple leaves were just beginning to turn and would soon be brilliant yellow. I wore a cardigan over my cotton dress and trudged up the sloping street toward a school day that would find me preoccupied. As much as I loved the atmosphere of chalkboards and reading circles and the smell of purple ink on mimeographed papers still damp from the copier, I had less than my usual acuity for snatching up ideas and fitting them into the knowledge I had already attained.

Finally, the long day over, I made my way home among all the children eager for after school snacks and outside games. Chattering and trading friendly punches, they were oblivious to the turmoil inside my head as I mulled over what it would mean if my parents were no longer married. Mother had told me I might have to visit my father wherever he lived, and the uncertainty made me shiver with nerves.

When I reached the house, I could hear voices coming from the back porch, so I went around the side to where my Hosom grandparents were seated in the buggy seat swing and Mother was sitting on the floor boards, her bare feet swollen and sore as they rested on the section of cement separating the porch from the shop. Her cigarette glowed red as she took a drag, and the smoke, released through her nostrils, made its way upward in a slow gray coil. She had been crying, so I knew that she and Daddy were still married. I wouldn't have to visit him on Olivet Ridge or anywhere else. Feeling guilty at my intense relief and sorry for my mother at the same time, I sat down next to her and snuggled against her side. My grandparents' expressions were grim, as they anticipated the next installment in the Raymond versus Leona saga.

"The judge dismissed the case on lack of evidence," she

said. The words weren't for me, but for her, as if through repetition they would somehow lose their intensity. "According to Mr. Hollingsworth, Raymond's attorney and the judge are Lodge buddies. Even though I lost, he says I don't have to cook for him or wash his clothes or sleep with him—I don't even have to talk to him if I don't want to. Isn't that a fine how-do-you-do?" She hiccupped on the last word, a sort of laugh turned into a sob.

Grandpa chewed his tobacco thoughtfully, and then shifted the wad to his cheek, got up from the swing, and spit into the gravel which caught the rain run-off from the porch roof. He squared his narrow shoulders, waiting for Grandma to hoist her considerable weight out of the buggy seat. Grandma's parting remark, "Marry in haste, repent at leisure," made my mother angry enough to get up from the porch floor, dust off her backside, and go in to start supper.

Chapter 8

HAVING DADDY BACK in the house added a level of tension. He reclaimed his upstairs quarters, but didn't reopen the barber shop. Instead he hired on at a shop in Zanesville and daily thumbed a ride to work to save the cost of driving. Mother didn't follow her lawyer's advice about not cooking for him or refusing to do his laundry, and of course they talked—not much maybe, but civilly. What I never understood was why Daddy fought the divorce. If he really didn't want to live with us, why not welcome the chance to be rid of us? Either way, he would have had to support me and maybe Mother too. On Saturday nights, my parents sat down at the kitchen table, and he counted out money for household expenses. Mother was able to get herself some much needed clothing and shoes by saving what was left over after she bought groceries, and she was no longer dependent upon Grandpa Hosom for her smokes.

Even though Grandma Hosom avoided the house when my father was there, she kept in close contact, knowing as well as I did that Mother's stiff upper lip was all for show. Visiting Mother and attending church were all the social contacts Grandma desired, but Grandpa liked to get out and take in the sights. Early in the evening when the weather was nice, I sometimes joined him. Grandpa's favorite hike was across the bridge to the railroad tracks. At five o'clock a commuter train passed through Philo on its daily route from Parkersburg to Zanesville and back. We could hear the Doodlebug's whistle long before it came into view. Sometimes it made a quick stop to drop a passenger or two. Grandpa and I always waved at the engineer and watched the red caboose disappear around the out-going curve before we headed back across the river.

Summer and fall, Grandpa escaped Grandma and the stuffy green trailer by working at Carter's farm and apple orchard a mile north of Duncan Falls. Rooted in country ways, he walked to and from work until the autumn weather turned unpredictable. Then Mother gave him a lift and I rode along. The original Carter farmhouse, a one-story dwelling with vertical siding and a continuous porch encircling the front and both sides, fascinated me. Lace curtains hung at the long, low windows, and through them I could make out silhouettes of furniture. Mother told me that the house had twelve rooms. One day, I promised myself, I would have a house that vast.

At Carter's, autumn meant grading apples and cider. A long conveyer belt passed through the sorting area, which was in the basement of the old house. Less than perfect fruit was plucked off the belt and tossed into a box. Those were the apples Mother bought, saving out the best for eating fresh. Others she pared and turned into applesauce and pies, scenting the entire house with cinnamon and nutmeg. If the cider press was in operation, we lingered so I could watch. A bucketful of aromatic apples was dumped into the top of the machine and dropped to a pressing table which squeezed out pure, golden cider to be funneled into glass jugs and sealed with corks. Mother kept a jug of cider around the house long after it had lost its sweetness and relished the tartly sour nips she took from time to time.

No longer troubled over how divorce might change our lives, I could put my mind to other business. At school, I watched the teacher walk up and down the aisles handing out an armful of workbooks, and I thought that had to be the coolest thing ever. I wanted a big wooden desk and a chalkboard just like hers. As my father started spending his evenings beside the fireplace, I snared him to play school with me, and that's when I learned that Grandma Rippey had wanted to be a teacher too. Daddy scavenged a chalkboard and put it on an easel, and I was elated. As a second grader, I had no idea the significance of this make-believe role. I knew teachers controlled their classrooms and vaguely realized that some people could do that and some could not. Since I hadn't yet learned words like self-assurance, the elusive entity which I recognized in my teacher but failed to see in my mother had no name, but I wanted it.

About the same time, I learned what it was like to lose myself in a book. I brought home a library book one afternoon and curled up in a rocker beside the fireplace. The story was about an abandoned lighthouse and the mysterious lights which appeared there. Before I knew what was happening, Mother was telling me supper was ready. When I'd started reading, the room had been bright with daylight. To my amazement, it had grown dark outside, and the lamp on the library table cast its light on my page. Returning from the world of the story was like coming home from a far, far place.

———————⊷«◉»⊶———————

On the surface, things at home were better, but several afternoons when I came in from school, bringing cold air and cinders, I found Mother lying on the sofa, her cigarette smoldering in an ashtray, along with a cup of coffee gone cold. Close up, I could see the pulse pounding in her neck. "It's just nerves," she assured me each time. Sometimes the spells ended quickly; sometimes they lasted for hours. Barbara was aware of the problem, and Daddy had to be suspicious, although Mother was up and in the kitchen when he came home, regardless of how she felt. Why didn't she see a doctor about what she called her palpitations? Anyone ever committed to a mental institution would never ask that question. The boundary separating a physical defect from a mental one is easily breached, and the admission of any irregularity may prove a slippery slope leading to the loss of freedom. Distrust of my father was deeply ingrained in her and with good reason.

Mother was also in dire need of dental care. Fillings fell out, teeth broke off, gums became inflamed and roots abscessed. Her teeth had so long been neglected that there was only one solution, extraction and dentures. About that time, Daddy had his teeth extracted and dentures fitted, so it stood to reason that Mother should follow suit. But when she brought up the subject, his response was short and sweet: No money for teeth. She could have hers extracted if she chose, but he wasn't buying dentures. When she asked him why he'd bought them for himself, he said he had to look presentable for work. The importance of her appearance and health and her value as a human being could not have been made clearer. Mother had seen enough people whose mouths were shrunken and withered from lack of teeth, so she opted to keep what teeth she had, even as they continued to poison her.

Quite honestly, I don't know how my mother endured for as long as she did. A trooper, she attended PTA meetings, mother-daughter banquets, awards programs—all of it. A lover of movies, she took Barbara and me to Zanesville, where we would see a show, shop a little, and have lunch at Katsamps, a family-owned restaurant that catered to the lunch crowd. A wizard with the budget, Mother financed these outings by accumulating left over grocery money. As a child, I could appreciate some of what Mother was going through and wish she were happier, but the resiliency and self-centeredness of youth allowed me the semblance of a normal childhood. Barbara, older and aligned with one side exclusively, hated my father for his cruelty, served up under the guise of twisted reasoning. If there had been any way for her to live with either our grandparents or Aunt Edie, she would have left the premises.

As long as they moved in separate circles, my parents could tolerate each other. When they collided, it usually involved me. For example, when Mother received notice from the school that I was to be inoculated against polio, she made the mistake of telling Daddy. He threw a fit. No child of his was going to be a guinea pig for science. Instead of going public with his objections, he ordered Mother to send a note refusing permission. Mortified, she did as she was instructed. I was the only child who didn't have a sore arm on shot days, and this put me in an awkward spot too. Being Raymond Rippey's daughter wasn't as difficult as being his wife, but it was no walk in the park either.

My father's lack of judgment showed up in other ways. While working in Zanesville, he heard about a foreman job on a crew clearing right-of-way for power lines. The money sounded good and the chance to be the boss sounded even better. Imagining himself a leader of men, he interviewed for the job. Well-spoken and not above dissembling as he saw fit, he convinced the superintendent and was hired. At first, he was full of bravado, but soon came the complaining and the excuses. Everything that went wrong was someone else's fault. The job lasted a month. A talented barber with a load of entertaining verbiage and a strong client base, he talked the shop owner in Zanesville into taking him back, and most of his regulars returned.

<hr/>

An annual distraction refocused my mother and grand-mother's attention each summer, as a roving band of strangers paraded down Main Street in gaudy old trucks and trailers, men at the steering wheels, women in colorful shawls and scarves, children barefoot and skinny. Vigilant residents of Duncan Falls watched askance as the gypsies made camp along the Muskingum River, where those on the lowest rungs of the social ladder lived in run-down houses as insubstantial as their livelihood.

I heard the stories over and over how gypsies were inclined to steal children, slip merchandise off the shelves, and cast spells in an unintelligible language. They could appear at your backdoor bartering trinkets for food, or they might just help themselves to corn and tomatoes from your garden. If you raised chickens, you'd better pen them up early. In some towns, they were escorted right on out by keepers of the peace.

Eventually, the gypsies always moved on, as suddenly and unexpectedly as they had appeared. My mother and grandmother would breathe a sigh of relief as the caravan emerged from the dirt road along the river, entered Main Street, and headed out of town. The drivers and passengers looked exactly as they had when they arrived, bare-limbed children still thin and brown. No freshly killed chickens hung from conveyances, and if vegetables or store goods had been stolen, the evidence was well hidden. Instead of relief, what I had begun to feel when the gypsies left town was a vague sense of sadness. I hadn't seen the gypsies do any of the things people said they did. Were they bad people just because they were different?

There were so many things I wondered about as I observed the behaviors of adults. One of them was money, something that bothered Mother a lot. Even with Daddy working regular hours in Zanesville and thumbing a ride to work and back, her budget was limited, yet a lot more money than she ever saw passed through his hands every week. Where was it going? Despite his stinginess with Mother, he liked to appear a man of generosity, handing out money to random strangers if they had a bleak enough story. And there was no one he more wanted to impress than his mother and his sister. Irked as she was with his tight-fisted hold on the strings, Mother made sure that I had decent clothes and sufficient supplies for school before he got a chance to hand his money off to either of the women she saw as her competition. She didn't have to worry about money for Barbara. My sister used her ADC checks wisely and supplemented her income with babysitting. As for her own needs, Mother managed to stay one step above disreputable through genius level budgeting.

Daddy, on the other hand, reveled in being a natty dresser. He headed off to work every day in a crisp white shirt, necktie, and sharply creased pants. I remember one time when he made a big production of purchasing what he called a suit of clothes, more commonly known as a business suit. At a men's store in Zanesville, Mother and I watched as he decided on the weight and color and cut. He was in his element, sounding off as one who knew a great deal about gentlemen's attire. Mother observed it all in her bargain basement shoes and the green wool coat that had served her for all the years I could remember. I didn't know the word yet for what bothered me about Daddy's brand new suit beside Mother's old, worn coat. But the impression was similar to what I had begun to feel about the gypsies. I guess you could say that injustice was an emerging concept.

Chapter 9

PEOPLE WITH NO more worldly goods than we had usually have a hard time finding people with less. Grandma Rippey's brother, Albert Jenkins, lived on a run-down farm out back of Philo. Albert looked the part of grisly old hillbilly, and his raw-boned wife, Mamie, carried the load of gardening, cooking, washing, canning—all the labors of a farm wife even if the farmer didn't farm. For some reason, Mother had taken a liking to Mamie and her daughter, Bernice, who was only a few years older than Barbara. At fifteen, Bernice had given birth to a baby boy, Tommy, three years younger than I. Tommy had bright red hair and tons of freckles, the very picture of the man who had impregnated Bernice and then disappeared. A high school dropout saddled with an illegitimate child, Bernice found herself with zero prospects of either job or husband.

By her senior year, Barbara had lost her waif-like thinness and acquired a well-rounded figure. Wondering what to do with the clothing she had outgrown, Barbara thought of Bernice, who remained skinny as a broom. So she carefully packed the garments in a couple of brown grocery sacks, and on an oppressively hot August afternoon, she asked Mother to drive her out to visit Bernice. Naturally, I tagged along.

No breeze at all stirred the ancient trees shielding the farmhouse as Mother shifted down and turned into the driveway. Albert was on the front porch, chewing his tobacco, his long-sleeved flannel shirt and bib overalls defying the heat index. Dangling his legs over the edge of the high porch sat Tommy, red hair glowing as if lit from inside, freckles in sharp relief against white skin. The whine of the Plymouth's engine and the rattle of cinders against its fenders brought Mamie and Bernice to the kitchen door. Both women were streaked with sweat, and tendrils of dark hair clung to Bernice's face. Heat from the kitchen flooded toward us as we approached the door, seeking to dissolve itself in the comparative coolness of August shade.

A big pot of tomatoes bubbled front and center on the coal and wood range. On the right hand side, away from the firebox, sat a row of Mason jars upside down on a dish towel, waiting to be filled. Custom demanded that Mother join in the kitchen work. Custom also prompted Mamie to send Bernice to fetch fresh water from the well and offer us cold drinks while she ladled the jars full and topped them with one of the flats floating in water. Mother took each hot jar from Mamie, held it in a folded towel, and twisted the metal ring tight enough to ensure a seal.

With nothing else to do, I took in the kitchen. Soot darkened the ceiling and wall near the cook stove, and the board floor sagged. Rain-streaked windows were propped up with sticks, but the faded curtains were as motionless as the trees outside. A wooden table and mismatched chairs, a kitchen cupboard that used to be white, and a stand beside the back door under a wavy mirror made up the furnishings. There wasn't even an ice-box, and I wondered where they kept cold things, but I knew I'd get a jerk on the arm from Barbara if I voiced my curiosity.

At our house, we stocked the ice box with a huge, frozen rectangle from the ice house up the street at least once a week, more often in summer. Sometimes we took the car and the ice man transferred the block to our towel-covered trunk. If the weather was cool, we used my wagon and wrapped the ice in a blanket for its trip home. I was allowed to step into the ice house and help myself to a chunk to suck on. The cold, steamy air smelled of closed space and metal.

Mother wasn't a stellar housekeeper, but she was meticulous about the kitchen. Hot, sudsy water in an oval dish pan turned dirty dishes to squeaky clean, even before they were scalded with boiling water from the teakettle. Dishtowels were changed out frequently. By contrast, in Mamie's house, a long-standing film had attached itself to all the surfaces, and the odor of mildew combined with a sour staleness permeated the atmosphere. I would learn to associate this smell with a kind of poverty as different from ours as daylight from dark.

After the women had finished the tomatoes, we joined Albert on the front porch. He acknowledged our presence with a nod, and Tommy scurried to Bernice and buried his face in her damp lap. Mamie pulled Tommy away from his mother and gestured the girls into the front room of the house. I was beyond surprise when Barbara grabbed my hand and included me in the business of girls and clothes.

Anticipation made two red spots burn in Bernice's cheeks. She stripped down to a slip translucent from many washings and tried on her new clothing, turning this way and that to pick up the reflection in the glass door of an ancient, loose-jointed secretary, the grandest piece in the room.

I hadn't yet learned much about the human need for dignity and respect, but my sister's generosity, not only in dispensing her hand-me-downs where they would do the most good, but in the way she shared the garments—not as cast-offs, but as pieces she regretted having outgrown—taught me a great lesson.

⸺•◦•⸺

It was 1953, and Barbara had just begun her senior year when she started dating Russell North, adding another twist to the plot of our inexplicable lives. The quiet, dark-haired boy pulled up in front of the house a couple of times a week and waited in the car while Barbara grabbed her sweater and purse and sailed out the door before my father could offer one of his put-downs. My mother remembered when the North family had lived near her parents and Edie in McConnelsville. Russell's father had deserted his family, so at sixteen, Russell quit school and took a job with Bartlett's Tree Service, becoming man of the house and fully supporting his mother and two younger sisters. Where Russell was concerned, Daddy's nasty remarks were way off base.

Following her graduation from Philo High School, Barbara took a secretarial job for a jeweler in Zanesville.

When Daddy wasn't home, Russell would come into the kitchen for a cup of coffee and a cigarette with Mother. I stopped worrying about Barbara; Russell wasn't the kind of guy to cause problems. The following summer, he gave her a diamond ring. You hear it said that people in love have a glow; well, Barbara had a glow. At nine years old, even I could see the change in her. Making her own money, Barbara began filling an old trunk with dishes and linens and tableware. She would begin her married life living in the same house as Russell's mother and sisters, but her hope chest bespoke a time when she would be mistress of her own space.

Naturally, there had to be a downside. Grandma Hosom and Aunt Edie had predicted that Barbara, given her condition at birth, would never be able to have children. With marriage imminent, Aunt Edie showed up to insist that Barbara be examined by a gynecologist. Barbara had never told Russell about any of this, and bringing up the subject was beyond her. Mother, in one of her finest moments, not only took Barbara to see Dr. Daw but spoke to Russell privately when he showed up that evening. Instead of running out to Russell's car at the curb, Barbara sat nervously behind the bedroom door, and Mother motioned him into the living room.

Mother explained about Barbara's premature birth and its aftereffects, the scarred belly and lack of a navel, along with the concerns Grandma and Aunt Edie had harbored for nineteen years. Thankfully, she was able to tell him that Dr. Daw had pronounced Barbara fully capable of giving birth. Russell listened patiently until Mother finished.

"Is that all?" he asked, his features smoothing. Who knew

what the poor guy had been thinking, pulled aside for a tete-a-tete with his soon-to-be mother-in-law. Mother disappeared into the kitchen, Barbara emerged from the bedroom, and she and Russell headed up Route 60, another tragedy averted. Mother always said Grandma could make a mountain out of a molehill, and I had no trouble believing it.

Until Russell came along, happiness had been in short supply in my sister's life. With him, she finally had the home and family she'd been denied growing up, and she never forgot how blessed she was in her choice of mate. Steady as the sunrise, Russell North provided the finest example of a good husband.

Chapter 10

WHILE FAMILY AND neighborhood dramas were playing out, I was developing a social life. A few doors up the street lived Janet, two years behind me in school. Our friendship was based on proximity and my love of television. Because of Janet, I got to see *The Lone Ranger*, *Roy Rogers*, *Howdy Doody*, *Zorro*, and *Superman*—essentials for a kid in the fifties. We adored *The Mickey Mouse Club* from its first airing and arranged our afternoons around it. Janet also had a bedroom full of well-cared-for dolls. The few I had were left in pitiful stages of neglect, a fact which didn't bode well for future offspring, if conventional wisdom was to be believed.

Despite the TV and the dolls, Janet's life wasn't any more perfect than mine. Every morning, her father could be heard coughing up the phlegm of emphysema. Her brother had muscular dystrophy and lived in a wheelchair. A hoist made of steel bars and a cranking device transferred him from bed to chair to toilet seat, saving wear and tear on his mother's back. Their plight made me thankful, not so much for what I had as for what I had escaped.

You could say I made friends at school, but there was a difference—sometimes subtle, sometimes obvious—between me and the other girls in my class. For one thing, they had nice homes, fathers nobody laughed at, mothers who could smile and show their teeth, and siblings with the same last name. My mother did a good job of making me look like the others, but even when I was included in activities, a cultural gap remained. If I complained to Mother, all she said was, "Life isn't fair." That answer never failed to tick me off. *Why wasn't life fair?*

The most defining event was my first and last slumber party. Six girls invaded my classmate Joan's house and did all the normal, sleeper-over things. Then it was bath time, and girls paired off, leaving me odd-girl-out. Two by two, everyone stripped and giggled and splashed. When my turn came, I closed the door and bathed alone. No one knocked on the door; no one wanted to hang out and talk; no one cared. If I had ever hoped to be included, the party at Joanie's was the capper to that.

My favorite friend from Duncan Falls, though, saw only one difference between us and since I never suggested he play girl games, the difference did not matter. An inventive thinker, Stevie was a misfit too. He looked at the playhouse Daddy had constructed out of the abandoned chicken coop and saw a ship, the sloping roof the deck in high gale. Inside was the engine compartment or, some days, the belly of a submarine. Stevie and I were alternately buccaneers, pirates, and commanders of a World War II naval operation. The playhouse also gave us a venue for revisiting the movies. The director perched on the roof for a panoramic view of the studio set. On the ground below, the cast of one acted out the scenes. I was supreme at shouting orders, and Stevie was by far the better actor. He nailed the Little Tramp's stiff-legged gait and twirling walking stick. Imagining a bowler hat, mustache, and black suit was no trouble.

During bad weather, Stevie and I transformed the living room into the newspaper offices of the *Dailey Planet*, with you know who playing Clark Kent, aka Superman, and Jimmy Olson. I, of course, was Lois Lane. Production of the *Planet* required a stack of newspapers and the piano bench. Slamming the lid down on old newspapers morphed their headlines into news bytes of colliding meteors or alien invasions. Other times, we placed Mother's two overstuffed rockers front to front and safety-pinned a blanket over the top. Piano bench in front, we braved dangers of the Old West in stagecoach or covered wagon. Stevie drove the horses while simultaneously shooting bad guys. I screamed a lot and kept both chairs in motion. About the time Stevie fell to the floor in the throes of death, Mother surrendered and offered food. That always worked for Stevie. He would eat anything and everything. A skinny, tow-headed boy with wide gray eyes, he had what my mother called a bottomless pit for a stomach.

———•((●))•———

The Carter girls across the street, Carrie, twelve, and Charlotte, slightly older, introduced me to another subculture the summer I turned eleven. Together, the sisters babysat for young mothers who entrusted their babies to them for an entire day. Still adolescents themselves, those mothers were desperate for a reprieve. Carrie knew all about babies, not just how to care for them, but how they were started in the first place. Before sharing the details, she informed me that nobody my age could possibly be so stupid. I guess I was pretty naïve; it took me a while to figure out why Carrie wanted to associate with the chubby, unpopular kid across the street. The answer to the riddle was simple: Carrie enjoyed nothing so much as a patsy.

Charlotte hung out with a street savvy bunch that operated from a different set of standards. People who got good grades were an alien class. Sneaking cigarettes and smoking in the girls' bathroom at school was way cool. Climbing through a window in the dead of night to meet a boy guaranteed a hike in status. Boyfriends, of course, were wannabe tough guys with cigarettes hanging from their lips and long hair slicked into DAs. Any reference to boys or men spawned knowing looks among those girls. But under their sophistication lurked suspicion and unease. Something dark had left its mark. Something I would not understand until years later when I worked with girls who had a similar look.

One afternoon, Carrie introduced a new game. She tied a scarf around my eyes, grabbed my arm, and pulled me up the street. The ding of a gas pump signaled the filling station. The close-up smell of diesel and the hiss of air brakes meant we were passing the bus stop. But the purr of power mowers and the whoosh of cars were familiar sounds on any Duncan Falls street, and I soon lost my bearings. Then we headed downhill, and the sound of rushing water and the hum of tires on grating grew louder. When I felt grass under my feet instead of pavement, it was game over for me. I yanked my arm free and the blindfold off my face. Overhead was the bridge leading to Philo and below the frothing waters of the dam. Just how much closer to the river had she planned to take me?

My mother didn't approve of the Carters, and that was unusual since she seldom criticized anybody except Daddy and Grandma Rippey. Mrs. Carter, she said, was coarse. You could hear Mrs. Carter yelling at her daughters clear across the street. Evenings and days off, she wore a housecoat and high-heeled mules. And since she worked, a fact that made her suspect anyway, she left a lot of household chores to the girls.

I wandered over to their house one Saturday just as the family was finishing supper. Mrs. Carter hustled upstairs and Mr. Carter sat at the table, smoking his cigarette and reading the sports page. The girls were clearing the table and filling the sink while they argued over who would wash and who would dry. Carrie handed me the dish towel, dispute resolved. Mrs. Carter reappeared. "You look pretty, Mommy," Carrie said.

"Thank you, Baby," Mrs. Carter responded off-handedly, running fingers through slightly damp curls. She shook a cigarette out of her husband's pack, lit it with his butane lighter, and inhaled deeply before listing off what the girls were to accomplish while their parents were out for the evening: Mop the kitchen, scrub the bathroom, vacuum the carpets. Both girls groaned. "Just wait until you get married. Then you'll find out what work is," she said, tapping off ash into a saucer.

The first thought that entered my mind was this: "Maybe they will have kids to do all the work for them." To this day, I'm not sure whether I said the words or kept silent. I can only hope I exercised a level of discretion appropriate to the moment.

With Barbara married, I had claimed her single bed and dresser and created my own space. When Carrie came over, we hung around my end of the room, and she asked personal questions like why my parents didn't sleep together and if my sister had been pregnant when she got married. She fingered my possessions aligned on the dresser top, including a jar where I kept my allowance money. The day she asked for a glass of water, I was pretty sure what had happened while I was in the kitchen. After she left, I checked my money jar, and sure enough, several dollars were missing. That cooled the friendship for good, and I finished the summer before the start of my sixth grade year rereading my favorite books and pondering some of the changes I knew were coming. Other changes I could never have guessed.

Chapter 11

ONE SIGNIFICANT CHANGE had already taken place. Since my father worked in Zanesville, the only sign of life in the shop was when he went over to letter a sign or work on a landscape. A year earlier, a stranger, Harry Mason, had come to our house, asking about the vacant building. Mason said he had a contract with Ohio Power to supply chip wood, and he paid other men to do the cutting and hauling. The shop would give him a place to handle payroll and take business calls. My parents saw no reason to pass up a few extra dollars, so Mason hauled in a desk, had a phone installed, and posted a sign, "Mason's Contracting." After that, he seldom showed up, so wood haulers expecting payment came to our house. Mother had no idea what to tell them.

A month or so in, Mason offered Mother the job of paying the haulers. While she didn't mind earning a little money, she wasn't about to sit in an empty building waiting for drivers to show. So Mason's phone appeared in our living room, and chip wood haulers started showing up at irregular intervals, their huge trucks idling out front. Grandma Hosom declared the arrangement insane and forbade Mother to let the men in the house. Mother's kind heart wouldn't allow her to leave a hard-working laborer outside in rain or blistering cold. As the weather worsened, tired men warmed work-reddened hands at our fireplace while my mother smoothed out delivery slips, calculated their share of the haul, and wrote checks. In addition to the drop in room temperature and the influx of fresh air, there remained in their wake the scent of trees and gasoline and outdoor labor.

Then Mason had another idea. At no cost to us, he would build office space onto our house. It sounded fishy, even to me, but Daddy gave the go-ahead. Mason could have burned the house to the ground for all he cared. No one signed anything, but the footer was dug and the foundation was laid. The back porch disappeared, and wall studs went up, forming a space twice as large as the porch and boxing in a vacant spot between one kitchen wall and the rest of the new structure. Mother saw that space as ideal for the bathroom she had never had, and Mason obliged. It seemed too good to be true, a real bathroom! Daddy refused to use it, preferring the outhouse and a sponge bath in his upstairs man cave. It was just one more irony in the life and times of the Rippeys: Through a virtual stranger, we had finally gained a telephone and now a bathroom. Mother and I had no way of knowing how brief a time we would have to enjoy these conveniences.

———◦((◦))◦———

Other changes were more personal and more troubling. Even before the obvious signs of pubescence began, my thinking processes went through a transformation, opening possibilities at odds with what I had accepted as absolutes. At eleven, I became aware of scientific reality in a more immediate sense. I already knew about the Earth's rotation, the Sun at the center of the system, the planets and moons following in elliptical orbit—stuff to memorize for a test. It didn't become personal until my concept of the physical world changed from a reassuring amalgam of houses and streets into a whirling sphere blasting through black nothingness on a path which, if altered, would end existence. Galaxies stretched for unknowable distances. The night sky, heretofore a brilliant tapestry where I searched out the Big Dipper, became a dizzying reminder that nowhere in the universe existed a true *terra firma*. As if these realizations were not mind-boggling enough, an unsettling episode opened a frightening dimension to my newly shaken world view.

I was lying across my bed one summer evening, musing on whatever thoughts came randomly to mind. Outside the screen, light traffic passed through town. Once in a while someone walked by the house, feet crunching on cinders. My parents were reading in the next room, daily dramas on pause. Suddenly the room, its furnishings and its shadows, withdrew, leaving me engulfed in an utter awareness of self, singular and alone. A decision not my own had placed me in time and space. *I* existed. *I*, unique and separate, and yet part of a huge company of individuals sharing the same reality.

Heart racing, I was off the bed, through the door, and into the lamp-lit living room before I even knew I had moved. I stopped short of throwing myself against Mother, of burying my face in her shoulder. If I were to do that, she would know something was wrong, and I had no words to tell her. In matching overstuffed rockers and reading glasses, my parents were intent on their sections of *The Times Recorder*. From the ashtray, Mother's cigarette sent a diffusion of smoke into the shadows beyond the lighted circle. The sense of separation began to ease and I felt my heart-rate slowing.

Again, I was part of this place and these people who seemed surprised by a daughter's sudden appearance. No, I answered Mother's question, nothing was the matter. Daddy invited me to read the funnies with him, an activity that I had declared myself too old for. But that evening, I perched on the arm of his chair, not because I cared about Dagwood or Dick Tracy, but because I needed the reassurance of his barber shop smell and the familiar commentary he added as he read. I wasn't sure what to do with my new experience or where it fit in my understanding of things. Mental equilibrium returned, I put my encounter into the back of my mind, hoping it would never return.

⸻ ◈ ⸻

Overweight, hypertensive, and always in a tizzy, Grandma Hosom made a textbook case for a heart attack or, in her case, a stroke. The stroke was fairly mild, so following a short stay at Bethesda Hospital, Grandma returned to the green trailer, and my mother shared caretaking duties with Grandpa, even though her own summer hadn't been that great. The spells of tachycardia had become more pronounced, and writing checks for the wood haulers at uncertain hours limited her chance to rest and recover when the spells hit. And, as anyone who knew her could have predicted, invalidism made Mishie Hosom excessively demanding, and Grandpa bore the brunt of the challenge. But even a man as longsuffering as Grandpa needed a reprieve now and then, so he was slipping out one afternoon, when Grandma's voice halted his escape. "Where are you going, Claredon?" His reply, "I'm going down to piss in the river and watch it raise," didn't score him any points, but it did give him time to clear the door while Grandma thought of a comeback.

Despite the upheavals and the fact that my inactive summer had forced me into the next dress size, I was glad to be back in school. Until sixth grade, I'd never seen myself as a smart kid, possibly because the girls who visibly occupied that position had excluded me from their clique. Now, when my homework and test papers came back with A or A+ at the top, the smart kids took notice and asked me to join them at lunch and in group work. They must have hoped some of the fat girl's knowledge would rub off.

My short-lived popularity ended midway through September, on a day hot enough to be July. Classrooms were steamy, even with windows wide open. Teachers broke the rules and allowed drinking fountain breaks. The last period of the day, my music class was seated in a semi-circle of folding chairs, looking about as alert as slugs. The teacher stood beside the chalkboard, explaining note signatures.

I had been half-drowsing along with the rest of the flock, when it suddenly felt like the floor was sliding right out from under me. The outer range of my vision shrank, and my heart tried to jump out of my chest and then began to pound so hard I was sure everyone heard it. I must have looked stricken, because the teacher hurried to my chair and ushered me outside. My imagination went crazy: Was I dying? Was I going to pass out? Since the day was almost over, the principal covered the music class and the teacher walked me home. Mother met us at the door and agreed it was probably the heat that had caused my strange sensations.

That should have been the end of it. Instead, my fear of passing out went phobic. Every day, I asked teachers to open windows, and when the weather turned chilly, I carried wet paper towels in a plastic purse. If a dizzy spell hit, I pulled out a dripping towel and put it on my face. If the attack was bad, I ran from the room. When hysterical begging wore my mother down, I stayed home, if not for the whole day, at least until noon, cutting the risk of another panic attack at school in half.

As if I needed another complication, I began having strange visual episodes too. Everything would appear normal one moment; the next, my world became sepia-toned and glaring. Fluorescent lighting and cloudy days were nearly certain to trigger The Glare, affecting venues other than the classroom. Whenever it struck, I hid my face or ran to the shadows. In a matter of weeks, a model student became an incomprehensible neurotic. Looking back, I wonder if the disturbing episode of self-awareness I had experienced that night in the bedroom had somehow generalized into a hypersensitivity to my surroundings, including variations in lighting. Maybe there was a connection. Maybe not.

One thing was certain: I wasn't getting any sympathy from the primary teacher of sixth graders. Her responses to my strange behaviors were pursed lips and reprimands. Pleasing my teachers had always been a point of pride with me, but that was before my world had come crashing down. As things stood that fall and winter, a teacher's disapproval no longer fazed me. With more time at home, inactivity, and free rein on the fridge, I edged closer and closer to obesity.

My weight finally got Daddy's attention, and he felt compelled to tell me that fat was an ugly word for an ugly condition. When the rest of the story—panic attacks, poor school attendance, and The Glare—came out, he blamed Mother for neglecting me and insisted I see a doctor. He started with the optometrist and found I needed glasses, but even though the chalkboard cleared up, not so the inexplicable optic effects.

Grandma Hosom took time from her personal tragedy to comment on mine: She'd seen girls go off the deep end when facing the perils of imminent womanhood. But it would only get worse, she assured me. Pregnancy and childbirth endangered a woman physically, and melancholia and hysterics put her mind in jeopardy too. In its turn, The Change caused insanity in those whose minds were weak. If you could believe Grandma, a woman's lifespan was a gauntlet of terrors only the strongest survived. A good dose of Lydia Pinkham never hurt, either, she concluded, referencing a tonic for female complaints laced with forty-proof alcohol.

For Mother, overwhelmed by Grandma's care and interrupted at all hours by Mason's drivers, my situation was the last straw. She managed until February. Then the chest cold that landed her in bed came along and left her gaunt and lethargic afterward. Mason had to make other arrangements for his wood haulers, and Grandma and Grandpa had to fend for themselves. Barbara and Little Rusty spent a few days at our house, trying to bolster Mother's spirits, but she seemed no better. Once he heard about his sister's illness, Uncle Jim made speedy alterations to the sun porch on his house in Malta, creating a bedroom where his parents could stay while Grandma finished her recuperation. The first of March, Grandma Rippey came to help out. Her presence brightened my father's outlook, if not my mother's. Emotionally, physically, and psychologically, Mother's energy was spent. And in my heart, I knew that it was my irrational fears and bizarre behaviors which had tipped the balance against her.

Chapter 12

IN MID-MARCH, 1958, Daddy loaded clothing and necessities into the pick-up truck and transported the shreds of his family to Olivet Ridge. Grandpa Rippey had died four years earlier, and Grandma divided her time between the Ridge and McConnelsville, where Aunt Joyce had installed a bedroom and bath for her parents when Grandpa was ill. Grandma welcomed the chance to be needed.

It was cold and blustery and sunless when we arrived at Grandma's house, where the only sign of spring was a reddish cast to the tree limbs and a hint of budding on the weeping willow they had planted the spring I was born. Winter-dead grasses and neglected perennials cluttered the fence line, and the tulip poplar showed no attempt to renew itself. Marking the western boundary, gnarled apple trees appeared bleak and tortured in the overcast. Between house and barn remained piles of Grandpa's collectables—wooden spools, stacked crates, rusted machinery—still waiting for a purpose. If not for smoke issuing from both chimneys, no one would have guessed the house was occupied. But Grandma was there and had prepared bedrooms. Mother's was right off the living room. The rest of us would occupy the upstairs. Everything smelled of camphor and cleanliness.

As we settled in, Daddy's mood swung from stern to buoyant. This was no visit. Our clothing stuffed into grocery bags and my withdrawal from Duncan Falls Elementary School made this an official change in residence. Mother was worn out and took refuge in bed. Stepping into her room, I edged through the narrow space to sit beside her. She opened her eyes and made an effort to smile, but the bleakness of her situation wouldn't allow it. I kissed her cheek. "I'm sorry, Mommy," I whispered, the sense of guilt overwhelming me.

"It's not your fault, Honey. None of this is your fault." Exhausted, she closed her eyes against the gloom of evening, deepened by the green window blind.

In the kitchen, Grandma was pulling a pan of biscuits out of the oven, her cheeks pink from heat and exertion. On the stove top simmered a pan of pinto beans. In one skillet potatoes browned, and in another jowl bacon sizzled as much as its coating of flour would allow. This was typical of Grandma's meals, adequate, plain fare.

The first Monday on the Ridge, my father visited Windsor School, his alma mater, and enrolled me in sixth grade. He explained the reasons for changing schools and requested a week of transition. I had not expected a reprieve, but I was glad to have one. But if I had expected a vacation, Grandma was soon to set me straight.

During my first week, I learned about housework, Grandma-style. Everybody I knew had a wringer washer, even Mother. Not Grandma; she scrubbed clothes on a washboard and was determined that I learn the process, start to finish. Wash water came from rain barrels under the eaves or the cistern behind the kitchen. And in winter it was heated in big kettles on the coal and wood range. During warm months a black kettle over an open fire served well. Water for drinking and cooking, on the other hand, came from a spring below the barn, a hearty trek I was expected to make twice a day. My father leaned toward the notion that carrying water was woman's work, but since Grandma was up in years and I was a newbie, he pitched in.

If I wasn't helping Grandma with meals and dishes, washing clothes, or ironing, I trailed after my father as he cut firewood, purchased a hundred chicks, and bargained for a Jersey milk cow. All the activity gave my mind a reprieve, and while it wasn't what I would call fun, it was engrossing. The only reminder that our turn of events was tragic occurred when I was with my mother. She ventured out of her room for meals, the outhouse, and a cigarette on the front porch, but that was it. When the flat of fluffy yellow chicks was placed under a warming lamp in the barn, I tried to coax her out to see them. She declined, no less exhausted than the day we arrived.

Friday, I was down near the spring helping Daddy cut lengths of firewood with a crosscut saw. I had a hard time keeping the blade in position and my rhythm in synch with his. Frustrated, I dropped my end of the saw and announced, "I quit!"

He picked up the saw and motioned for me to take my end. I backed away, sudden hot tears threatening to spill over, turned toward the path that led back to the house, and started up the slope. Sobbing as I topped the rise, I yelled back at him, "I'm going home!"

Even as the words tumbled out, I wasn't sure what they meant. Did I mean I was going back to the house? Or back to Duncan Falls? Where was home anyway? Within minutes, Daddy appeared on the hill behind me. I expected him to order me back to work, but he followed me into the house. "Wash your face and meet me outside," he said, his voice calm.

I poured teakettle water into the metal wash pan and cleaned the tears and snot from my face. I took the pan to the back door and gave its contents a sling. Then I met him on the stoop beside the east door and followed him across the yard to the driveway. By the time we reached the road, we were side by side.

The weather had turned. What had earlier in the week been wind gusts were good clean breezes that caused the awakening tree branches to sway. The fields we passed were greening and leaf buds on maples and birches had begun to open. As we walked a mile down the road and back again, Daddy talked about how to recognize trees by their bark, and the harmless creatures I would run across when I found my way to the woods. The notion that I would need this information seemed highly unlikely. On the way back, I realized something. I had started out sad and resentful. As we passed farm houses and fields and I half-listened to my father's monologue, I felt a gradual lightening of my spirits. My improved mood must have shown because Daddy smiled. "It's the fresh air and exercise. When you're down in the dumps, a walk is the best medicine."

Daddy had not applied this advice in Duncan Falls.

Evenings, he either dozed in a rocker or went upstairs early, his snores loud enough, as Mother put it, to wake the dead. But here on the Ridge, he was a different person, eager to work and cheerful. Only when talking to Mother, did his old personality reemerge. According to him, her depression was a cop-out, a choice. During her first illness, I had been three years old, and my memories of the time were vague, but I had sensed his harshness then too. For the eight years following, I had observed Mother's strength of will, and I believed a remnant of it existed still. And I saw a capacity for kindness in my father, with me and with Grandma. Why not show Mother the same compassion? Would less blaming rekindle her desire to get well? These were the questions I pondered as we returned to the farmhouse and I set the table for noon dinner.

Since I had left Duncan Falls, I hadn't been troubled by The Glare or the feeling I would pass out. Of course, I hadn't been to school yet. Imagining a classroom, a whole new set of observers, and another disapproving teacher caused uneasiness to flutter into my throat. All week, the school bus passed the house on its way to pick up the Hartley children at the next farm. As a town kid, I had rarely ridden a school bus. But one unforgettable ride had taken me to Zanesville.

Lily, one of my classmates, had gotten off the bus on a winter afternoon, slipped on the ice, and slid helplessly behind the huge front wheel. Clutch disengaged, the bus drifted back, and Lily was crushed. The tragedy itself was horrifying enough; the way the adults handled things made it worse. The entire fourth grade class was taken to the funeral home by school bus and made to troop past the open casket. Vivid still is the memory of Lily's body on display, her straight blond hair limp on her shoulders, white hands unnaturally clasped, and her long, sweeping eyelashes resting against waxy cheeks. This was my first encounter with death, and it was awful. Riding the bus to school in Stockport would be a benign experience by comparison.

Saturday afternoon, Grandma and I walked up the road to call on the Hartley family. Mr. Hartley and John, a heavily freckled ten-year-old, met us in the yard. Mrs. Hartley had been a war bride, and her British accent remained crisp. Their daughter, Lyn, had just turned thirteen and sat politely while the women chatted over their tea cups. She wore dungarees and a plaid flannel shirt. Her silky dark hair was cut short, and her skin was pink and white with a faint sprinkling of freckles. She wasn't a bit like the girls I knew in Duncan Falls, either the top tier snobs or the street smart set.

When she took me outside to meet her pony, her little sister, Liz, tagged along. Babe was part Shetland, swaybacked and mild-natured. Lyn invited me to ride, but I declined, glancing down at the skirt Grandma had made me wear to go calling. Lyn grinned. "Next time, then."

On the way back to the house, Grandma asked what I thought of her. "She's nice," I said.

Monday morning, Lyn sat beside me on the bus. She took me to the sixth grade classroom and said, "Good luck," before going to the seventh grade room across the hall. Had my Duncan Falls demons followed me here? I wondered. Mrs. McConkey led me to a row of desks nearest the wall of windows. She opened each sash a few inches. "It's a little close in here," she said, and I could have kissed her.

During lunch break, a girl in my class asked, "What's wrong with your mother?" From the way she kept looking at her companions, I could tell she had drawn the short straw.

"Nothing," I replied.

Prodded on by looks, she persisted, "I heard she went crazy or something."

I'd already answered the question, so I went over to the swings. Nobody was bold enough to pursue the issue, so that was the end of it.

Chapter 13

IN SOME WAYS the first month on Olivet Ridge seemed like a lifetime. I tended the fluffy yellow chicks which rapidly lost their charm and turned into scraggly, bird-like creatures that wandered around the straw covered barn floor amidst their droppings, pecking each other for the inevitable chicken lice. Lyn had introduced me to the woods just below our barnyard where we hopped across the creek from stone to stone. She gave me a ride on Babe, whose plodding gait made me think of camels in the desert, broad feet insensate to burning sands. A pony was okay, but nowhere near the top of my want list.

Watching my maiden journey on pony-back, Daddy had an idea. One evening a few weeks later, he returned from Beverly where he was barbering part time, with a sway-backed pony in the bed of his pick-up. Silently, I watched as he led the shaggy, black and white equine down a couple of planks. This pony made Babe look like a show horse. His heavy, matted mane had broken over the musculature, and his head drooped dejectedly. Worst of all, the unfortunate pony's left eye was a mound of sightless pink tissue with a translucent iris suspended at its end. Daddy said he had had a run-in with a barbed wire fence.

Torn between pity and revulsion, I climbed obediently on its back and took the rope ends dangling from the halter. Around the cluttered space between house and barn we lumbered. "He can trot. Put your heels into his sides." I obeyed, and sure enough, he picked up speed. On the pony's blind side was some haphazardly stacked junk wood. I was too inexperienced to steer away, and he was too blind to avoid it. Colliding with jagged pieces of lath and broken crates, he bucked me off into the middle of the pile.

Henceforth, I treated the pony with the same indifference I gave our milk cow, Pet, whose mean Jersey horns kept me at a safe distance. The nameless pony departed as suddenly as he had come, and I never stopped feeling guilty for rejecting so pathetic a creature. The only excuse I can plead is immaturity. The same excuse which I offer for bearing the scratches and bruises I received from my tumble as badges of martyrdom.

As May approached, forsythia and dogwood appeared. Evidence of passing time, they reminded me how long Mother had lain, curled on her side in the small bedroom, the dark window blind blotting out the glorious weather. She looked no stronger than she had in March. My father presented me with a diary for my twelfth birthday. Grandma baked a cake, a rare concession since Jehovah's Witnesses didn't celebrate birthdays. The yellow layer cake had a raspberry jam filling and white confectioner's sugar frosting. On top were colored sprinkles. Given our dearth of fancy foods, the cake was a treat. Mother's back was toward the door when I took her a slice; when I returned for the plate, the cake was untouched, and her position unchanged. Daddy had begun threatening her with Cambridge State Hospital, and change was looming; I could feel it. If not in Mother's condition, then in the course events were about to take. But first, I had an event of my own to deal with.

During recess a few days after my birthday, I was met with a surprise. I had started my period. Mother had told me last fall it could happen any time and that it was nothing to worry about. On the way home, I wondered whom I should approach with my news. If I told Mother, I couldn't be certain she would request supplies from my father, and I had no intention of asking him myself. That left Grandma. She was upstairs when I got home, sorting through clothing from a trunk. I had learned why there were so many old clothes in the house. Grandma believed that during Armageddon, discarded items would come in handy. I didn't care to ponder theology just then, so I burst out with my news.

"You know about menstruation?" She pronounced all four syllables. Even the most distasteful words in Grandma's vocabulary deserved proper enunciation.

Having just crossed the Rubicon into womanhood, I felt the power of my status. "Mother told me," I announced, willing to share the credit for my adult knowledge. Grandma disappeared downstairs, undoubtedly to find my father. Shortly afterward, I heard Daddy's truck bump down the driveway toward the road. Only she could make such a request, however random or embarrassing, and have it handled with dispatch. And except for his role as errand boy, my father left the rest of this business up to the womenfolk.

"I wouldn't mention this to the other girls," Grandma cautioned the next morning on my way out the door. "They might make fun of you." I promised I wouldn't. No way would I share private matters with kids I hardly knew. How naïve did she think I was?

—————=((•))=—————

With the ending of the school year, I could feel tension building again. Mother remained in her private space twenty-four seven. Occasionally, Grandma would roust her out to change sheets and sweep the floor. My attempt at pep talks had petered out. Several times a day, she crept like a shadow onto the porch and sucked the good out of a Kool, feet bare and blue on the linoleum. I was learning, as I could not have from my observations as a three-year-old, what an eerie and persistent beast depression is. The inevitable came in June. Daddy had arranged for Mother to see a doctor in Beverly, and departure was set for Cambridge. The intervening days were perpetual limbo, like Grandma's expectation of Armageddon.

Woodpeckers at work on the shed and the sound of Grandma's pans in the kitchen usually woke me, but that morning, the day Mother was to leave, I'd been awake for a long time. I lay upstairs on a mattress that swayed in the middle, listening to Grandma's reedy voice in the kitchen, singing as she stoked the coal and wood range. Usually the aroma of coffee and bacon enticed me downstairs, but this morning my stomach was in knots.

When I appeared in the dining room, Daddy was finishing his eggs, ready for the trip to Cambridge, black hair slick and shiny, white shirt freshly starched. Grandma hustled back from the kitchen to pour more coffee. When she saw me, still rumpled from the bed, she pressed her lips together. Using his bread, Daddy cleaned the yolk from the ancient earthenware plate; then he heaped strawberry preserves onto his bread, covering the yellow remnants of egg with red.

I'd had trouble with eggs since Daddy had explained that by the end of the summer, we would have to cull all but two or three of the roosters from the flock I was attempting to raise. During the last month the chicken population had sprouted glossy red feathers and taken on adult form. They roamed freely over the property, scratching up worms and bugs, but they always came running for their graining twice a day. Outside the screen door, a couple of pullets pecked at the egg shells Grandma had thrown out. Laying eggs would make them productive members of the farm community. Not so their unfortunate brothers.

I'd heard how chickens were slaughtered, scrawny necks stretched across a stump for the ax. If you failed to hold onto the legs tightly, the headless carcasses would run their last circles in the saw dust. The killing stump was also used for splitting kindling. Faded brown streaks from long ago bespoke its more grisly use. How many hapless roosters or hens past the age of productivity had met their end there, blood spurting and pooling, leaving tell-tale ribbons? I wasn't sure how brave I would be when the day of slaughter came, or how helpful I would be in the kitchen, packing Mason jars with deboned chicken parts, ready for the granite cold-packer.

Checking on Mother, I found her ready to leave, right down to hose and shoes and purse. Her eyes were open, bright blue in the gloom, and her readiness gave me immeasurable relief. This time, *she* had made the choice. No black sheriff's car would come. No strong hand would lead her out. While compliance was the sensible route, the situation was not fair by any means. As with the young roosters facing the blade and the canning pot through sheer bad luck, Mother had received the short stick again. For the second time in a decade, she faced uprooting and separation at a level I could scarcely imagine. It proved the fundamental truth that she had always tried to teach me: Life isn't fair.

Chapter 14

UNTIL THE SUMMER of 1958, my first on Olivet Ridge, I thought of forests as a bunch of trees. But with Lyn, I discovered a place where fallen leaves of many seasons silenced footsteps, and moss carpeted the stones. Shafts of sunlight penetrated high, interlacing branches, and huge rocks jutted from hillsides as if they had paused, mid-tumble, and wedged themselves into the slopes. In the creek, water spiders took long strides across the surface while crawdads scuttled backward underneath.

One humid afternoon in mid-July, Lyn and I ignored darkening clouds and distant rumbles of thunder. When the boughs above us tossed and heavy drops bombarded, it was too late to make a run for home, so we sheltered under an oak of tremendous girth. When the storm abated, we went home soaked, slip-sliding up through the pasture. Snug in her stable, Pet chewed her cud and watched as we straggled past.

I hardly thought about Duncan Falls or the kids there anymore and was content with my new lifestyle. I rarely complained about chores. When necessary, I could handle the housework and most of the cooking. Feeling adventurous one day, I gathered early apples from a tree below the spring, pared and cored them the way I'd watched my mother do. I also knew the ratio of flour to lard and how to add cold water until the pie crust dough was ready to roll out. Firing Grandma's oven, I created a tolerable apple pie. I just wished that Mother could have enjoyed it with us.

Even though my father worked in a barber shop part time, he had no intention of giving up farming. There were two approaches, he believed. Big time farmers, like his uncle George Rippey in Indiana, owned many acres, produced large crops, and raised lifestock to sell for profit. They relied on tractors and mechanized tools. Some reached the level of gentlemen farmers and paid others to do the onerous tasks. Their families lived as comfortably as folks in town. When he spoke of this class of farmer, his tone carried an edge, as though they had missed the point.

The second approach to farming, his ideal, became clearer when, after his death many years later, I found among his possessions a card titled, "Utopia—Plans for," dated February 20, 1933. Here he had listed, along with the price of each item, the necessary components to achieving agricultural perfection. The list included saws, an ax, a hoe, a blanket, seeds, and other simple tools. Interestingly, along with a Bible, he felt the need for a book of English composition and grammar, a dictionary, a pen and ink, plenty of paper, and a dog. Two addenda were jotted on the side of the card. The first, added September 23, 1949, read, "I now have a wife and 3-year-old girl. Can Utopia come true?" The second, dated October 10, 1971, updated the status of the dream again:

"Yes, but it's too darn lonesome for Grandpa."

———=))(()(=———

In 1958, escaping Duncan Falls for Olivet Ridge provided the opportunity he had been hoping for. Unlike the
big time farmers, he would do his farming by hand. Hay cut
with a scythe, corn stocks with a machete-like corn knife.
There would be no mechanized implements on this farm,
but horse-power, in its original form, was a necessity. So that
summer, Twila, a giant work horse with mammoth feet and
a huge belly, arrived in a truck with wooden sideboards and
took her place in the stall next to the milk cow.

Putting this beast to hard use would have to wait,
though, because Twila was close to giving birth. Lyn and
I were ecstatic at prospects of a colt or a filly, but intimidated by Twila's bulk. We tested the waters by offering her
apples and grain and gently untangling mane and tail with a
curry comb. Twila accepted our overtures with good humor
and usually met us at the barnyard fence in anticipation of a
treat. Debating names for her offspring, we finally settled on
Charles, Prince of Wales, for a colt and Queen Elizabeth for
a filly. Nothing was too grand for this barnyard. As the days
passed, Lyn and I agreed: Twila was either going to give birth
soon or explode. Then, one morning, the waiting was over.
Sitting at the breakfast table, ready for barbering in town,
Daddy gave me the news: A healthy colt had been delivered.

"Prince Charles!" I charged through the screen door and
pelted toward the barn. For once, Daddy overrode Grandma's

commandment that I get properly dressed before going outside. Sure enough, standing on spindly, shaky legs, wet from his mother's tongue, the tiny colt nuzzled the mare's milk sack and pulled impatiently at her teat. When she saw us, Twila rolled her eyes clear to the whites and snorted her mistrust of the intrusion. I thought to amend things by reaching out to her, but Daddy grabbed my hand before it cleared the barrier to the stall. "Keep your hands to yourself," he ordered. "And don't get into that stall, no matter what."

"But she likes me," I insisted, as Twila turned back to her colt.

"Mares are different once they give birth. She will defend that colt at any cost." He left the barn, heading out to the pick-up, and I mused over his warning. It seemed unreasonable to fear this gentle giant whom I had befriended for well over two weeks. But out of an abundance of caution, I decided to give her a few days to get used to motherhood before I got too friendly.

Back in the house, I jumped into my clothes so I could run up to the road and give Lyn the news. Grandma nixed my plan by placing a bowl of Purina, a tasteless brown porridge, on the table. I was not to leave the property until I had hauled water from the spring, carried in wood, and given the chickens their corn. Every morning, it was my job to open their coop so they could wander about the farm, as was the right of all living creatures unless there was an extremely good reason to restrain them.

Lyn and I followed my father's orders for several days, watching the pair of equines as they meandered around the hilly pasture behind the barn. Prince became better looking every day. By contrast to his mother's dark brown coat and even darker mane and tail, his coat bore a golden sheen and his mane was lighter still. When would it be safe to venture inside the fence, to extend a friendly hand and touch the warm, wet nose? Well, we were about to find out.

One day, returning from a ramble in the woods and nearing the barn, Lyn and I spotted Twila and Prince not far from the path we normally took. So far, good sense had made us choose the less direct route past the barnyard and adjoining pasture, one closer to the bordering fence. But that day, we could no longer resist. Using our most obsequious manners, we approached the mare and colt. In less time than it takes to tell, a mammoth beast whirled in our direction and huge feet thundered toward us; the enraged Twila was all set to bite and kick the stupidity right out of us. Lyn headed straight for the fence and topped it. I had hesitated for what seemed only a second, but it was too long. There was nothing between me and a savage mare except a smallish walnut tree. I skirted the trunk, trusting its spindly protection to keep me breathing.

"Run for the fence!" Lyn shouted, but no way would I trust my speed against Twila's.

After several trips around the tree, Twila seemed to tire of playing cat and mouse, so I took off like a shot, barreling onto the closest post, ignoring the barbed wire that bit through my jeans and shirt, and swung myself into the weeds on the other side, where Lyn was jumping up and down and screaming encouragements. Having made her point, Twila ambled back to her colt. Lyn and I debated telling Grandma about our great adventure, but only for a second. What little sense we had left told us this was one story that could wait.

＝⇒((●))⇐＝

Our adventure with Twila was not the only excitement Lyn and I had that summer. A week or so later, after checking Twila's stall where she and Prince Charles sheltered from the ferocious sun, I nearly stepped on a mottled, heavy-bodied snake stretched out in one of the ruts we called a driveway that led up from the road. Lyn and I froze, but only for a second. Then we dashed to the east door. "Grandma!" I shouted. "There's a snake in the driveway!"

Grandma was lifting a pan of ginger cookies out of the oven. Anyone else would have been dripping sweat; she had a beading of moisture on her upper lip. "You'll wake your daddy," she shushed, transferring the cookies to a towel on the table. From the living room came loud and steady snores.

"I almost stepped on it. I think it's a copperhead!" I'd been warned to steer clear of copperheads and alerted to pay attention to the description Daddy gave.

Grandma put on her rubber galoshes, a long-sleeved jersey, and a pair of gloves, the outfit she wore for berrypicking. Lyn and I followed her to the shed where she chose a long-handled hoe, then around the house under the tulip poplar and the sweeping willow. Except for the hum of insects in the hayfield behind the house and the occasional call of birds, there was silence. In the midday heat, the world of Olivet Ridge had shut down. It was just Grandma, Lyn and I—and the copperhead, lying exactly where we'd seen it.

Grandma edged to within three or four feet of the snake and brought the hoe down hard on its neck. Had she been younger and stronger, the blow would have severed the head from the body. Barely stunned, the snake whipped into a coil, and on the next blow, began to wrap the hoe handle. Most people would have dropped the hoe and retreated to safety. Instead, Grandma repeated the short, steady blows, ignoring the snake's bared fangs less than two feet from her gloved hand. The snake's lower body split and bled, and its resolve wavered. Slowly, it slipped down the handle, exposing its upper body to the steady beating. Barely writhing, the copperhead was beaten, but Grandma didn't stop, and then I saw why. From the wounds on the underbelly, tiny replicas of the copperhead wriggled out, a dozen, maybe, new and pale. Grandma's hoe dissected the mass and continued to strike until all wriggling stopped.

As odd as it seemed, I felt sorry for the copperhead. The excitement of the kill was gone; the mangled remains were left for scavengers. Grandma climbed the short bank into the side yard, her face red from heat and exertion, her shoulders stooped. She leaned the bloodied hoe at the door and went inside. Wordlessly, Lyn headed up the gravel road toward home. Daddy continued to snore in the darkened living room, unaware he had missed the slaying of a dangerous viper. While I admired my fearless grandmother, I had no desire to become the snake killer she was. Her coolness under pressure, though, was something else.

Chapter 15

WITH MY MOTHER out of the house, Grandma took it into her head that the small bedroom she had occupied would be a more suitable place for me than upstairs with Daddy. So we emptied the room of its clutter, leaving a small chest of drawers for my clothes and the single bed. There was room for the metal typing desk and swivel chair that Daddy had retrieved from Duncan Falls on his way back from taking Mother to Cambridge. He had stopped to make sure the house was intact and picked up a few items we wanted.

Of the many things I hadn't thought much about before that summer, housekeeping was one, except to realize that our house in Duncan Falls never looked as nice or as well-kept as others. My mother wasn't a fussy person by nature, but a few amenities and encouragement from Daddy might have made her an entirely different housekeeper. I know she envied Aunt Betty and Aunt Gladys their attractive and comfortable homes on those rare occasions we visited.

As for Grandma Rippey, as particular as she was about personal hygiene, dishes, and beds, clutter didn't faze her. Crates and boxes, stacks of *Watchtowers* and *Morgan County*

Heralds, and piles of tools were everywhere. Apparently, nothing had been sorted or discarded in years. About the time Grandma decided to change sleeping arrangements, Aunt Joyce arrived on the scene with intentions of performing a major house-cleaning. I had never seen anyone attack anything the way Aunt Joyce attacked that house.

She began in the kitchen by removing every non-kitchen item we unearthed. I made a hundred trips to the barn that first day, lugging out her cast-offs. Then she handed me a broom, its straw end covered in an old pillow case, and instructed me to sweep the walls and corners, leaving not a single cobweb or trace of dust. Curtains came down dirty and went back up clean once the windows were crystal clear. In two days we invaded all but the collection of treasures Grandma kept upstairs, pending Armageddon. Grandma stifled objections and obediently washed long-stored dishes from the tall walnut cupboard and glass-fronted cabinet. Junk, if burnable, went into a bonfire that Daddy helped tend. The rest of the time he stayed out of his sister's reach by pretending to straighten and organize the barn. Joyce's instruction wasn't lost on me, nor was the reward of de-cluttered space and shining surfaces. Right then, I made myself a promise: This is the way I will keep house when I have one.

<hr />

Grandma left the ridge now and then for a few days so she could attend Assembly and catch some rest. During those times, I was chief cook and bottle washer, according to Daddy. That simply meant I did most of the cooking and clean-up. Sometimes, Grandma and I reversed roles; she stayed on the Ridge and I went to McConnelsville. What a luxury was Grandma's room at Aunt Joyce's—ruffled curtains, chenille bedspread, adjoining bath!

Aunt Joyce worked at Kate Love Simpson Library, so I tagged along and glued labels and shelved returns. Despite her conservative lifestyle, Aunt Joyce was open-minded when it came to reading, so no sections of the library were off limits to me. Later on when I selected books at the library, she might look at a title and ask, "Do your parents know what you are reading?" But the question was pro forma. And even if I had sought approval, it's doubtful either parent would have objected.

Aunt Joyce's daughter Darlene was enrolled in business school in Columbus and had begun dating Leslie, a young man studying in the Jehovah's Witness equivalent to seminary. Through Darlene, I was introduced to the proper way to set a table and to present food. Aunt Joyce and I would come in from the library and Uncle Robert from his electronics repair job to find the round kitchen table set with matching tablecloth and napkins, separate plates for bread, and extra forks for dessert. Robert Childs was a gentle soul, tall and skeletal and fragile. Not long after he and Joyce were married, he suffered a nervous breakdown. In that era, the routine policy for male inpatients was vasectomy, so Darlene was destined to be an only child.

Another break from Olivet Ridge was time spent with my sister. She and Russell and Little Rusty still lived with Mrs. North and his two sisters, Shirley and Dianna. Shirley was engaged to a short, skinny guy who looked mean, and time would prove my impression accurate. Dianna was two years older than I was and seemed to resent my being there; nevertheless, I loved hanging out with Barbara. She and Russell took me to see two movies at the drive-in, *High Society* and *Cat on A Hot Tin Roof.* Both were to leave lasting impressions and reinforce a concept that I was beginning to grasp: My world was small and limited. I returned to Olivet Ridge with plenty to think about, knowing that if Barbara hadn't already had a houseful, she would have taken me in.

That summer, I stopped using food to assuage the turbulence in my life as I had the last couple of years in Duncan Falls. By August, the clothes that had been snug last year hung on me, so Daddy took me shopping for school clothes, and Lyn went along. Never having been shopping with my father, other than to stop by the A&P for ice cream, I had no idea what to expect. In Marietta, we visited dress shops and J. C. Penny. For the first time ever, I chose grown-up clothes, and my father seemed oblivious to the expense. Lyn was impressed by the number of items he bought; she had two younger siblings who also had to be clothed. When we went to lunch, Daddy asked us what we wanted and then ordered for us. His exquisite manners impressed Lyn too. As for me, at that point, my father could do little that surprised me.

———※《●》※———

I had been writing Mother all summer, and during the weeks following our shopping trip, I began receiving replies.

Brief, penmanship shaky, her letters were proof she was getting better, and Daddy said it was time to visit her. I feared she might be a stranger, possessing neither her full personality nor the diminished one I had come to know since late last winter. Given my uncertainty, the drive to Cambridge took forever, allowing me time to wonder also about what the hospital would be like. A prison of gray stones and barred windows, overhung by gloom?

In contrast to my imaginings, the view from the highway was replete with hay fields where wire-bound bales shot from spouts on the baler onto the freshly mown stubble. Tractors followed, pulling wagons, and gangly boys slung the bales as effortlessly as pillows onto the wagon beds. Summer harvest was in full swing and the voice of cicadas loud, urging the gatherers on.

We turned onto an innocuous gravel lane marked by a sign indicating Cambridge State Hospital was ahead and bearing the official seal of the State of Ohio. A long building of yellow brick, flanked on three sides by green lawns with white chairs and benches, emerged from the trees. People milled about, patients and visitors, nurses and orderlies. We entered through large glass doors and put in our request at the desk. Soon, a door opened and a nurse's aide appeared, and behind her, my mother. Mother's face lit up when she saw me, and it was the best possible reaction I could have received. We hugged fiercely, and my anxieties calmed.

On one of the benches under a maple tree, I filled her in on my summer, the short version since visits had to be brief. Mother's eyes checked me over, taking in the shiny, clean pony tail brushing my shoulders and the new dress. And yes,

I informed her, I had everything I needed to start school. Ever cautious, her restless eyes wandered toward those who passed, and I recognized the lack of confidence, that old bugaboo made worse by depression. But gone was the haunted, vacant look, and she responded to the back and forth of conversation. Her cotton dress was belted at the waist and her graying hair trimmed to emphasize the natural waves that lent elegance to her appearance. She had made strides in her ten weeks here. How much longer was full recovery going to take?

Even at twelve, though, I could understand how this time was different. If it had taken serious grit for her to recover in 1950, it would take even more this time. Then, she had returned to the home she knew as hers and to relative convenience: post office and stores within walking distance, familiar neighbors a dooryard away, and the elementary school close enough to hear the squeak of swings and shouts of children. This time, her house and furnishings lay abandoned, and "home" was temporary and alien territory. Would she, or could she, reclaim the life she had had in Duncan Falls? And then there was the issue of treatment. In 1958, medications were favored over electric shock treatments, but barbaric or not, shock treatments had reordered her thinking and sent her home from Columbus. Would the new wonder drugs be as successful?

Until later, when I experienced my own battles with depression, I had no idea how stubbornly she had fought to overcome the odds. And just as shock treatments alone had not returned her to Duncan Falls, neither would anti-depressants, however effective, return her to Olivet Ridge. Before, it had been a displaced four-year-old she must rescue. Eight years later, her daughter was twelve, and who knew what influences Belle Rippey and Joyce Childs might be exerting on her impressionable mind?

Even when Mother's thinking was otherwise rational, she suspected both women of harboring intentions to proselytize me. In reality, Grandma and Aunt Joyce never pressured me in the slightest about anything. And while they might have preferred a different mate for my father, they respected Mother's position in regard to me. During the months of her illness, I depended on Grandma and Aunt Joyce as fill-ins. But no one possessed the power to alter my loyalty to my mother or to what she had taught me. Her worries were unfounded, but if they influenced her recovery, I am grateful for them.

The morning Daddy left for Cambridge to pick up Mother, I headed to school with a million butterflies fighting for space against the slice of charred bread which masqueraded as toast in Grandma's kitchen. As soon as the bus door opened for Lyn and her brother, my friend shot me a look that clearly showed she had read my face. Instead of showering me with questions, she just settled into the seat and opened a book. After a long day, the big yellow bus let me off amid a puff of brown dust. Mother and I met about halfway through the yard and got most of the hugging taken care of on the spot. I could tell by the spicy smell of chili sauce coming from the kitchen that she was preparing supper, and even before I noticed Daddy's truck wasn't in the driveway, I knew he had taken Grandma to Aunt Joyce's.

Over the next few days I watched for signs that Mother

wasn't completely herself, but she seemed fine, more than fine, by all appearances well again. Finding that working two or three days a week was insufficient to finance the homestead, Daddy took a full-time spot at Wilson's Barber Shop in McConnelsville. Once they had retrieved the Plymouth from Duncan Falls, Mother began a daily routine of chauffeuring him to and from McConnelsville, so he could postpone taking his morning stay-awake pills and skip the afternoon dose. With Mother in charge, life in Grandma's house was less Spartan. She cooked my favorite foods and insisted the washing machine be brought to Olivet Ridge. Good-bye, wash board! Whenever Grandma came down to spend a day or two, she looked around to see what else Mother had changed. To her credit, Grandma kept her opinions to herself.

Sometimes I overheard bits of conversations between my parents about Duncan Falls, and I wondered when we were moving back. One Saturday, we drove up to check on things. Going through the cold, closed house was like revisiting history, yet nowhere in the emptiness could I find ghosts of my life before we moved, and in a way, I was glad. The bad times spent there were too recent; it would take a long time before I could view the Duncan Falls years objectively. I could tell Mother missed her own things, though, even if they were worn and shabby. If we were to stay at Grandma's, what would become of them?

Chapter 16

AT STOCKPORT, JUNIOR high students had one class-room, one teacher, and recess, just like elementary. But seventh grade was a change for me from the start. I didn't need anyone's reaction to know I was no longer the roly-poly sixth grader who expected the sky to fall on her head. Two seventh graders were my third cousins, both grandchildren of Ethel Porter, Grandma Rippey's sister. Ethel and Jimmy Porter's sons played fiddles and banjoes and called square dances. My cousin Larry insisted I join him on the dance floor during the Fall Festival. After that, I was ready for a square dance, anytime, anywhere.

Saturdays, after chores, Lyn and I wandered through goldenrod and purple iron weed in the meadow and beneath the reds and yellows of oaks and maples in the woods. We collected dark red sumac and fallen walnuts and watched Prince Charles advance from awkward colt to handsome young stallion, bucking and kicking in the crispy autumn grass. Once again, Twila ate apples from our hands, but neither of us forgot our close encounter with her maternal instinct. On week-ends I watched *Wyatt Earp*, *Bonanza*, *Wagon*

Train, and *Perry Mason* with Lyn and her family.

Remembering how I had loved my playhouse in Duncan Falls, Daddy built another one behind Grandma's vegetable garden, a twelve-foot square building with real glass windows and a gable roof covered in tar-paper. He ran an electric line from the house so we had power. I say "we" because Lyn also benefitted from our "club house." We furnished it with cast off chairs and a table and used it as a retreat. Even when my family moved to a house farther down the road, Lyn and I met there. Again, as when my father had taken me shopping and given me *carte blanche* in my purchases, I was struck by his generosity. When he wanted, Raymond Rippey could be a superb father.

I wasn't sure how things had turned out so well, when just a few months earlier, if I dared think about the future, I could imagine nothing but disaster. Mother seemed surprisingly content in a place she had sworn she could never tolerate. Daddy was the man I remembered from earliest childhood, and they were getting along better than ever. There were arguments, especially on the subject of money, when he grumbled about the increased cost of living now that Mother was at the helm. But she stood her ground, and the drums of war receded.

———◦《◉》◦———

A minor complication that fall involved a pair of shoats which Daddy and Aunt Joyce had purchased early in the summer. I was used to carrying out the bucket into which all kitchen scraps and leftovers were deposited and slinging the contents into the hog trough, while holding my breath against the stench. Extra field corn and withered root vegetables were added to their diet as they approached the fattening up stage. The nearly identical, healthy-looking specimens had me wondering what butchering day would be like and whether I would be spared the grisly parts.

In September, I had worried about killing the young roosters. We had been tardy in dispatching the extras, and nasty fights had broken out, resulting in bloodied necks and flying feathers. I'd been spurred by over-sexed roosters, so I didn't wish to save any of them; I just didn't want to witness their demise. When I discovered Daddy had done the deed while I was at school, I was grateful. All that was left when I came home was removing pinfeathers from the shriveled white carcasses with yellow feet left attached as hand-holds. Instructed in the art of plucking, I popped out pinfeathers as slick as blackheads. By the time I got home from school the next day, the last jars were processing on the coal and wood range, making the early autumn kitchen feel like July. The best part was eating the odds and ends, rolled in seasoned flour, fried in lard, and served hot and crispy.

The hog slaughter, however, didn't work out so well. One Saturday in November, Aunt Joyce came down to pick up Grandma for Assembly the next day. The air was snappy enough to remind us that our days of comfort were ending, and a long, cold winter was on its way. I was returning from slopping the robust porkers when Aunt Joyce appeared around the corner of the barn, carrying a bucket full of coal. "Coal is good for pigs," Aunt Joyce informed me. "And we want these two nice and healthy."

She heaved the blue-black delicacy over the fence and the hogs attacked, razor sharp incisors cutting through the hardness, molars grinding it up like Christmas candy. Aunt Joyce and Grandma left, and at dusk my parents showed up in the Plymouth. I told Mother about the coal while Daddy went upstairs to change clothes. She agreed that a little coal was fine, but when I said bucketful, she threw on a cardigan and grabbed a flashlight.

Nearing the pen, we could hear one hog munching and the other drinking noisily at the water trough. "You say that bucket was full?" Mother asked. I nodded. She shone the flashlight beam into the pen. Only a chunk or two were left, but Mother and I picked up long sticks and poked at the gluttonous pig to discourage the feasting. We threw rocks and shouted, but the jaws continued to pulverize the coal to the last morsel. After snuffling around on the ground, the pig made its way to the lean-to shelter and settled into the hay, ready for an after dinner nap.

That's when Daddy showed up. I repeated my explanation about Aunt Joyce and the coal. "How much?" he asked, and he was no happier than Mother with the answer. "Well," he said, "it's done. I guess we'll wait and see what happens.

What was to happen, happened quickly. The next morning, while one hog rooted around in the mud, the other lay still and cold in the lean-to. Daddy walked up to the neighbors and got Aunt Joyce on the phone. They would be down soon, she said, not that there was anything to be done. The pig was history. By the time they arrived, the dead hog had been dragged outside the pen and lay sprawled on the ground, its belly distended.

Seeing the results of her handiwork, Aunt Joyce teared up. Until that point, Daddy had been miffed at her stupidity, but seeing his little sister in tears, he backed off from delivering reprimands. Still, what about the hog? A slaughtered animal had to be bled out immediately, so we were looking at a useless carcass. I could see my parents calculating the loss of half of their investment, and I felt the next statement out of my father's mouth was more than generous. "We'll split the other hog and call it even," he offered.

My aunt blew her nose and walked around to where she could get a better look at the hog. "But *your* hog is the one that died, Raymond."

It was obvious my father was having trouble with Aunt Joyce's sense of fairness. Still he couldn't challenge her. My mother, on the other hand, wasn't buying Joyce's naiveté any more than she had bought her tears. Her eyes narrowed to blue slits, and she opened her mouth, but my father put his hand on her arm to forestall what was certain to be a blunt observation of Joyce's character.

Throughout this exchange, Grandma Rippey stood silently with her hands in the pockets of her coat, a small Sunday hat holding her hair perfectly still and her eyes on the ground. Likewise, Uncle Robert, funereal in his black suit, said nothing. Finally my father took control. "You womenfolk go in the house. Robert and I will take care of things here."

I assumed I had escaped the unpleasantness of hog butchering, but I was wrong. Aunt Joyce made the generous gift of the head and organs in return for Daddy's work, and to my horror, when I returned from school on a blustery December afternoon, I discovered the hog's skull, hairless and boiled with bits of meat clinging to the bone, sitting in a large enamel dishpan and waiting for me to pick it clean. The pork would be ground, combined with apples and spices and raisins and then baked in a piecrust. When the delicacy was served, aromatic and still warm from the oven, I passed on the chance to sample it. All I could see when I looked at the lovely pie was an ugly, stripped skull with empty eye sockets and teeth grinning from a lipless mouth.

We might not have had an abundance of meat that winter, but we had plenty of snow and nights when the wind howled down the chimneys as if determined to smother the fires. The school bus traveled over some dicey roads, chains digging their way through snow blown into the wheel tracks. During the worst of it, we had a few days off. Then Lyn, John, and I got out the sleds and hit the cow paths in the Hartley's pasture that wound down the hill to the creek bed. The long pull back up was worth it for the exuberance of the ride down. We found a wooden sleigh in Lyn's barn designed to be pulled by a horse. After our shameless begging to take it down the hill, Lyn's mother relented. And did that thing travel! Dragging the monster back up the hill proved more than the three of us could handle, but when Lyn's mother asked us how the ride went, we didn't let on we'd had to abandon the bobsled. Lyn's father towed it back to the barn with the tractor.

That winter I split my first kindling and wheeled in firewood and coal to keep the boxes and shuttles full. Trips to the spring were treacherous, and my father went with me, broke the ice on the spring pool and walked at my back as we ascended the hill. Pet and Twila and Prince kept close to the barn, despite their shaggy coats. Their stalls were warm and fragrant with straw, and sometimes Lyn and I hung out there, perching on the cross pieces that separated the mangers from the rest of the barn, talking to the horses and each other.

My winter was free of illness, except for a mild case of the flu. Not so for Mother. She seemed to go from one toothache to another. One time, she had an abscess on her gum that my father opened with a darning needle sterilized in the fire. Once the infection was drained out, her pain eased. Otherwise, though, she stayed in good spirits and we spent many evenings lying across her bed upstairs, toasty warm from the small wood heater in the room and the quilt we shared, reading aloud from books which I stocked up on whenever I got a chance to visit the library. That became my favorite way to read that winter, trading off chapter by chapter. How lucky I was to have such a mother.

<hr />

Come spring, Lyn and I ventured into our favorite spot in the woods where the old logging road rose sharply from the creek and huge rocks remained anchored in primeval stability. Nothing had changed, save for branches lost to winter storms. I could almost believe in permanence here. Things were changing in my family, though, and I told Lyn we would be moving soon but only half a mile farther down

Olivet Ridge.

The property was owned by an elderly man of dubious reputation. Years before, his wife had become ill and left home for a time to recover. During her absence, the older of their daughters, barely fifteen and timid as a mouse, became pregnant. She gave birth to a boy whose over-sized head and mental disability supported the consensus that the girl's father had sired him. By the time we bought the house, the man no one trusted was stooped and aging, thin strands of hair combed across his scalp and hands moist and nervous. The following year, when I read *David Copperfield* in English class, the old man became forever linked in my mind to the despicable Uriah Heep.

Early that spring, my parents began work on the house. A large, flat yard and garden space, along with an area off the backdoor paved with fieldstones and surrounding a deep, dependable well were bonus features. In the front yard stood two pear trees perfectly aligned for a swing, and once their blossoms appeared, the air was filled with fragrance. One downside was the board and batten siding hadn't seen paint in forever; another was size. There were four small rooms to begin, not counting a long, open upstairs. Daddy removed the wall between the smallest room and the kitchen to make space for a table. That left the living room and a bedroom across the front. My parents insisted that I take the downstairs bedroom; they would share the upstairs in their separate beds.

There was a lot to be done before we even thought about bringing our furnishings down from Duncan Falls. Walls needed repair before mother and I could apply the first strip of wallpaper or a single stroke of paint. Boatloads of junk had to be disposed of and grime removed from windows and floors. It was well into summer before we began moving our furnishings to Olivet Ridge. Then there was the challenge of selling the Duncan Falls house. Months and months went by before a couple, down on their luck and desperate for a place to live, purchased the house through land contract. The house was sold, Mother's things were back in her possession, and my parents seemed to have buried the hatchet, at least for the time being.

Chapter 17

WE HAD BARELY settled into the new place when another complication asserted itself. Uncle Jim and his family were moving to Florida where he had purchased a tire shop. My grandparents' trailer had been sold, and they had no desire to move to Florida. Although Grandma had recovered from her stroke, you'd never know it from her complaints. Grandpa was growing frail, couldn't hear well, a blessing in some ways, and spent his days sitting in his chair and ignoring Grandma. A family council was called to decide how best to care for the aging couple. The meeting place was Olivet Ridge, so Mother could show off her refurbished house.

Jim and Betty, along with their stair-step children, came to the meeting, but their focus was clearly on the move to Florida. Hank and Edie drove down from Canton. Homer and Gladys arrived late, neither entirely comfortable in the presence of the family. Before we left Duncan Falls, Uncle Homer had opened a gas station and mechanics shop in Vincent, Ohio, but he wasn't the businessman his brother was, and the service station went under. A few weeks afterward, Homer came up missing. Sometime later, he called

Gladys from Albuquerque, New Mexico, saying he was out of money and remembered nothing since leaving Vincent. My father, no stranger to ducking responsibility, was openly skeptical, but Mother bought the story. More importantly, so did Gladys. At least, she wired him money enough to come home.

Seated around the yard on the grass and kitchen chairs, Mother's siblings discussed the possibilities for their parents' housing. Everyone had disclaimers, whether spoken or understood: Edie, her childlike husband; Jim, the move to Florida; Homer, his emotional instability. So unless my grandparents moved in with us, they were destined for the poor house in the most literal sense. Just below McConnelsville, the Morgan County Home sat amidst several acres of farmland, where the homeless could reside and work on the farm or inside the facility to help pay for their keep. Everybody knew it was charity, a dreaded concept to proud people like my grandparents, but the choice now came down to our place or the County Home. As distasteful as it might be for them, living in the same house as Raymond Rippey did not carry the stigma of public assistance. And my father, for all of his faults, would never turn away his aged in-laws.

What had once been the accumulation of a lifetime had dwindled with each previous move, from Hackney Ridge to the house on Kennebec to the little green trailer to the makeshift bedroom at Uncle Jim's. My grandparents' possessions now consisted of their clothing and a box of memorabilia. And that was a good thing, because in our house, there *was* no extra room. The sofa-bed in the living room was opened for Grandma, who needed plenty of space, and for Grandpa, who needed only a little, a reclining lawn chair was padded with comforters. Those two pieces occupied most of the floor space. Mother's library table and two upholstered rockers were crammed into the other end of the room. The player piano took up what remained of the front wall. In the center of it all stood a Warm Morning heater, our heating source.

Within days, my world shrank to my room and the outdoors, with quick runs through the crowded space to the kitchen and the privy. I still felt shell-shocked when August ended and eighth grade began. Winter would have taken eons to pass if I hadn't discovered a way to fill the long evenings. Sequestered in my room due to darkness and inclement weather, the unwelcome stirrings from my near neighbors my only distraction, I began writing a novel. By that time, I was well-versed in the appealing styles of Betty Smith, Rosamond du Jardin, Phyllis Whitney, and Grace Livingston Hill. And I had plenty of words to put on paper, all products of wishful thinking: a house peopled by two parents who spoke lovingly to each other and a fourteen year old daughter, Marcie, whose bedroom opened into an empty hallway. When grandparents entered Marcie's world, they were entertaining and mobile. My reality was far different. Even with my bedroom door closed, I received the benefit of every turn and sigh and groan and snore, every voiced complaint, every voiding of Grandma's bladder into the slop jar. So if writing did nothing else for me that winter, it took me to a place far more bearable.

Whether to free up space or in search of solitude, Daddy removed himself to the farm. He also offered to drive his truck to and from work to spare Mother the long days. But she insisted on chauffeuring him, and I had no trouble understanding why. If I hadn't been able to escape to school five days a week, I would have gone crazy myself. How disappointing it must have been for her, stealing a moment to sit at her table and smoke a cigarette, two needy parents so close she could hear their breathing. Or driving through gray mornings and evenings on her rounds to and from McConnelsville, contemplating how convenient she had made it for her siblings to unload the needs and distresses of their parents on her, arguably the one least able to care for them. None of them would tolerate the conditions she lived under in the best of times: no phone or indoor plumbing, inadequate heat. I should have known she was calculating, if not revenge, then certainly a solution.

At Christmastime, Uncle Homer showed up with a used console television for his parents. He wedged it into the crowded space and positioned the antenna outside the front window, giving my grandparents a close encounter with the fuzzy image. Daddy's means to mount the antenna above roof level was the trunk of a slender maple from Grandma's woods. High as we were on Olivet Ridge, the picture was great. The problem was, the pole warped and spent its life looking like a bow without a string, bent over the roof or alternately out over the yard, the antenna along for the ride. It was just the touch our substandard housing needed to catch the attention of anyone who passed by. As for the television, there was no practical way for anyone besides my grandparents to watch it in their crowded quarters. Seldom did they vacate their beds, and neither saw value in bathing. Our living room had begun to smell just like the little green trailer, not a place in which I wanted to spend a minute longer than I had to.

Uncle Homer's visit forced him to confront his parents' housing situation. Mother had written to him, Uncle Jim, and Aunt Edie about the crowded conditions, made worse by winter confinement, sparing no detail. But words on paper are one thing, seeing is another. A small addition built onto the rear of the house would make our space livable, Mother said as they sat at the kitchen table, sharing a smoke, the noisy chatter from the newly installed television giving them a modicum of privacy. And the cost, split four ways, wouldn't be excessive. Uncle Homer agreed to approach the other two. When he did, Aunt Edie's reaction was predictable: Put money into Raymond Rippey's property? But she realized the impossibility of the present arrangement, as did Uncle Jim.

They all chipped in, and in April the footer was dug, and not long after school was out, I was helping Mother paint the new room and hang curtains at the windows. Furnished with second hand beds, a pair of rockers, and a coal and wood heater, their room was adequate and a considerable upgrade from camping out in the living room. It took two full days of airing and scrubbing to rid the living room of the smell and the grime, but the results were worth every minute and every effort.

⊸•((◐))•⊸

That summer Lyn and I resumed our friendship as if

nothing had changed and got together with a couple of other girls within bicycling distance. We fooled away summer afternoons in the club house deciding which boys we thought were cute. I joined 4-H and made a skirt and blouse as my project. Unfortunately, Daddy took me shopping for the material. I settled on a green stripe for the skirt. He insisted a tiny pink and white check was perfect for the blouse, so I made the mismatched outfit but never wore it.

When Lyn's parents took their kids to drive-in movies, I was invited. Mom and I went to a few, just the two of us. That's the summer I saw *Gone with the Wind* for the second time. Old enough to understand it then, I found the book in the library and reread it as many times as I had *Little Women*. Most Sundays, Mother and I attended the Fairview Church of her childhood. A spare, clapboard building, hedged by leaning, weathered gravestones and low-branched maples, it sat at the highest point of Olivet Ridge, the surrounding landscape softened by summer. My personal worship was tied up with the glory of a summer morning, the rustling of leaves outside, and the pungent scent of communion wine. What I may have missed in religious content, I made up for in sensory experience.

Grandma and Grandpa Hosom spent a lot of time in the shade of the pear trees in our yard. It wasn't a bad lifestyle, with mother supplying meals and laundry service. Health restored, Grandma become adventurous. Mother and I found evidence of her snooping through drawers and cabinets. We had nothing of value hidden away, but the intrusion was irritating. Then one morning, Grandma's curiosity got her into trouble. Sitting at the kitchen table with her coffee and cigarette, Mother heard Grandma leaving for the privy but didn't hear her return. Checking, she found Grandma lying on the cement floor of the abandoned chicken coop, having caught her heel in a crack and gone down. Fearing a broken hip, Mother sent me running to fetch Daddy. An ambulance took Grandma Hosom to Good Samaritan Hospital in Zanesville, Mother at her side.

Late that night, Barbara and Russell delivered Mother home, thoroughly exhausted and wondering how we were going to cope with Grandma's latest mishap. Her hip reset, Grandma renewed her role as impossible patient, and Mother added another duty to her roster, convalescent care. Grandma moaned and groaned without ceasing and prayed to die in tones loud enough to convince her audience that God was as deaf as Grandpa. And, thank God, Grandpa *was* nearly deaf. Given the peaceful look on his face, he could sit a few feet from Grandma's bed and hear little more than a rumbling of bees.

There is one side note on the television. The world depicted through the strange new medium was foreign to my grandparents, so they left the TV in the living room. Having earned our privilege the hard way, Mother and I watched it guilt free. And on Saturday evenings, Daddy made sure he was there in time for *The Lawrence Welk Show*. Uncle Homer's gift did not go unappreciated.

Chapter 18

THE NIGHT BEFORE my first day as a freshman, it was after two before I finally fell asleep. I had wanted to make a good impression to begin the year, but when I left for school, my eyes were gritty and my stomach threatened to up-chuck the slice of toast Mother had insisted I eat.

High school meant I had a bevy of new teachers. Mrs. Wade's homemade suit made me think "country," but her knowledge of algebra and science bespoke a sharp mind. And Mrs. Harrison might have looked like a sweet little grandmother, but she knew all the endings to every Latin verb and expected us to know them too. Then, there was English, and word was out that Mrs. Gage never smiled before Thanksgiving. She assigned a one-page autobiography that should have been a piece of cake for a writer of my experience, but by the time I got off the bus, I had convinced myself I could write nothing that would please her. After several false starts, I gave up trying to sound like I knew anything and just wrote. At least I had no trouble falling asleep that night.

The next day in English class, Mrs. Gage skimmed

through our homework. When she came to mine, she glanced my way. Oh, boy, I thought. After class, she motioned me to her desk. Before I could make excuses, she said the essay was well written. Then she proved that she could smile, regardless of the date on the calendar. I sailed out of the classroom, overcome with relief.

Having begun under a cloud, the start of my freshman year continued to be problematic. I spent the first six weeks trying to decipher the secret code to algebra. Other students raced ahead while I limped behind, my status as exceptional student sliding toward oblivion. Why didn't Mrs. Wade just give up on me instead of patiently explaining each equation, yellow pencil held in dry fingertips pointing out my errors? Thanks to her perseverance, the basic concept eventually made sense to me. Actually, it made a lot of sense. Through the manipulation of known factors, unknown factors were revealed. I broke through my mental block in time to score decently on the six-week exam, and Mrs. Wade did her own manipulation to turn my sorry homework scores into a B. I was still on the honor roll, but more crucially, I had my groove back.

I had signed up for home economics because that's what girls did in 1960. Our first undertaking was to complete an outfit from pattern selection to finished product. When Mrs. Harrison, the home economics teacher as well as the Latin teacher, produced catalogs of patterns, she brought out a tape measure and bathroom scale. She was nothing if not discrete, so weighing and measuring were conducted in private. Still, I could not believe my numbers. Just under five feet tall, I weighed one hundred fourteen pounds and required a size twelve dress pattern. All around me, girls ranging from petite to tall, skinny to plump, shared weight, height, and pattern sizes. I said nothing.

That evening, I related the shocking news to Mother, unleashing the tears I had kept under wraps all day. Given her height of five-one and her solid muscular build, she saw nothing amiss. But she was surprised that I was taking the news so hard. "I don't want to be fat," I sobbed, remembering my overweight years in Duncan Falls and my father's pronouncement about the ugly word "fat." I had been smugly satisfied that first summer on the Ridge when the pounds fell off, and the mirror reflected a trim, petite shape, but those days were no more. The mirror in my room confirmed it; my short, stocky body was a far cry from the figures I saw on the covers of *Photoplay* and *Teen*. Those bodies were perfectly proportioned for skinny slacks and fitted pullovers. The fashion world had yet to embrace the pencil-thin Twiggy, but the ideal figure in 1960 was *not* mine. No way could I be talked into eating a single bite that evening.

The next morning, I refused breakfast. On the way to school, I made up my mind to drop the class and hurried to the principal's office. Mr. Harkins was seated behind his desk, an older version of his son, also a freshman, right down to the freckles; his once-red hair was thinning on top. My excuse was the need for another study hall. He gave his permission and so did Mrs. Harrison. If she had an inkling of my real reason, she kept it to herself. By lunch time, the cafeteria meal smelled and looked so enticing I broke my fast. I had escaped the embarrassment of a size twelve dress pattern, but I wasn't finished with body image issues.

That winter, it was my turn to suffer from toothache. Once my teeth had all come in and assumed permanent positions, their appearance was disappointing. Back then, the only kids who wore braces had calamitous dental issues. And unless the tooth fairy had been especially kind, we lived with less than perfect dentition. During my second grade year in Duncan Falls, I had been subjected to a dental screening which revealed a shocking number of cavities, and my parents were advised to take me to a dentist. After one look in my mouth, the Zanesville dentist wheeled out a tank of nitrous oxide, slapped a mask over my face, and proceeded to extract seven teeth.

The aggressive approach created more problems than it solved. The lateral incisor on my upper right never appeared, and the one on the left was a dwarf which developed a painful cavity my freshman winter. An ancient dentist who practiced in Stockport tried filling the tooth, but the filling fell out. Back I went, and this time he administered a shot of Novocain and extracted the tooth without waiting for the painkiller to take effect. Small wonder I confuse that old man with Dustin Hoffman's nemesis in *The Marathon Man*.

There I was, nearing fifteen, hyper-sensitive about my image and embarrassed to tears by the gap in my teeth. And by spring, the left central incisor was drifting farther left, attempting to fill the space vacated by the missing tooth. Horrified, I showed Mother. Forget that she had been denied dental care herself. Forget, too, that repeated oral infections continued to poison her system. Arming herself with the fierceness my welfare always brought out in her, she made an appointment with Dr. Kishler in McConnelsville. Thanks to her, I was fitted with a one-tooth bridge anchored to the capped central incisor. Daddy offered no objection, recognizing a superior force when he met one. If only Mother could have stood up for herself with the same ferocity.

Even though Daddy appeared to have mellowed, he hadn't abandoned the hope of replacing barbering with an equally lucrative means of revenue. The summer before my freshman year, he had attended auctioneering school and returned home with a bona fide certificate and recordings of his auctioning prowess, before and after. While he could produce a monologue on any number of topics, he was no auctioneer. That didn't stop him from advertising in the *Morgan County Herald* or attempting to associate with experienced auctioneers in the hope they might toss some crumbs his way. When Windsor School held an auction of old furnishings the following spring, Daddy volunteered as co-auctioneer with a polished professional, whose son just happened to be in my class. As Daddy stumbled painfully through what was supposed to be a lightning fast spiel, everybody knew it was *my* father holding the mike. We both survived the ordeal, and he stopped imagining himself a silver-tongued devil.

⟞⟩⟨◉⟩⟝

Then, as suddenly as my freshman year had started, it was over. The last day of school, I marked the courses I would take as a sophomore—biology, geometry, Latin 2—all college prep. But on the way home, a fleeting vignette forced me to take a second look at my future. First off the bus was Carlin, a boy in Lyn's class. His mother stood on the front porch, broom in hand, as her son made his way up the driveway. Carlin's mother was forty-something; her face and figure showed a life of hard work, typical of East Windsor residents.

That's when it hit me. What if that's me at her age, with nothing to show for my efforts except a vegetable garden, a clothesline of clean laundry, and kids with a future no brighter? But wait, I was taking college prep courses. I would be a teacher, and maybe a writer. My life would be nothing like hers. And then, common sense told me it was time for a reality check. No one in my family had ever gone to college except Great-Uncle Owen Rippey, the lawyer in Michigan, now as old as my grandparents. Aunt Edie had earned her RN in nursing school. The truth was, my parents had the poorest financial standing among the Hosoms and Rippeys combined. How likely was it that *their* daughter would be the one who made the leap to higher education and all its benefits? Of all the "smart kids" who took higher math and Latin, I was the one who didn't belong. I should be taking business classes, so I could at least work in an office after graduation.

The trouble was I didn't *want* to work in an office. Since falling in love with the classroom and the idea of meting out knowledge to a roomful of students, becoming a teacher had been my shining hope. Observing Mrs. Gage for the last nine months, I now imagined myself teaching high school

English—*Silas Marner*, gerunds, dependent clauses, iambic pentameter—everything I had absorbed as a freshman and everything I knew I would absorb from her future classes. I envied her ready knowledge, the ease with which she managed the classroom and presented her lessons. Her stride down the hall was confident and purposeful. She had a husband, children, and a house to manage, yet in her classroom, no other world existed, and I could never imagine her burdened by regret or dissatisfaction. The dichotomy between the two women who were having the strongest impact on my life at the time was only too clear. While I adored my mother and valued her sacrifice, I could never endure the level of disappointment and neglect that was her lot.

While the other kids on the bus celebrated the last day of school by singing and hollering out the windows, I sat deep in thought, thoroughly unsettled by the direction those thoughts were taking me. As I left the bus that afternoon and watched the huge tires roll on down Olivet Ridge, spitting dust and gravel from their treads, I realized if I were to have the life I wanted, I had hurdles to leap I could not yet imagine. And even then, would it be enough?

Chapter 19

WORRY OVER THE future gave way to warm summer days and a chance to sleep in. At fifteen, I felt a difference in myself, the proximity of adulthood urging me to assume more responsibilities. With Mother still making her twice-a-day trips to deliver and retrieve Daddy from the workplace, I took it upon myself to prepare supper most evenings. Within the limitations of her budget, Mother let me select ingredients for dishes I wanted to try. And now, in addition to my own things, I ironed Daddy's shirts and clothing for Mother and my grandparents. Mother was glad for the help, maintaining as she did the hefty workload required by the care of her parents and other chores.

Events which defined the passing of time began with a request from Grandma Rippey. She had decided to spruce up the farm house, including wallpapering and general cleaning, and she offered to pay me for my help. It was just the two of us, and I discovered we were similar enough of mind to make good work partners. We worked mornings, then took a break for lunch and Grandma's nap, and continued into early evening. I handled the heaviest work, hauling water and climbing the ladder to place strips of wallpaper at the ceiling, but Grandma hadn't lost her mojo. We soon had both rooms papered and clean-up underway.

Toward the end of the week, I went back to her house after mid-day break to find her still upstairs, and I went up to check on her. She lay on her bed, stockinged feet crossed at the ankles, chest rising and falling in gentle rhythm, cheekbones prominent and ruddy. Absent the wire-framed glasses, her face in repose revealed an old lady, tired and vulnerable. Downstairs again, I stoked the cook stove, put water to heat over the fire, and dived into cleaning the living room like a whirling dervish. I was back in the kitchen washing up when I heard the squeak of the stair treads. Checking the antique clock on the dining room mantle, Grandma looked annoyed. "Why didn't you wake me?"

I carried the dishpan to the back door and broadcast the water onto the grass. Long rays of afternoon sun, diffused by the apple trees, slanted across the wooden stoop. The scent of mint was strong, the plants beside the kitchen door warm from the afternoon sun, and I pinched off a cluster. Noting how fresh and clean everything looked, Grandma agreed we were finished for the day. Walking up the graveled slope toward home, I thought of her there in her rocker, a cup of fragrant mint tea on a saucer in her lap, and her work on the house nearly finished—a strong and competent woman despite the hand she'd been dealt.

Grandma Rippey had a couple of reasons for fixing up her house that summer. Donald, known as Babe since high school because he batted with his left, was driving in from California with his wife and daughter, and they would be staying in Grandma's house. "Camping out" was the way Uncle Babe had put it when he and Grandma talked on the phone, and Grandma did not appreciate his choice of words. She didn't say so, but then she didn't have to.

Prior to that event, Aunt Joyce's daughter Darlene and her new husband Leslie would be moving to Illinois near his family. Before they left, Darlene planned to throw a barbecue at the old home place. For people on Olivet Ridge, barbecuing was an up-town idea, and according to Daddy, who told Mother and me all about it after the fact, the whole thing was an ordeal. Leslie transported a charcoal grill, thermos coolers of food, and lawn chairs in Robert's pick-up. From set-up, to lighting the charcoal, to cooking the meat was a long, drawn-out process. Everyone bragged on the tough, blackened, half-raw meat. My imagination filled in the rest.

Mother and I had declined the invitation, and our absence probably raised a few eyebrows. For one thing, Mother's teeth were in a sorry state. No way would she attempt barbecued meat. And it went without saying she had little use for the crowd that would gather, although she may well have said it anyway. Knowing how she felt, I couldn't leave her to the role of odd woman out, even if I was tempted to see how the shin-dig went down. We sat in the swing under the pear trees with Grandpa and Grandma Hosom for as long as we could stand Grandma's complaining. Before the sun had set in the west, we tucked her in for the night, complaining still.

Since Grandpa's presence was required wherever Grandma was, he stood at the exterior doorway to their room, chewing his tobacco and spitting into the grass beside the step. And, as usual, whatever his thoughts, they were known only to himself--and to God.

———————

The other event of the summer was one I could hardly wait for. My cousin Patsy and I had been pen pals since my Duncan Falls days, and I was finally going to meet her. Aunt Lillian had been unable to have children, so she and Uncle Babe adopted a baby girl the summer before I was born and named her Patricia Ann. Voices dropped when Patsy's birth mother was mentioned; "Mexican" was the term for any-one of Hispanic or Latin origins. A series of school pictures showed a gangly, dark-haired child gradually transforming into an exotic beauty. The family arrived on Olivet Ridge late in the evening, and my mother advised me to wait until the next morning to visit.

Nine-thirty was late enough, I decided, as I headed up the road, double checking my white shorts, tennis shoes, and sleeveless blouse for any flaw. Nervously, I knocked on the eastside door, noting that my father had recently mowed the grass. The car in the driveway had California plates, and nig-gles of excitement flicked through my stomach. Uncle Babe answered the door, a taller, younger version of my father, who seemed amazed that I had grown since he had seen me years ago in Duncan Falls. Aunt Lillian, wearing her housecoat, gave me a restrained hug, a worry line dividing her carefully shaped eyebrows. Uncle Babe went to the bedroom that had been mine and spoke to Patsy. She emerged, abundant dark hair wild from the pillow, dark eyes tilted at the corners, lips pouty, and a sleepy frown on her face. "Sorry," I said awkwardly, "I guess I'm a little early."

Uncle Babe reassured me they were all being lazy. He, too, had inherited Grandpa Rippey's ability to converse with anybody, anytime and carried the show on his own, with preoccupied responses from Aunt Lillian as required. Patsy, in baby doll pajamas, sat in Grandma Rippey's sewing rocker, legs crossed beneath her and feet tucked, arms crossed, her scowl unrelenting. Fifteen minutes was as long as I could maintain the charade, so I excused myself and went back home.

After Mother left for McConnelsville that afternoon, a soft knock sounded on the screen door. To my amazement, it was Patsy, and what a transformation. The crazy hair from morning was now a chignon, and she wore white shorts, tighter and shorter than mine, but she could carry it off with the body she had. A hot pink halter top emphasized the enviable combination of full breasts and tiny waist, and the sandals she wore had not come from the clearance rack at Stiffler's. The combined effect was so beyond Olivet Ridge she might as well have come straight from Hollywood.

For a minute, we just looked at each other through the screen. Then I opened the door and we went outside to the swing. Wasting no time with small talk, Patsy dived into the real story. Her parents had no idea who she was or what she wanted. She hated school, had been suspended, and hung out with the wrong crowd. I could tell she wasn't making a play for sympathy or approval. She needed to set me straight, I guess, feeling she owed me that after our years as pen-pals. For how long, I wondered, had her letters been pure fiction, filled with mundane news to match mine?

They had stopped in Cincinnati to visit Aunt Lillian's parents. Next door to Patsy's grandparents lived nineteen year old Pete. Sparks had begun to fly from their first meeting. "I can't wait to get back," she said.

I guess I was pretty dense. "Back to California?"

Patsy picked up a miniature green pear from the ground beneath the swing. She examined it as though the aborted pear held the mystery of life. She looked up and shook her head. "We were in Cincinnati for a week. Pete and I fell in love. We're getting married." A slight rustling of leaves overhead and the distant growl of farm equipment failed to fill the silence. "The way I look at it, I've tried everything else. I might as well try marriage."

I couldn't fathom a suitable response, but I must have said something. After we hugged good-bye, I waited there in the swing until she disappeared around the bend, feeling bereft over the loss of my imaginary cousin and pen-pal, another girl, a lot like me, who happened to live in California, a Patsy who had never existed except in her letters and my imagination.

The summer had started with a sobering realization that the future was going to catch up with me before I was ready for it. It ended with resolve to stick with my college prep classes. Maybe I was just a rebel, stubbornly believing that I would be luckier than I deserved, that the chance of a lifetime would somehow fall to me.

Chapter 20

A REVELATION DAWNED on me in homeroom one morning at the start of my sophomore year, September, 1961: Boys liked me. All four desks surrounding mine were occupied by boys, who at the moment were competing for my cryptic comebacks to their remarks. I was behind schedule in finding boys an odd but intriguing species, but daily notations in my diary showed I was catching up. One boy's name appeared there more often than others'. Brash and edgy, Chuck seemed an unlikely candidate for a studious girl to take an interest in, but the fifteen year old mind defies logic.

Besides diary updates, I continued writing my novel. Another means of escape, of course, was reading. Of the several books I read that winter, one especially caught my attention, Alan Le May's *The Unforgiven*, which had been released as a John Huston film in 1960, starring Burt Lancaster and Audrey Hepburn. It would make a great high school play, I thought. Too bad we weren't juniors yet because at Windsor High School the junior class produced a play in the spring and the senior class in the fall.

Nobody had ever produced a sophomore play *or* one

written by a student, but I decided there was a first time for everything. With Shakespeare as my playwriting guide, I created a monstrosity of three acts broken into nine brief scenes. I took the script to Delmar Medley, the history and government teacher, who also directed the junior and senior plays. Rather than telling me I was crazy to attempt such a project, he suggested I reduce the number of scenes and forget Shakespeare. When I gave him the new version and asked if sophomores could put it on, he told me my playwriting expertise wasn't quite up to an evening audience, but he would support a day-time presentation for younger students.

All I had to do was convince enough sophomores to jump on board. The idea of running around the stage shooting each other appealed to the boys. The girls were more reluctant, but since there were fewer female roles, I soon had a cast. Each character with a speaking part needed a script, but back in the day, you couldn't run to the Xerox machine and make copies appear. I coerced two friends, Nancy and Ruth, and any other half-willing girl to become scribes. Paper and pencils flew during study hall. Initial practices had to take place in empty classrooms or the hallway, since a bunch of sophomores on the loose in the gymnasium didn't strike adults as a good idea. We soldiered on, delivering lines in undertones, stage directions left to the imagination. This was not much fun, so the grumbling started. When I consulted Mr. Medley one last time, he agreed to chaperone an evening practice if we were ready for a stage rehearsal. I said we were, fingers crossed behind my back.

The Unforgiven is the story of a pioneer family who adopts a baby girl taken from the Kiowa Nation and raises her as theirs. The father dies, so only the mother knows the truth until a deranged old man shows up and exposes the fraud. The Zachary family is alienated from the white community, which is rife with racial prejudice, and when the Kiowa discover that one of their own is masquerading as a settler's child, they don their war paint and proceed to take her back. No one was willing to play the leading lady, Rachel Zachary. The script called for a kiss in the final scene, and while the leading man was all for the idea, the girls were not so eager. Even when I down-graded the kiss to a hug, there were no takers. Ruth had dark hair, dark eyes, and a dusky complexion, but no amount of begging got me anywhere.

So there we were in the high school gym. Props waited on stage: a table, an oil lamp, a cot for the mother's death scene, a make-believe window through which the Zachary family could defend themselves. Boys with cap-guns and empty bb guns were pursuing one another indiscriminately, while Chuck, as Ben Zachery, attempted to woo and win someone to take the role of Rachel. Girls ran squealing around the gym with Chuck in hot pursuit. I, director and producer, stood helpless in the midst of chaos. At this point, Mr. Medley entered the gym, set up a metal folding chair on the free-throw line, and replaced me on the spot. "Cast, on stage," he ordered, his deep, tobacco roughened voice sounding forth in the melee with god-like authority.

Chuck took center stage. He had been the first to volunteer as Rachel's older "brother," who shares the secret of Rachel's origins and whose feelings for her are more than brotherly. When he chose to annoy, Chuck delivered his lines in the voice of Pepe le Pew. Using my list of characters,

Mr. Medley called the roll. One line was blank. "Rachel Zachary!" he roared.

I looked at Ruth imploringly, but she shook her head. Being chased around the gym by Pepe le Pew had sealed her resolve. Worse yet, she took my arm and proceeded to drag me to the stage. "She wrote it. She knows all the lines."

Mr. Medley failed to hide his skepticism: A blue-eyed, pale-skinned Kiowa? But his objections were drowned out by the cast. "Rachel! Rachel!" they chanted.

It wasn't that I hadn't considered the part, but I was no more comfortable hugging a boy on stage than anyone else. Mr. Medley acquiesced, and I took my place, scowling. Chuck gave me a wicked grin. What had I gotten myself into?

At long last, we put on the play for junior high and freshman students. I can't judge how well it went based on the exuberance of our audience. They had escaped the monotony of the classroom in favor of painted savages, cap guns, and plenty of screaming. Uneasiness about the final scene in which Ben and Rachel Zachary seal their status as a couple proved completely unwarranted. Chuck gave me an appropriate hug, appearing a bit embarrassed himself.

Mrs. Gage must have slipped into the gym for the performance because she made it a point to remark on what a good job I had done. Even so, I was more than happy to leave the life of playwright, director, and producer behind. At the very least, I had learned a valuable lesson: Never expect someone else to do what you won't do yourself.

April 1962, along with my sophomore year, was nearly finished. A week after our illustrious performance, Chuck followed me from the bus to the nearly empty homeroom one morning, looking like he had something on his mind. He had become friends with Allen and his side-kick Roger, both seniors and holders of all the academic honors possible at Windsor High School. A wiener roast in honor of graduation was planned for Friday night at Luke Chute Island, accessible from one bank of the Muskingum River by a sand bar. A few under-classman were included, and Chuck was asking *me* to join them. "It's a group thing," he said, trying to sound casual.

"I'll have to ask my father," I replied, hoping my attempt at casual was better than his. Group thing or not, I had been informed there would be no dating until I was sixteen, and that was ten whole days away. Mother wasn't a legalist, and together we talked Daddy into relaxing the rule. Ruth, Nancy, and Lyn all had the same basic response when I told them: "He's been dying to ask you out." How did they know this? Again, the content of their words was identical: "Anyone can tell he likes you."

The evening finally arrived, and six of us scrunched into Allen's car, including dates for Allen and Roger. It was my first time on the sand bar, and I may have looked hesitant as we approached it. Chuck took my hand, and the natural gesture gave me reassurance. On level with the calm, glassy water, we approached a huge bonfire which sent sparks and smoke into the evening sky and the music blasting in stereo from transistor radios. Of course, there were looks of speculation as Chuck continued to hold my hand once we had reached the party. Instead of taking part in the wild Frisbee game or some other kind of horseplay, Chuck stayed with me. Through the hotdogs and marshmallows, we sat together on one of the logs arranged around the bonfire. A light fog drifted in, casting a chill outside the bright circle, and an almost full moon rose enormous from a bend in the river.

Standing, Allen drained the last of his Coke and held the bottle high, shouting, "Spin the bottle!" He smoothed a spot in the sand and gave the bottle a spin. It was only a matter of time until it was Chuck's turn to spin, and mine to be the recipient. For a first kiss, it wasn't what a girl dreams of, but it wasn't bad either.

Later, at my doorstep, I could honestly say I had had a great time. With a final squeeze of my hand, Chuck trotted back to Allen's car and they were off down the road. By that time, the round, haloed moon had risen above the trees. Observing it, I remembered the feel of Chuck's hand and the brief touch of his lips. The deferential way he had treated me stood in sharp contrast to his past torments. Only one explanation made sense. My friends were right; he did like me. And under the bad-boy pretense was someone I liked too.

<hr />

Until Chuck and I became an item, Allen was just a brainy kid two years ahead of me and known for his wide range of talents and try-anything personality. His father had become successful in the oil business in Weston, West Virginia, and the family moved there. Allen stayed in Stockport with a retired teacher for his senior year. Allen had a car, plenty of spending money, and way more freedom in Mr. Hindman's house than he'd had in his parents'.

One Saturday evening, Allen drove Chuck, Roger, and me to the top of Water Tower Hill where we could look down on Stockport and track the headlights going through town and across the arching one-lane bridge above the Muskingum. Below the far end of the bridge, the rectangular loch which allowed boat traffic to navigate the river was only a darker shadow. Frothing white water appeared iridescent in the scant light as it spilled over the dam. From where we stood, the town appeared well protected by the hills that crowded in from both sides.

Before going back to the car, Allen disappeared around the side of the tank. "Up here," he called, and then we saw him, circling the high outer rim.

"You're crazy," was Roger's assessment, even while I sensed Chuck's desire to join him. Chuck watched Allen continue his circuit, but he stayed where he was.

On the way to Olivet Ridge, we hit a straight stretch. His foot on the accelerator, Allen let go of the steering wheel. Roger screamed, "Oh, God!" and grabbed the wheel. Once on the gravel road, Allen turned off the headlights and drove by moonlight. It felt like flying, with the wind from open windows whipping into the back seat where Chuck and I watched the silvery fields flashing past. March pipers could be heard even above the whoosh of the air. This was as close to danger as I had been since my unfriendly encounter with Twila, but the familiarity of the landscape and the warmth of Chuck's hand cancelled my fear.

By far, the craziest thing I ever saw Allen and Chuck do was climb the framework of the Stockport Bridge. As Roger and I watched for a deputy marshal who might be out prowling, the other two scaled the bridge girders clear to the top. Any misstep could have landed them on the bridge deck or in the Muskingum River only yards from the dam.

<hr />

At the end of May, graduation arrived. When I walked into the gymnasium, things were in an uproar. Allen, class valedictorian, hadn't shown up, and nobody—his parents, Mr. Hindman, Roger—had seen him since early afternoon. All around the gym, people held hushed conversations, an eye on the door, expecting Allen to charge in, mortarboard askew and robe billowing behind. Allen's parents, the principal, and the town marshal claimed one corner of the gym as command center, while Roger hovered on the periphery, his face as white as the tassel which he kept flipping from side to side, his nervous hand revealing a prescience that this would not end well. After an hour, the graduates lined up, and the organist began the overture to "Pomp and Circumstance." Roger delivered his salutatorian's speech by rote and too softly to hear, even if anyone had been listening.

What was supposed to be a graduation party turned into a vigil with all the booths at Bob's Pizzeria packed. Everybody had a theory. Allen was somewhere on a Greyhound bus laughing his head off for giving everybody the slip. One of the winos from down by the river had knocked him over the head and buried him in the flood debris. He had been kidnapped and was being held for ransom. I couldn't imagine any of those things. But when somebody reminded us how Allen had bragged that he could climb down the loch wall as easily as he had scaled the Stockport Bridge, I remembered him and Chuck swinging up those cables. I remembered the Tarzan yell when Allen reached the apex of the arch, arms spread wide as if ready to fly.

They started searching the river the next morning. Emergency vehicles, county and state police cars, and Army Corps of Engineer trucks made deep grooves in the grassy bottom which extended from road to riverbank. Out of curiosity, Mother and I drove over there midmorning, and the place was crawling with onlookers, all in fearful expectation, eyeing the two rescue boats at work in the river. From where I stood, the uneven stones in the loch wall were plain to see, and I could imagine Allen thinking what fine footholds they would make. It felt obscene to associate Allen's animated face with the choking, greenish water moving toward the dam, carrying bits of debris. Mother and I didn't stay long.

Searchers didn't find Allen that first day, or the next. The third day, recovery hooks finally snagged Allen's body and hoisted it out of the water just below the dam. Three days later, when I should have been with the others, paying my final respects, I sat in the swing under the pear trees, hedged from the gravel road and the passing cars by tall lilac bushes. If I didn't actually see the casket and the mountains of flowers banking the front of the church, I might postpone deliberating the adage, "The old must die and the young may." Knowing something and facing its stark reality are two entirely different things.

Even as I kicked my feet back and forth in the soft grass, I knew also that this present state of limbo, like good times and life itself, wouldn't last forever. I would ride my bike past Fairview Cemetery and see the mound of dirt sticking up higher than the others. I would read the headstone and look at the graduation picture Allen's parents had sealed in glass and placed there. I'd hear people talking about Allen and his wasted potential. For that one afternoon, though, I chose the fragile security of my own front yard.

And later still, I would understand exactly why I avoided Allen's funeral on that first Saturday in June, 1962. And it went deeper than avoiding irrefutable proof of his death. The credo I depended on back then was this: Taking risks is dangerous, so stick with the tried and true. Unlike me, Allen wasn't satisfied with the status quo; he disdained a paradigm that would deny adventure or challenge. Instead, he embraced risk, invoking youth and health and high spirits as bulwarks to danger. But even the best of intentions can invite the worst of ironies. Dragged dead from the Muskingum River at eighteen, Allen became a symbol of the most tragic results of taking foolish risks.

Chapter 21

LIFE DIDN'T STOP with Allen's death. Things in the country and the world continued their transformations in the summer of 1962. Radio, television, and the press provided news about the Beatles, the JFK White House, Viet Nam, and Civil Rights. And yet I paid little attention to what was going on outside my personal universe. It was easier to drift into an exclusive relationship with Chuck, and if a persistent, niggling doubt warned me to take a closer look at my motives, why upset a storybook romance?

Following Allen's funeral, his parents and two younger sisters returned to Weston, and the rest of us went on with our summer. A gentle, thoughtful soul, Roger was lost without Allen, and Ohio University looked less inviting now that he would be going there alone. He and Chuck spent more time together, and my third cousin and classmate, Kathy, completed a friendly foursome. In July, Allen's father invited us to visit the family in Weston. The presence of a youthful group who shared their loss would bring Allen closer, if only for a few hours.

Going to Weston was another first, an overnight stay

miles from home, accompanied by three other teen-agers. If Allen's father hadn't made a showing through financial success, it's unlikely my father would have allowed me to go. We took scenic West Virginia roads through dense valleys chiseled out between mountains. Harmless, mid-summer rivers eased over rocks, placid little streams that during flood season uprooted trees and ripped away top-soil.

In Weston, we were treated like royalty and escorted through the small town to offices and oil wells that Allen's father had leased. We were his proof that Allen's short life had engendered loyal friends. An afternoon visit to Stonewall State Park gave us a chance to rent rowboats before heading back to Ohio. Drifting on calm waters, with Aker Bilk's "Stranger on the Shore" playing across the lake, was the stuff of dreams. Moments like those and extended time with Chuck heightened the budding romance. Before I knew what was happening, my sense of who I was became all tied up with Chuck and my personal version of the Cinderella fantasy.

⋯⋯◉⋯⋯

My life, in most ways, though, had not changed. Our housing remained sub-standard, and Grandma Hosom continued to complain with volume and consistency while Grandpa Hosom heard less and less. Mother's palpitations came and went, and Daddy's time was spent at Grandma Rippey's except for meals. There had been a development in the Duncan Falls property. The couple who purchased it on land contract had defaulted and left the place a pigsty, complete with human excrement and every other kind of filth. My parents cleaned out the worst of it and argued about their options, but nothing was decided.

My outlook, however, had changed, due in part to Allen's death. The year before, I had worried that the money wouldn't be there when time for college came. This year, my desire for higher education, once a flawless standard, had developed a wrinkle. With college came all sorts of challenges—new surroundings, new expectations, new people. My personal catch-22 involved preparing for an opportunity that might never come and, if it did, lacking the courage to meet it.

No wonder I chose to focus on the here and now—one positive, Chuck; one negative, my body image. I had not yet achieved my ideal, a slender physique. By the scales, the clothes I wore, and every other indicator, I was well within normal parameters, and yet I stressed about pounds and inches. Instead of confronting my obsession, I memorized calorie tables, reduced food portions, and checked my progress on every scale available. Worst of all, I saw nothing abnormal about what I was doing.

The week before school started, though, food became the farthest thing from my mind. Daddy came straight to the house from work one evening, instead of stopping first at the farm.

"Chuck's father was in for a haircut today," he announced. Just those words made my stomach seize. "And we had a talk about this 'going steady' business." He gave me time to digest his words. Chuck must have been more open with his parents than I had been with mine, because the words "going steady" had never passed my lips with either one. A rush of tears blurred my vision and threatened a torrent. "You two need to take a break from each other."

Mother looked on uneasily as she took out bread and butter and lifted the pot of beef stew off the stove. "You just said she couldn't go steady, Raymond, not that she couldn't see him at all."

"Doesn't matter," he said. "She needs to spend time with other people. No more Chuck. That's that."

I might have spoken if an emotional avalanche hadn't swept the words from my head. Choking tears had no relevance to my father, who seated himself at the table, heaping beef stew onto his plate, buttering a slice of bread. I fled to my room and buried my face in a pillow to muffle the sobs. If not for those essential gulps of air, I could have maintained absolute silence until he left for the farm. Mother came to check, bringing a cool cloth for my face, and her touch brought on another tsunami. When she came again, with offers of toast and tea, I refused.

However unreasonable my reaction was, dismissing it as melodramatic trivializes my distress. How could I go back to school displaced from my identity? The daydream which had been my reality was perfect. Chuck and I were perfect. Why did my father have to ruin the best thing in my life?

By the time Mother returned from taking Daddy to work the next morning, I was in the swing under the pear trees, toes maintaining a gentle rhythm. Back then, I was subject to persistent nosebleeds that knocked me out of commission for an entire evening. The morning after a nosebleed I always feared a sudden move would bring on more bleeding.

That August morning, I felt just as fragile, and it took nothing at all to start the tears again. I sobbed intermittently for most of the day. By evening I was exhausted, despondent, and so thirsty my mouth felt like it was lined with cotton.

When Daddy came over for supper, I retreated to my room, and if he had wanted me out, he would have had to drag me. Looking back, I can see that my self-imposed isolation would have been the perfect time for reflection. Why was I in shambles over a father's natural concern about his daughter's exclusive relationship? How had my identity become so quickly dependent on someone else? And this obsession with achieving a svelte figure—how did it figure into the equation of the "new me"? But I was young, ignorant, and stuck like a barnacle to a fragile life raft in a great big sea of uncertainty. What issues mattered more than those facing me at the moment?

The next day I was free of crying jags, and that evening, Mother told me about pleading my case to my father on the drive back from McConnelsville. She had characterized my teen-age romance as completely natural for a girl my age. As a couple, Chuck and I were seldom alone; we went everywhere with Roger and Kathy since Chuck wouldn't be driving until the end of the year. By the time they reached home and Mother had run out of steam, Daddy longed only to fill his empty stomach and retire to his solitary quarters. And he had had two days to cool down. "All right," he told her. "Just so she keeps her head on straight."

"Oh, she will," Mother assured him.

This time, though, Mother's help in making the unpleasant go away was to prove less beneficial than she and

I believed, enabling the postponement of a serious reckoning until much, much later. But, true to her heroic impulses, Mother had once again taken on the giant.

———⊷⊶———

With classes resumed, homework piled on, and there wasn't much time for social activities. Every couple of weeks, Roger came home from OU, and we would all get together for a movie or just to hang out. A perpetual sadness had become an integral part of Roger's personality. That was one reason Kathy backed out of our foursome. The other was a bit more complicated. Roger had never once kissed Kathy good-night or shown an interest beyond the most casual friendship, she said. Mulling that over, a bizarre idea came to mind: Maybe Roger didn't like girls. Maybe Roger liked Allen. That would explain his intense and prolonged grief. Stockport, circa1962, didn't concern itself with those possibilities unless they became glaringly obvious, so I didn't either.

Although I had a heavier schedule that fall, I settled into a predictable routine. That wasn't to say my junior year passed without incident. One challenge came from following Mrs. Gage's advice. Most college papers, she said, had to be typed, so I signed up for Typing I. My typing teacher must have been a hundred years old when I took her class and had spent all those years honing her technique. Shoes squeaking on floorboards, she paced the room as we typed, eyes darting everywhere, at her side a heavy wooden yardstick. Only in my imagination did she smack the yardstick against the palm of her hand like a billy club. Also, I am sure she smiled, sometime.

Never having been blessed with natural dexterity, I couldn't make my fingers behave on a keyboard, a serious disadvantage in typing class. There I would be, creeping through my exercises, avoiding the cardinal sin of the over-strike, when some offender would whisper or peek at the keyboard. Down would come the yardstick, smack across a desk, the sound reverberating throughout my spine and straight to my fingertips. Even if I hadn't made mistakes yet, I was doomed. Before many weeks, I had resigned myself to reality. The best I could hope for was to achieve rudimentary typing skills and escape.

On the home front, another problem became apparent as soon as the weather turned cold. No matter how hot a fire we built in the Warm Morning heater and the kitchen range, the house was never warm. There wasn't a single strip of insulation in the walls, and every door jam, every window sash, and every joint in the floor had shrunk with the dryness of winter. Outside air battled inside air, and it was no mystery which side was winning. No wonder Mother and I developed lingering colds, hers worse than mine, its severity due to her staying up half the night to tend fires. On top of that, the car heater malfunctioned, so she carried a quilt during her McConnelsville runs. This was, she informed my father, her last year on Olivet Ridge.

———≡»«(»)«≡———

Besides warmth, spring brought events of importance. New to Windsor High School that year was the National Honor Society. Grade-wise I knew I was a shoo-in, but scholarship was not the only consideration. How would I show up in character, service, and leadership? It wasn't until the induction assembly when Mrs. Gage, the first to take the ceremonial scepter, touched my shoulder that I fully believed I was in. I assumed Chuck would be proud of me, but he sat through the ceremony, arms crossed. It wasn't until the junior play was pronounced a success that I was able to make sense of his reaction.

Another unexpected outcome of the ceremony came when photographs taken the day of the induction came back. How thin I looked! That can't be me, I thought, heading into the girls' restroom where the mirror was hung on a slant that allowed a full-length view. Something had to be wrong with the photo. My legs did not look skinny; the mirror showed full, rounded calves. Nothing on me could be considered thin. I puzzled over the anomaly, never guessing that the skewed image I saw in the mirror could be one more aspect of the distorted thinking I had experienced in my childhood. BDD, body dysmorphic disorder, could probably be found in medical texts in the sixties, but it wasn't commonly recognized. Certainly, it wasn't in my case. Back then, anorexia nervosa wasn't a widely known term either, but I was living proof it existed. Unable to see my body as it really was, I edged closer and closer to a dangerous condition.

The eating habits I had acquired throughout the winter and spring were Spartan bordering on bizarre. Mornings, I started with cereal, fruit, and a glass of skimmed milk. Lunch, the tray at school, minus the buttered bread and dessert; those I slid onto Chuck's tray. Evenings, I allowed myself one slice of dry toast, one apple, and a glass of skimmed milk. This I ate alone and always in the same order. First the toast, along with small sips of milk. The apple I ate one side at a time, creating a nearly perfect half before proceeding to the remainder. By bedtime, I was usually ravenous but seldom gave in. I kept a seamstress tape in my room and routinely measured my waist. Throughout the winter, the circumference grew smaller and smaller. By spring, I had an eighteen-inch waist, the same as Scarlett O'Hara's after Mammy had pulled the ribs of the corset into the smallest possible circle. Such insanity I accepted as necessary to achieve an equally insane ideal.

———————

As juniors, we chose *Ask Any Girl*, a play based on the 1959 movie starring David Niven and Shirley McClain. Having watched my handling of *The Unforgiven*, Mr. Medley selected me as the female lead and Chuck to play the role opposite. The play and all it entailed was the highlight of my high school experience. I loved rehearsing, dressing for the scenes, and perfecting my lines and delivery. When it was all over and the final performance was behind us, Chuck *was* proud of me, of *us* actually. That was it, I realized, comparing his pride in our joint success to his reaction to my NHS induction, an event in which he was an onlooker and I was a central player.

Looking back, I see the nearly impossible odds I faced. It was 1963, and I was living in Stockport, Ohio, a time and a place in which gender equity was a long way off. A woman was secondary to a man, her role supportive. People as liberated as I imagined Mrs. Gage to be lived by the universal code. Her husband, she said, "allowed" her to teach. And it was she who said a woman should never use the title "Mrs." with her own first name. "Mrs." stood for "mistress of," and what woman was mistress of herself? No woman I knew—at least not yet.

In his defense, Chuck was playing a role as ingrained in his psyche as my role was in mine. We were products of our culture and destined to make the same assumptions as those who had taught us. If Chuck ever questioned our couple's dynamic, he kept it to himself, and I can't fault him for that. I kept my questions quiet too.

Chapter 22

DADDY'S OPENING SALVO was predictable: He was not paying rent in Stockport when he already owned two houses. Mother wasn't about to let that deter her, but she had the larger issue to consider, finding a place that would also house her parents. Unless one of her siblings stepped up to take a turn, Grandma and Grandpa Hosom would move with us.

With battle lines between them drawn, I started a project of my own. It began when Mother came across a vanity perfect for a girl's bedroom, a nice piece, but scuffed and water-marked. A can of stripper, a scraper, some sandpaper, and a lot of hard work revealed a lovely walnut finish ready to varnish. A chest and low dresser showed up next, and I refinished those also. My hands were a wreck, but the beauty I'd uncovered made it worth the sacrifice.

Because of the fumes and the mess, I worked outside on the paving stones beside the back door, and Daddy observed my work as he came for supper each evening. Realizing my masterpieces deserved a home, he softened enough to consider moving. Then, in a show of grudging consent, he agreed to sell the corner property and rent a two-story house on Broadway Street beside the Stockport Hardware. He would remain on the farm, making Mother's daily trips longer, but she agreed to the deal. Yet the problem was only half-solved; one bed would fit into the larger downstairs bedroom, but not two. And no way could my grandparents share a bed.

During the winter, Grandma Hosom's care had become onerous. She left her bed only to slide onto a potty-chair and turned bath time into an Olympic event. Mother reached her limit the morning Grandma upended a pan of bath water in her bed. Even the mattress had to be hauled outside to dry. As for her complaining, Grandma had upped the volume so that with windows open, her voice could be heard from the road. If she were to join us in Stockport, neighbors, hardware store patrons, and passers-by would be subjected to marathon moaning and groaning. Together, these concerns sealed Grandma's fate. A van from the nursing home arrived one morning in late June. Grandma begged and promised, but Mother was finished with her role as doormat. Once the van left, though, she sat down and had a good cry. And she never quite forgave herself for abandoning her mother.

The previous December, Chuck had received his driver's license and taken a job as projectionist at the Opera House, a vintage movie theater in McConnelsville. Roger no longer had to be part of the equation when we needed transportation. And that was just as well, as he became more involved in life on campus.

Another friend I saw less of was Lyn who had begun dating seriously her senior year. She had graduated in May and was set to begin business school in Columbus. Just before she left, she appeared at my door, face radiant. On her left hand was a diamond solitaire. My jaw dropped, and I grabbed her amid mutual squeals. I had to wonder how long business school would last, with her fiancé a hundred miles away. When I saw her again the following spring, she and Gary were happily married and a baby bump was visible. The message was simple and predictable: Mixed feelings about college are sometimes resolved by Mother Nature.

All through my junior year and well into the summer, I stuck to my eating program; that is, until Chuck voiced concerns. I had ignored pleadings from teachers, friends, and my sister, but Chuck's mentioning my thinness got my attention. I dreaded regaining the pounds and inches I'd fought so hard to lose, and yet I dreaded his dissatisfaction more. I finally compromised and began adding once-forbidden foods to my regimen. But the months of minimal eating had so worn me down that small increases took a long time to show.

If my food obsession had an upside, it came when Mrs. Gage told us to start thinking about topics for our research papers, the mammoth project all seniors complained about. I already knew what mine would be. I had a title before I wrote the first notecard: "The Way to Good Nutrition." I had read everything available at the Kate Love Simpson Library on diet and nutrition and scoured magazines for articles, amassing considerable knowledge of food groups and nutrients, a common practice among anorexics.

For so long, I had flirted with a serious eating disorder. And I was a perfect candidate with my unstable home life, the desire to control my universe, and a fear that my whole house of cards could fall flat at any moment. I would like to think good sense caused me to choose safer eating habits. Far from it. Fear of losing a seventeen year old boyfriend who knew only the outermost layers of my personality caused me to turn the corner. Just one more of life's little ironies.

Settled into the house in Stockport, I gave full attention to senior activities. Our drama production was *A Teen on a Tangent*, a play about a boy who faced over-simplified temptations. Plays written for high school were notoriously lame or so watered down from the original they were barely recognizable. In the senior play, I was the bratty little sister with a smart mouth. I could identify with that role.

Then on November 22, 1963, at 1:30 p. m., EST, normal activity halted. I was between classes in the upper hallway at Windsor High School when Mrs. Gage, composure shaken, relayed the news: President John Fitzgerald Kennedy had been shot. Before the bell rang for the next class, the solemn voice of Walter Cronkite bore even worse news through the open office door: The President was dead. Word spread throughout the building, where everyone stood immobilized, and many began to sob. Numbly, as grim details continued to pour out, we headed toward our classrooms, seeking familiar patterns.

School dismissed early, and as Chuck and I took to the uneven sidewalks, bulging and cracked over encroaching roots, I stared into the cloudy afternoon. Even with my fingers intertwined with Chuck's, I felt more vulnerable than I had thirteen months earlier when the Soviets put their missiles in Cuba. When a U-2 plane was shot down by the missile crew, everybody feared the worst, war with Russia. Then, as now, I had felt the outside world crowding in. Overhead, branches already bare or clinging belatedly to their leaves reflected the somber events in Dallas and the grim realities I allowed myself to face only in the rarest moments.

———⟫⟨⟪⟩⟫⟨⟪———

Early in May, 1964, I once again took the English scholarship test. When results came back, I had placed sixth in the state, a record for Windsor High School, but of no consequence otherwise. Chuck announced he was joining the Air Force and heading for basic training that summer. After two years of exclusive dating, we were destined for the next step, the informal engagement. Without much actual discussion, assumptions were that I would remain in a holdling pattern while he was at basic, and college, should the opportunity arise, would be extraneous. I had said nothing to rock the boat. It was as if two separate people lived in my body, the devoted girlfriend and the hopeful academic. I had a pretty good idea who would win, if for no other reason than I lacked the courage to embrace the more daring one. Other senior girls had been showing up with engagement rings. One girl married, reportedly to keep her fiancé out of the draft. In my heart, I did not envy any of them.

When Mrs. Gage bluntly asked if Chuck and I planned to get married after graduation, I said no, hedging the truth.

We *didn't* plan to get married after graduation, at least not *right* after graduation. If marrying Chuck was the dream of my life, why not answer the question honestly? Why not wish for a diamond ring like the other girls were wearing? I blame deliberate blindness for ignoring the warning signs flashing all around me like neon.

What I couldn't completely dismiss, though, was a sense of my life being out of kilter. Never was that feeling more evident than during our senior trip, a whirlwind journey by train through the nation's capital and on to New York City where the World's Fair was being held. So much of the experience still remains a blur. There are flashes of Radio City Music Hall where we saw *The Pink Panther* and of my aborted elevator ride in the Empire State Building. A panic attack sent me right back down while the others went on to the observation deck.

My clearest memory is of going to dinner alone following an argument with Chuck. The other girls had already left, so I was on my own. Green as grass, I walked into the dining room on the ground floor of the hotel and seated myself at a small table in front of the windows. A waiter hustled over and took me to an obscure location near the kitchen. A lady, he said, did not sit by the windows without an escort. Unabashed, I ordered. At the next table, a mother and daughter were having an early dinner before meeting someone for a show. The girl had trouble dismantling her chicken; the mother drank Manhattans and chain-smoked.

"Tell the girls you'll be sitting with them on the way home," Chuck announced as we gathered in the hotel lobby the next morning. Everyone around us looked shocked, and

I felt numb. Had he just broken up with me?

During the entire trip, I had felt uprooted and stranded in the unfamiliar, going through the motions while everybody else had a great time. I hadn't been the best of company for Chuck, and the strange environment brought out sides to our personalities that we weren't expecting. There was plenty of time to evaluate things as the commuter train made its way south to D.C. and then as we headed west on the Baltimore and Ohio. What if this break-up with Chuck was permanent? What if I *did* go to Ohio University in the fall? My application had been accepted. I could get student loans, and Daddy might scrape up some money; a daughter in college should be worth something. On campus, I'd settle into a dorm, learn my way around. Managing alone in an environment I knew nothing of would require a serious level of self-assurance, something I had made few strides in the last couple of years. But if Chuck and I were finished, decisions were upon me.

Watching the green blur of Maryland from my window, I felt the chill of the unknown in all its bleakness. And I remembered a recurring nightmare that had started about the time Mother filed her unsuccessful claim for divorce, the spring I turned seven. In my dream, I was alone in a great, dark void, clutching for a handhold on a smooth circular disc, my only alternative to sliding into blackness. As I stretched to my limit, an eerie presence assured me I would never catch hold, no matter how hard I tried. At this point, I always awoke ice cold and crying. And even though I remembered every detail, I would never tell Mother what I had dreamed.

Then, from a few seats away, I heard Chuck's voice, responding to someone's remark. Its familiar timbre registered deep in my awareness, interrupting the memory of the nightmare. I didn't have to venture into the unknown. Or reach for the unattainable. Everything could continue as planned, my future in the hands of someone who had promised to be there. Without a second thought, I was out of my seat and snuggling in beside him. Chuck's startled but relieved expression gave me assurance that I had chosen correctly, and his arms around me banished the last of the dark images. Good-bye, Ohio University. Hello to everything that followed.

⸺•《◉》•⸺

What followed almost immediately was Mrs. Gage's pulling me aside after our last English class and informing me that she had something to say. "I'm not supposed to tell you this, Lois." Her snappy brown eyes were as serious as I had ever seen them. "But I'm afraid you are going to throw away the best opportunity you will ever get." I tried to swallow, but my throat was too dry to function.

"Tomorrow night at the honors banquet, a representative from Ohio University will award you a full tuition scholarship." She continued to hold my eyes with hers, steady and unblinking. "If you show up, it is yours. If not, I will know you are turning it down."

"Thank you for telling me," I managed to squeak out, my feet ready to bolt, but she caught my arm. "Are you going to attend?" I couldn't tell her the truth, but I softened the lie. "I don't know," I mumbled, as the bell rang. The look she gave was far more eloquent than further words would have been, and I could feel her eyes following me as I barreled down the hall toward my final class at Windsor High.

Mrs. Gage had already called Mother and explained the offer by the time I got home, and Mother was leaving to pick up my father. "Don't tell Daddy," I pleaded. Always my staunchest ally, Mother hesitated before agreeing to take part in so serious a crime. "Are you sure?" she asked. "Really sure?"

"Yes, yes, yes!" The last word came out as a wail. I took the steps to my room two at a time and threw myself on the bed. If only I could block it out, all of it. No more decisions, no more choices, no more chances to change anything. Every racing thought and every swirling doubt just gone! Nothing in my head but peaceful, silent oblivion.

The next evening, while I pretended to be entirely satisfied with my decision, my imagination created a split screen of events going on back in Stockport and in Zanesville where Chuck and I were celebrating my choice. About the time baked steak, mashed potatoes, and green beans were served on cafeteria trays in the high school auditorium, Chuck and I were entering a Chinese restaurant. By then, I figured, Mrs. Gage would have given up scanning the tables and keeping one eye on the door, finally believing that I *could* be this stupid. The awards ceremony would have begun by the time Chuck and I finished our chicken chow Mein and egg rolls. When we were seated in the ornate Liberty Theater where the opening credits of *From Russia with Love* rolled across the screen, I envisioned Mrs. Gage congratulating Kathy and her parents and leaving the auditorium, her heart heavy.

Theme music, the aroma of buttered popcorn, the familiar warmth of Chuck's arm around my shoulders—none of these could dispell my regret. In a dark, cold spot in my soul I knew I had made the most profound and far-reaching mistake of my life.

Chapter 23

WITH MY SENIOR year wrapping up, another upheaval was upon us. Daddy had agreed to pay rent in Stockport through June, not one day longer. Since Mother couldn't face another stint on Olivet Ridge, particularly in the hated "home place," that left our only option the Duncan Falls house, which the couple who had purchased it through land contract had deserted and left in horrific condition. The day following graduation, Mother and I drove up Route 60, and I stared out the side window, my mind stuck in the evening before.

After the last strain of the recessional, the new graduates had lined up for congratulations. To everyone else, Mrs. Gage offered positive remarks and congratulations. To me, the one she had guided through scholarship exams and encouraged to write honestly and well, all she had to say was this: "I hope you find what you're looking for."

The Duncan Falls house was just as Mother had described it. No way would it be move-in ready by the end of June. The place smelled of mold, cat urine, and dirty human beings. Mother looked utterly disheartened, facing another round of sheer drudgery, just so she could have a place to call home. She had turned fifty-six that spring and looked every minute of it. Throughout her entire married life her most basic needs had been ignored: medical and dental care, shoes and clothing. But most debilitating of all, her opinions and feelings carried little value in my father's world. As we stood in the kitchen, crumbling newspapers and adding kindling to the range to heat scrub water, Mother took a Kool from her apron pocket and struck a match against the filthy cook-top. The tip of her cigarette glowed red as she inhaled, and I found music on my transistor.

By mid-afternoon, Mother's pace had slowed, but she hadn't quit. When I noticed the heavy pulsing in her neck, I took the broom from her hand and led her outside where she could rest in the shade. Back in the house, I forced myself to take a reality check. If by a miracle we could make the place livable, what would we live on? I could get a job, even two, but could we manage on that? Mother had to know the plan was a lost cause, but returning to Olivet Ridge would cancel out any dignity and self-direction she had gained in recent years. By early evening, we were back in the 1951 Chevy Fleet-line, headed toward McConnelsville to pick up my father at the shop. The gods of commerce must have been smiling on Daddy when he bargained for the Chevy; it wasn't a bad little car.

We were just beyond Rokeby Loch, when I noticed a flagman in our lane. Summer road repair had begun, and northbound traffic had the right of way. Mother applied the brake and brought the car to a stop. From directly behind us came the sound of screeching tires and then a solid thud as another car slammed into our rear bumper. My head hit the windshield, and the steering wheel drove into Mother's chest. Once I was sure she was only startled, I got out, checking the damage. Other than a dented bumper, no damage was obvious on our car.

The driver of the beat-up sedan behind us met me at the collision point and I caught a whiff of his breath. So did Mother when he stumbled up to her window. The drunk pulled out a roll of bills and started peeling some off. Mother's distraught blue eyes went to the money the man held out. "I don't want to get anyone in trouble," she said.

"Don't touch that money," I told her. Turning to the man, I said, "We'll see you at the sheriff's office." I forced the number and letter sequence from his dirty license plate into my brain and got back into my seat. The man continued to stand there, money out, as Mother restarted the engine and eased in behind the last car in the southbound string. The flagman gave us a salute as we passed.

When we got to McConnelsville, Mother still seemed disoriented. At my insistence, she pulled into a parking spot near a window bearing black lettering which read "Morgan County Sheriff." No way had the drunk followed us; he was headed for tall timbers as fast as his sorry ride would take him. Mother asked me to write the accident statement. She signed it and I recited the license number. The young deputy commented, "We've heard that one before."

Daddy took the news of our fender-bender in stride and was soon napping, chin on chest. He had brought the scent of the barber shop into the car, smells that never failed to take me back to times that seemed so long ago. When we arrived at the old home place, he jerked awake and climbed out into a soft spring evening. Grandma Rippey no longer spent much time there, and the life of the place was gone. No garden, no chickens, no welcoming smoke issuing from the kitchen chimney. There was just a solitary man, slightly stooped from years behind a barber chair, walking through tall grass toward an empty house.

Back in Stockport, Mother asked me to fix Grandpa's supper and went directly to her bedroom. While Grandpa ate his warmed-up meatloaf, I looked in on her, and she appeared to be sleeping, so I drew the quilt over her legs. The disheartening work and the accident had sent her for a loop. I could only hope she would sleep it off.

The next morning, she sat at the table, coffee and cigarette cold in front of her, the vein in her neck jumping worse than the day before. No way was she up to driving Daddy to work, so I got word to him by way of the neighbors. Not long after, his pick-up pulled up to the curb. For years, Mother had underplayed the palpitation episodes, but that morning, no one could miss the throbbing vein in her neck or the panic in her eyes. Daddy's reaction was immediate and his words abrupt: "You're going to the doctor."

The processing behind Mother's frightened eyes was only too clear: This could be the first step to the state hospital. "She's tired, Daddy," I intervened. "She'll be fine once she's rested."

He wouldn't budge, so I helped her dress. Once they had left, I gave Grandpa his shredded wheat and coffee and settled him on the porch where he could observe the comings and goings of the neighborhood, and passers-by could strike up conversations with him, little of which he heard. At the sound of a car horn, I turned toward the street.

The high school music instructor, twenty-five going on fifteen, had lived a few doors down from us for several months and had made it a policy to invite students into her house for parties. Chuck and I had attended a couple of those. That spring, a friend of hers from college I'll call Zephyr had shown up on her doorstep in a long, baggy dress and sandals, a guitar case and a backpack slung across her back. She had hitch-hiked from who knew where and lived on Alice's dime while she figured out how to get to San Francisco. That's where everything was happening. That morning, of all days, the pair drove by, Alice's car crammed with stuff and more strapped to the top. Zephyr's transportation issues had obviously been solved.

"We're going to California!" Zephyr shouted. Hanging out the window, ratty hair nearly dragging the street, she invited me to join them: "Come on! There's plenty of room." For one crazy nanosecond, I felt the urge to take her up on the offer.

———————

It was late afternoon when my parents returned. The doctor had prescribed medication to ease the tachycardia, but he wanted Mother to see a heart specialist. Once my father left for the farm, Mother told me that part of the afternoon had been spent house hunting, and Daddy had found a place beside the fire station owned by one of his cronies. Imagine that, I thought, he is coming through for her. I didn't know whether to laugh or cry with relief. If only she hadn't looked so lost, I would have been ready to celebrate.

The medication made Mother drowsy. She spent several days sleeping or resting. Daddy took me to see the house, and, as I had imagined, its present state of cleanliness did not meet my standards, but it was livable. The major drawback was space. The house had one sizable bedroom which would hold my parents' beds. The other sleeping space was a cramped L-shaped area off the kitchen. My single bed would barely fit. But Daddy was in hot pursuit of a bargain, so I didn't push my luck. Once Barbara saw the space I was to occupy, she offered her empty guest room. Russell's sisters were married, and his mother was staying with an older daughter. My sister's offer had one caveat: Should Mrs. North decide to return, she had first dibs.

There was no way to fit Grandpa into the Union Street house, and with Mother's health up in the air, it was time to make other arrangements. Who among the other Hosom children would take on a deaf old man who drifted in and out of senility and required considerable oversight? In the nursing home, he and Grandma could be together. After a lame explanation, I convinced myself that Grandpa was fine with the idea. I learned just how wrong I was when the attendants tried to escort him to the van. The passive old man let loose a string of profanity he must have been saving for just such a moment and swung at his captors with arthritic fists. Used to recalcitrant old folks, the men dealt with him in good humor and kindness. As I watched the van make its way up the street, my grandfather's head dropped forward in resignation, I felt as though I had been complicit in a criminal act.

As for Mother, my deepest fear was always another mental break-down. Having held up through caring for her parents, freezing in the house on the corner, worrying over where we would live, and watching her daughter throw away a scholarship worth thousands of dollars, a health problem should have been a walk in the park. Of course, it wasn't just the health problem. Each worrisome challenge had taken its toll, adding to the accumulation which now became sufficient to overwhelm any great spirit.

With less than a month before Chuck was to make his way to Lackland Air Force Base in San Antonio for basic training, I faced giving our McConnelsville digs a major clean-up, packing and moving as much of our stuff as possible, and doing what I could for Mother. I'll have to give Daddy credit. I didn't hear recriminations from him. He encouraged her to get involved in the move, but no more than I did. The doctor had her on supplements and insisted that she build herself up with good meals. But most of what I put on her plate stayed there.

If there was a positive aspect to Mother's illness this time, it was her doctor's refusal to mess around with it. After two months under his care and the consultation of a cardiologist, her physical problems were improving, but she still spent her days in bed, for the most part silent and unresponsive. Given her history of mental illness, the doctor recommended Athens State Hospital and the earlier the better.

As I knew she would, even before I had hung my clothes on the rod in my cubby hole, Barbara was on the doorstep insisting I move in with her. I put her off for a few days, knowing I would take her up on the offer, but wanting to stay with Mother until she went to Athens. This time, Mother recognized the road she was on as a dead end from the beginning. Submitting to the most dreaded scenario was ironically the first step to getting well. Delaying the move to Barbara's also gave me time to finish getting the house on Union Street closer to my standards of livability. Not to mention a chance to catch my breath. The summer had been readjustment after readjustment. And all too soon, Daddy's pick-up would pull away, just as it had six years earlier, with Mother packed and ready for treatment.

Chapter 24

BARBARA AND RUSSELL lived in a two-story house on the corner of Liberty and Second, and I insisted I would pay rent as soon as I had an income. They wouldn't hear of it, not after the room and board they'd provided for Russell's sisters. This was my first time living in a "normal" household in which a married couple shared a room and a bed and kept their disagreements private. And they talked. Following dinner most evenings, the pair lingered at the table, sipping their coffee, Russell smoking a Camel, sometimes holding Barbara's hand, companionable after a long day apart.

In my search for a job, I visited every business in McConnelsville and Malta: banks, restaurants, and retail establishments from clothing to hardware; dentist and doctor and insurance offices. Sometimes I was handed applications; most of the time, I was simply told they weren't hiring. If things went as Chuck intended, I would need a job for a year at most, depending on where he landed after basic training, so it wasn't like I was looking for a career. As I trod through both villages, I found myself tossing around thoughts I hadn't bothered with while Chuck was still home. Without his presence to cloud my thinking, the idea of joining him on some remote part of the planet where everything and everybody was utterly foreign seemed a high price to pay for security. Yet I made sure my daily letters to Lackland AFB expressed nothing less than ready compliance. I wanted so much to feel that way, and I tried. I really tried. At times, I almost had myself believing what I wrote.

Daddy was the one who found me a job. The owner of Central Super Market on Main Street, Bill Allen, was a patron of Wilson's Barber Shop. A cashier was soon to have a baby and didn't plan to return afterward. So after a brief interview, I was introduced to the basic cash register. No modern computer or handy scanner, this puppy had keys, a cash drawer, a display window for the total sale, and a receipt tape. Learning the register brought back memories of typing class, but at least I could look at the keyboard this time, and no one carried a yard stick. With September came the yellow buses passing in front of the store and the realization that at least four former classmates were now enrolled at Ohio University. I knew I didn't fit in a job that offered zero challenge, but I had ditched my chance for a real challenge in Athens. So I mastered the skill, got to know the other cashiers, and contented myself as much as I could with my situation.

Later that month, Little Bill, so called when he was out of earshot just as his dad was Old Bill behind *his* back, brought another newbie around to meet the check-out girls. Also fresh out of high school, Ron was clearly embarrassed by all the attention. Amid the usual nice-to-meet-you greetings, something totally unexpected fired in my brain. It felt as if I knew him from somewhere, and in his expression, I read a similar reaction. Then his eyes fell on Chuck's big, clunky class ring, and I returned to reality: I might not have the official diamond yet, but for all practical purposes, I was engaged and unavailable.

Perhaps it was for that reason, I told myself, as the weeks passed, that Ron remained aloof. With the other cashiers and everybody else, he loosened up. The cashiers, except for a former classmate of Ron's, were married with kids, and they all fell in love with his good manners and the even white teeth which flashed often in a grin as he became comfortable with his role as carryout boy. Privately, I had to admit he was easy on the eyes, and the fact that I was left out of his interactions annoyed me. One of the senior cashiers, Barb, who had taken me under her wing from the beginning, never missed anything. She summed up the situation as she saw it. "Too bad you're already taken," she said. "This one's a keeper."

Despite my loyalty to Chuck, it didn't take me long to enjoy a sense of freedom and independence. Other than the daily letters, my time and my thoughts were my own. The single life wasn't so bad, I decided. But having sacrificed any other future than one with Chuck, I realized this respite from a stronger personality overshadowing mine was temporary. And it was 1964; what girl who had opted for a cashier job over college wouldn't want to get married soon? It's just the way things happened.

For the moment, though, life was predictable. There was work, and there were chores at the house on Union Street where I met my father most evenings and prepared dinner. After that, I would go to Barbara's and write my letter to Chuck and then spend the rest of the evening chatting and watching TV. Rusty was a boisterous second grader and Teresa, Barbara's second child, a shy three-year-old; both were lovable kids. Even the weather seemed to be cooperating, as warmth and sunshine continued well into September. But since upheavals always seemed to hit when least expected, the timing was perfect for the next one.

First, a bit of background. The summer I was fourteen, I read *The Search for Bridey Murphy* by Morey Bernstein, based on Bernstein's questioning of a Colorado housewife, Virginia Tighe, through hypnotic regression. In a trance-like state, Tighe shared her incarnation as a 19th century Irishwoman, Bridey Murphy. During her regression, Tighe, aka Murphy, spoke with a brogue and gave specific details about places and events, "proving" she had experienced them herself. When I went to Mother in tears, frightened by the implications, she reminded me that I couldn't believe everything I read. Nevertheless, the images planted in my brain took a long time to fade.

More recently and bearing greater impact than I had realized at the time, Chuck had declared himself an atheist one day in senior English class. At first I thought his motive was the reaction an announcement like that would receive, but I was wrong. He explained that he couldn't believe in a God who allowed evil things to happen to innocents. Even so, the shock factor in the classroom was huge and objections erupted. Back in the day, in a school like Windsor High, a teacher could ban a controversial topic with no more than a statement of conviction. Mrs. Gage restored order with one sentence: "I cannot imagine a world without God, and I wouldn't want to."

The subject had been closed in English class, and I tried to close it in my own mind. Despite misgivings that crept into my consciousness now and then, I hadn't let myself explore what being married to an atheist would entail, and I certainly hadn't considered how complicated it would be when children came along. Regardless of what Chuck thought, I *knew* there was a God. I had been taught to believe, not only through Mother's words and Bible stories, but through a sort of spiritual osmosis. God was a fact, as real as the ground I walked on.

———————

And now, back to that unseasonably warm September evening in 1964, when my worldview took another hit, one that I wasn't sure I would ever recover from. So far that autumn, only the maples had begun to turn, and that evening as I left the store, their greenish yellow leaves remained motionless. After eating, Daddy usually retired to his workshop behind the house and told me to leave the dishes for later. That day was no different, but for some reason, I settled into the porch swing and lingered, vaguely aware that the innocent blue sky was darkening and the air had taken on the dampness of evening. When streetlights came on, I said good-night to Daddy in his shop and began the short trek to Barbara's, my mind continuing to drift without direction. On the way to Liberty Avenue, I watched a few stars appear in a sky, which by then had turned to navy. At that moment, the volley of doubts attacked.

What if God *isn't* out there somewhere? No all-seeing eye, no omniscient mind probing thoughts I haven't even formed yet. Just emptiness forever and ever and ever. And all the talk about a spiritual world and afterlife? Nonsense invented by men afraid of the dark. According to Karl Marx, "The opiate of the masses." Stopping, I tried to reign in the crazy thoughts. What was this, my personal revelation of cosmic irony? The twisted joke on billions of people looking skyward for help from a nonexistent Deity? Outrageous! How could I even imagine this? As if it were a charm, as if the cadence and imagery of the Lord's Prayer held the power to repel evil, I began to recite the familiar words but felt them evaporate into emptiness. I didn't realize I had stopped in the street until a car veered around me, the driver scowling and shaking her head.

Passing lighted houses where the dialogue and canned laughter of sitcoms filtered through screen doors reminded me the rest of the world was proceeding just as if I were not on the cusp of madness. I remembered the strange episode I'd had when I was eleven, back in Duncan Falls, when a hyperawareness of self had overwhelmed me. Was this crazy thinking another manifestation of whatever that was? Oh, that this would disappear as quickly. But inside I knew that what was happening this time was way more serious and lasting.

At Barbara's house, I escaped upstairs and faced my epiphany. Had I just become an agnostic? An atheist? Both, I knew from Mother's teaching, carried the condemnation of hell. And didn't people have to experience a life-altering crisis before they reached this point? Belief didn't just evaporate. On auto-pilot, I wrote my letter to Chuck, mentioning nothing about what was going on in my head. All night, my mind remained on its exhausting treadmill. I awoke after a couple hours of troubled sleep, foggy and confused, but as I left for work, foregoing breakfast, the pall of disbelief cancelled out the sunny morning. Just as The Glare had physically altered the way I saw my world, so did this latest cataclysm. While my mind trod in endless circles, I managed to mess up a check-out order, and when the customer returned to complain, I earned a sharp reprimand from Old Bill Allen.

That evening I stopped for dinner at the Blue Bell Restaurant so I could avoid my father's company, afraid my demeanor had altered to the point that he would ask questions. Starved from skipping breakfast and lunch, I felt half-sick after ingesting the heavy food, but I detoured by the house just long enough to grab a Bible. For the second evening, I stayed sequestered in my room. Starting at Genesis, I determined to read the entire Bible. Whatever switch had shut off in my brain would surely reset itself and expunge the doubts. I swore to persist until I either regained my faith or lost it entirely. However, constant digging for proof of God's existence only exacerbated what had quickly become my obsession.

For the remainder of the fall my life was schizophrenic. Outwardly, I worked and interacted as always; inwardly, my mind never shut down and yet found no way out of the quagmire of what-ifs. One moment, I would come up with a convincing argument for God. The next, a rebuttal, dredged from a mind split into pieces, "proved" it false. I could almost feel the synapses firing, burning the repetitive patterns throughout my brain. Since I'd done nothing I knew of to bring on the episode, I couldn't imagine why I was struggling with so basic a part of who I was.

The blitz of obsessive thoughts and compulsive searching now has a name familiar to everyone, obsessive compulsive disorder. At eighteen, I knew nothing of OCD, but I was no stranger to distorted thinking: fears of swallowing, passing out, gaining weight. The Glare had been as real as daylight. A frontal attack on long-held religious beliefs made the perfect *coup de grace* for a neurotic with my background. From another standpoint, I had reached a place in life where decisions about faith are pivotal. Heretofore, I had drifted, relying on a no-effort faith, unpracticed and untried. No wonder it could not stand up to questioning. Without discounting OCD or other psychological conditions to which I was certainly open, I know one thing for sure. The most desperate and chilling experience of my life was a wake-up call from God.

During this period, I accompanied Daddy to Athens State Hospital to visit Mother. Even though the trees were at their peak of autumn color, the day was gloomy and rainy. I wasn't about to discuss my struggles over faith with my father, so while the ping-pong match, belief versus disbelief, continued in my brain, I stared at patterns of water forming against the side window of the car. Even before that day, I had wished a thousand times over that I had gone with Mother when she was admitted, back when my mind was clear and I could be of some help to her.

Inside the imposing brick building standing high above the city, the security gate slid shut behind us with a startling clank. In a sitting area, plaintive strains of theme music and the intonation, "As sands through the hourglass, so are the days of our lives," signaled the airing of an afternoon soap. At tables and on couches sat a number of residents. Some appeared lethargic, others agitated, as though an inner battery had run amuck and excess energy found outlet in darting eyes and nervous fingers. Mother perched uneasily on the edge of her chair. Stories were circulating about patients who had disappeared, she whispered, and nothing Daddy could say dispelled her fear. Paranoia spread among this population as fast as the common cold. But who was I to judge? I had acquired a permanent pass on the crazy train and couldn't find the cord to pull to make it stop.

After Mother's stay at Cambridge, she had shared some of her observations. Many of the patients there were well-educated and well-spoken. "You can't lose your mind unless you have one to lose," was her take on things. In my case, was this altered state I found myself in tantamount to losing my mind? As for Mother, I knew she hadn't lost hers; I wasn't even sure her mind was the problem.

I pulled myself out of my own morass long enough to

kiss her softly wrinkled cheek and assure her that she would be home soon, maybe in time for Christmas. Would I have found my way back to sanity by then?

Chapter 25

IN OCTOBER, CHUCK completed his basic training and came home for two weeks. My charade that all was well fell short of convincing; Chuck knew something was wrong but didn't press me about it. His plans remained on track, and we window shopped for an engagement ring. I was somewhat reassured to see him, to remind myself there was one aspect of my life that hadn't tumbled off a cliff. We talked about living on Maelstrom Air Force Base in Great Falls, Montana, and he presented me with a diamond, its style the one I had pointed out in the window. He was gentler, more like the person I'd fallen in love with.

Once Chuck was gone, I decided to seek help with the spiritual abyss I found myself unable to climb out of. One Sunday evening, I attended Main Street Church of Christ, a couple of blocks from Barbara's house. The young minister, Charles Wingfield, seemed approachable, so I took the chance and asked if I could talk to him afterward. In the parsonage next door, three look-alike children passed through the toy-strewn living room to kiss him good-night. His wife, pregnant for the fourth, hustled the brood upstairs. While I skirted the edge of my dilemma, ashamed of doubts so severe as to undercut the tenets of his life's work, Charles was open to questions and offered suggestions for strengthening my faith. Over several weeks of sessions, Charles guided me into quieter waters.

With less noise in my head, I could reacquaint myself with the basics of my beliefs and read the Bible for its inspiration, not just to find concrete proof of God's existence. I was yet to discover that single, satisfactory piece of evidence that could withstand the rebuttal, "What if?" However, the orchestration of prophesy, history, and revelation in the Scriptures, along with the physical wonders of macro and micro creation, eventually stilled the awful doubts, transforming a childhood faith into one deeper and more enduring. Charles set me on a course of discovery that challenged mind and spirit. He was God's hand held out to me when I needed it most.

When an engaged couple fights via snail-mail, it doesn't take a prognosticator to see trouble ahead. One argument grew out of a custom at Central Market. When employees had birthdays, check-out girls took turns making cakes for them. So far, I hadn't made one, so when Ron's birthday came around in December, I volunteered. This was the kind of event I included in my daily letters to Chuck, and I had no idea it would light such a fire. What was I thinking, he wrote, baking a cake for another guy? How petty, I thought and told him so in my return letter. Another argument arose when Chuck wanted me to fly to Montana and find a job there. My life was teetering on uncertainty. Why complicate it further? I said no. He entreated. Back and forth it went.

There were other disagreements, but the most memorable involved my baptism. In the Church of Christ, baptism is a choice made by the individual, and while my mother had taught me its importance, she had never pressured me. Then, of course, the home situation had made it easier to ignore or postpone anything that could trigger controversy, and Daddy hadn't wholly bought into Mother's views on religion. At eighteen, I knew it was time to answer my convictions. Hoping to avoid another argument, I informed Chuck after the fact. Big mistake, I realized with the next mail delivery. Angry, slanted script filled the return letter, and the last words ran off the edge: "How could you…!"

At first, I was certain he would do something crazy. Then I forced myself to be logical. The envelope was addressed clearly and had made it to the mailbox. Therefore, I concluded, the dramatic finale portended no drastic measures. Fears laid to rest, I discovered I was furious. How dare he attempt to manipulate me by sending such a letter! My reply, in which I was probably expected to placate, was vitriolic. And so it went, through Christmas, New Year's Eve, and into January. Was the geographic distance between us that punishing, or had I changed? Chuck was expecting nothing from me now that I had not freely given while we were together. Dealing with job, self-maintenance, and a crisis of faith *had* made a difference. I no longer wanted or needed someone to direct every aspect of my life.

If we couldn't get along, he finally wrote, maybe we should call it quits. Emotionally exhausted, I not only didn't need the complication of a long-distance relationship, I didn't have the wherewithal to manage it. So I agreed. However dispassionate my final letter, the decision did not come without angst. At one time, I had loved him deeply, and part of me still did. For nearly three years, we had been a couple. Losing part of my identity was profound, and I cried into a pillow an entire night, mindful the walls at Barbara's house were thin. Letters postmarked Great Falls, Montana, continued to arrive, and Barbara asked if I was going to open them. No, I said, not out of cruelty or retribution but in the spirit of self-preservation, knowing that if I left a door open, I would eventually walk through it. By mid-January, the rings and the vanity set he had sent at Christmas were in his mother's hands. For better or for worse, it was over.

That's not to say my problems were over. The inability to concentrate had done my employee status at Central Market no favors, and Old Bill was not a forgiving man. While I was a good cashier, he put me in the back wrapping meat most of the winter and returned me to the register only during the busiest days. Then, too, I hadn't taken care of myself. Throughout the fall and into winter, I ate and ate and ate, trying to appease a need for stability and sanity in a world that had gone bonkers. I had lunch and dinner at local restaurants, sometimes eating a main course in one restaurant and dessert in another to disguise my gluttony. Evenings, I snacked on junk. My father, always with an eye for weight gain in his progeny, suggested I cut back, and I pretended to shrug it off. When I met a couple of high school friends in town for the holidays, their reaction as I walked into the Blue Bell Restaurant was comment enough.

My body, it seems, had more sense than my brain. It began with a stomach virus, one of those nasty twenty-four hour things. The second evening I was ill enough to bring Mother, barely home from Athens, out in the cold. My sister called the doctor, who told her to feed me toast and tea. That followed everything else I had attempted to eat for two days down the commode. Having Mother with me that evening was a comfort even if she didn't seem quite herself yet. Under Barbara and Mother's care, I increased my intake from a few sips of water to small bites of food over the next few days. If Old Bill questioned my absence from work, my appearance when I returned proved it legit. I had lost weight and looked wan and weak. Gradually, I regained strength if not weight because ordinary eating was impossible for weeks. Overeating had lost all appeal for me.

Even before the break-up with Chuck and the stomach issues, I had begun to rethink the idea of college. Through conversations at the check-out counter with elementary teachers, I learned about evening classes at the Ohio University Branch in Zanesville, and I enrolled in two courses, American History and Math for Elementary Teachers. I rode to Zanesville with a trio of teachers whose comradery was just what I needed. Tackling a challenge for which I had a natural affinity served as a distraction as well as reassurance that an important part of who I was had not entirely vanished.

Valentine's Day brought remembrance and a bit of melancholy as I rang up Whitman Samplers and greeting cards.

Snow melted and spring rains brought the Muskingum River out of its banks. Then came gusting March winds to begin the drying process and blow away the last of the dead leaves. Spring showed up in Easter lilies and forsythia. That year, the resilience of nature spoke to a corresponding resilience which I felt in myself, and I celebrated quietly and privately.

Yet, I could not miss the edginess Mother tried to hide under smiles. Time, I told myself, time will help. At least she could smile without embarrassment those days, showing new dentures so white they took some getting used to. She was also sporting a new wedding band, which replaced the one that she had worn down to a wire over the years. By all apparent signs, Daddy had had a change of heart. Amidst all the changes, Grandma and Grandpa Hosom continued to share a room at the nursing home, where she bemoaned the state of their affairs and complained about the food while he blessed his loss of hearing. In other words, they were as content as possible.

Chapter 26

ON A SLOW Monday afternoon in mid-March, 1965, Anna Grace, the head cashier at Central Market, slid to the floor, her face shiny with sweat, hands clutching her abdomen. A red emergency vehicle appeared and carried her to Bethesda Hospital, where she had gall bladder surgery within minutes of her arrival. The next day, Barb and Maybelle, another cashier, and I were discussing who would drive the three of us to visit Anna Grace. Ron wheeled in an empty carry-out cart and paused to listen to our conversation. "I'll drive," he volunteered.

Maybelle inspected the long, red nails which miraculously survived the punishment of cans and produce. "You wouldn't catch those guys doing that." She nodded toward the pair hanging out behind pet supplies with feather duster and broom at the ready in case Little Bill came snooping.

Ron parked his cart and, noting the lull in customers, headed toward the back. "In case you haven't noticed, I'm not one of those guys." He disappeared down the stairs for flats of cans to stock until we needed him again.

Barb tore open a carton of Marlboros and slid packages

into the slots above her register. As was her habit when Ron came by and I was there, she wiggled her eyebrows in my direction. "And you're a free woman now."

A harried shopper hustled up to my counter with a cart-load of groceries and a wailing toddler. It gave me an excuse to turn around so Barb wouldn't notice my reddening face and leap to conclusions. I had noticed the shape of Ron's long-fingered hands as he filled the brown paper bags. And the few dark hairs showing just above the white tee he wore under an open-neck shirt. I noticed how his brown eyes crinkled at the corners when he smiled. More impressive to me, though, was the courtesy he showed customers, taking time to carry even a single bag for the older ones, sometimes all the way home. However great a catch Ron might be, "a keeper" as Barb had said, I had been a free woman for barely two months. I was in no hurry to jump into the dating game.

Even though my sister was a loyal A&P shopper, she made a special trip to Central Market once she learned of our plans to visit Anna Grace. Involved was the guy whose birthday cake had caused a hullabaloo and whose name came up now and then at home. She had to see for herself this person who just might be more than a random blip on the radar. If she thought I wouldn't notice her pretending to shop while checking out the tall, dark haired carry out boy with the engaging grin, she was nuts. A private eye my sister was not. And she couldn't resist sharing her findings that evening.

As I spruced up for the trek to Zanesville, Barbara leaned into my room from the doorway. "He's really cute," she said. When a spotless blue and white Ford Galaxy pulled up out front, she hurried to the window. "Nice car, too."

"This isn't a date. We're visiting a sick friend—all *four* of us." I tossed my brush on the dresser and grabbed a sweater. "You're as bad as another Barb I know."

Barb and Maybelle waved at me from the back seat. My only option was to slide into the front. All three were in a festive mood that was hard to resist. We cheered up Anna Grace with news from the store and tales of Little Bill's attempts to spot shop-lifters, and then we went to Shoney's Big Boy where we lingered over burgers, fries, and Cokes. Ron insisted on picking up the check. Back in McConnelsville, he deposited Maybelle and Barb at the store parking lot before driving me to my sister's.

"Thanks for driving and dinner," I said. "Anna Grace seemed glad to see us," I added as filler, surprised that, alone with him, I was nervous. My sister was retrieving her kids' toys from the yard, a chore she would have insisted they do themselves any other evening and well before dark.

He seemed to be preparing his next words. "Would you like to see a movie sometime?"

"Sure," I said, just as if I had not promised myself there wouldn't be another guy in my life for a long, long time. But instead of taking back my embarrassingly quick answer, I reached for the door handle.

"How about Saturday night?" His voice sounded nervous too.

"Sure," I repeated and then amended the monosyllable: "That sounds like fun."

I got out of the car. "See you tomorrow," I said, heading up the walk to the porch steps, aware of his red taillights rounding the corner onto Second Street which led to the bridge to Malta.

My sister was lining up Teresa's tricycle and Rusty's bike against the porch railing. "How did it go?" she asked, as innocently as a nosey sister caught snooping could.

I should have kept her in suspense, but I had to share the news—and no way was I going to breathe a word to Barb or Maybelle. "He asked me out Saturday night."

My sister feigned amazement. Who did she think she was kidding?

My next sentence sounds so cheesy I hate to write it, and if it wasn't absolutely true, I'd never put these words on paper. I knew I was going to marry Ron Spencer on our first date.

When he picked me up on March 21, the first day of spring, the plan was to watch *Goldfinger*, the must-see James Bond movie of 1965. Now that the most awkward part of dating protocol, the asking, was behind us, we were more at ease. On the way to Zanesville, our conversation became absorbing enough to keep us driving around town. Thinking we were still killing time before the movie, we stopped at Frisch's for Cokes only to realize we would have to hustle to make the second showing, but that wasn't when I knew.

During the movie, Ron was especially skeptical when a baled Lincoln Continental dropped into the bed of a half-ton pick-up with only a moderate bounce of the tires. No fan of James Bond, I was less than impressed by the implausible stunts, but I did get a kick out of Ron's expecting Hollywood to play by the rules, and it felt perfectly natural when one of those hands I had admired reached for mine and held it throughout the rest of the movie. That wasn't when I knew either.

We were on the way home, having just turned onto Route 60, when the realization came utterly without preamble: I am going to marry this person. Recalling then the sense of recognition I had felt when we met, I wondered why it had taken me so long to acknowledge the obvious attraction.

Back in the day, another serious dating protocol involved the first kiss. It was bad form, and bad luck, to kiss on the first date. We had cleared that hurdle with a simple good-night and squeezing of hands on Barbara's front porch after *Goldfinger*. So when Ron walked me to the door the second time, there was an expectant pause. Then he opened the screen door, and as I stepped through and turned to face him, he bent to kiss me. I guess my response surprised him because he still says I almost knocked him through the door. I don't remember it that way. I do remember, though, the softness of his lips and the scent of shaving crème. In the distance, were sounds of cars crossing the bridge, tires humming on metal decking.

Not long after, Ron took me home to meet his family. He had already filled me in on family history. His father, Oran, had sustained a serious back injury a few years earlier. Full recovery came largely from Oran's stubborn refusal to become an invalid. While he was out of work, Ron's mother, Margery, took a job in a nursing home, and the oldest of the five kids took care of the younger ones. During Oran's recovery from the surgery, which had fused damaged vertebrae, he repaired cars, scooting around on a creeper. Twelve and the eldest male, Ron mowed lawns, put up hay for his uncle, learned to rebuild engines and to fix just about anything. Three years later, Oran went back to work. By then Margery had risen to head cook at the nursing home and decided to keep working.

Although Oran was slow to warm up to people, he was one of the kindest human beings I ever knew. Margery was a ball of fired-up energy, an insane housekeeper, a world class cook, and a fierce mother. I felt her scrutiny the minute I walked through the door. The first siblings I met were Larry, fifteen, and Roger, thirteen. And it didn't take long for me to meet his sisters, either, since they were more than curious about this girl their brother couldn't shut up about. The older, Charlene, and her husband, Joe, were expecting their first child in July. The younger, Donna, had married at fifteen and already had two little girls.

Ron came from a solid, salt of the earth family, and I must have passed inspection because they all treated me as if I'd always been there.

Chapter 27

AMIDST THE KINDLING of an unexpected romance came another shot of reality. Mrs. North decided to return to Barbara and Russell's house. Barbara was close to tears, and though I had been forewarned, I was upset too. Wedging into the over-stuffed house beside the fire station on Union Street was no longer an option I would consider. When my friend Barb got word of my dilemma, she said her father had an eight-by-eighteen-foot camper for sale. In my parents' side yard, I'd have my own space as well as the security of family nearby. I was shocked when Daddy handed me enough money to cut my outlay in half. A small loan at the bank covered the rest. The trailer was mine, mine, mine!

Ron showed up to help with the set-up and move, and while he and Mother took to each other on the spot, tolerance between him and my father was strained. There were hiccups running electricity and hooking up water and bottled gas, and discovering that Ron had mechanical skills my father lacked irked the heretofore alpha male no end. To Daddy, Chuck's sudden disappearance from my life had been good riddance, and he wished my new interest the same, only faster. He later complained to Mother about "that know-it-all boy Lois brought home." Of course, she lost no time telling me what he had said.

On the heels of my forced change of residence, another change came about when Ron hired on at Taylor Woodcraft, a factory which assembled industrial furniture. The pay was better, and it was a move upward for him, something he was clearly set on. But Central Market wouldn't be the same. I half expected Barb, his biggest fan, to show up wearing a black arm band on his last day. Despite the changes, I loved my tiny space, furnished with the contents of my hope chest. The best part was the kitchen. On my days off, I cooked lunch for Ron, who could make the drive from Taylor's to Union Street in minutes. I cooked my favorite meals for him—beef stew, fried chicken and all the fixings—and I became the dessert queen with cherry pie and German chocolate cake, just like the one that had gotten me into trouble.

I let myself be swept along that spring, shifting my focus, forging new patterns. Being together, whether watching TV with his brothers or seeing a second run movie at the Opera House, seemed the most natural thing in the world. Nevertheless, during my quieter hours, away from the whirlwind of a new and unexpected romance, I should have been taking careful stock of my motives, so close on the heels of a breakup. I should have been reminding myself that for months, I had scrutinized my relationship with Chuck, fearing commitment and dreading an uprooting from all that was familiar. And there I was, jumping headlong into another relationship without so much as a pause.

The vantage point of experience does wonders, and years

later I could admit that more than romance was at work at the time. At nineteen, I was a long way from attaining even the first of the goals that would drive my decisions for the rest of my life: security, self-confidence, and personal achievement. That spring, in particular, a raw and traumatized psyche was begging for reassurance, and it could have driven me into disastrous alliances. Yet a modicum of common sense, surely a gift from God, counteracted my short-sightedness. And while I marvel now at my naiveté, at my certainty that all would be well despite the odds, my instincts about Ron proved reliable. Ron Spencer was and is a good man, and our feelings for each other and commitment to our marriage have remained genuine.

———※(((◉)))※———

I don't remember exactly how or when the subject of marriage first came up. When asked later how Ron had proposed, my answer was always, "I don't think he did." Formal proposal or no formal proposal, our intentions got out fast. While my sister was crazy about Ron, she had misgivings. Firsthand observer during the final throes of my break-up with Chuck, she sat me down at once for a sister-on-sister grilling. "Are you sure you're not just on the rebound?" she asked.

I told her about my reaction when Ron and I first met, and how I had known with absolute certainty I would marry him on our first date. "I don't know how I knew," I said, "but I did." I hadn't been able to make sense of it to myself, so how could I explain the phenomenon to someone else? "It's like we've known each other forever," I finished, wondering if I would buy so lame an explanation from someone else. My sister gave me a searching look and then hugged me hard, as if to squeeze out any chance I was making a dreadful error.

Mother, too, wanted to know I was sure. I repeated what I had said to Barbara, and Mother seemed to understand. She, after all, had had more than one relationship, while my sister had discovered Mr. Right the first time around. Mother's first and last real love had been Henry, the boy in Parkersburg she couldn't marry because he was Catholic. And she had never felt for Barbara's father or mine what she felt for him. It's possible that she could have grown to love one of those men, had either man valued her as she deserved.

Less eager to share the news with Daddy, I waited until Mother had gone to Barbara's to watch TV one evening. Summer dusk was falling, and from outside the kitchen screens came the clicking of crickets and the honks of Canada geese that had migrated to the river bank just beyond the turn in the street. The hum of tires on pavement as cars rounded the corner and the muted tones of a radio playing next door accompanied them. I wasn't looking forward to this conversation, but there was no escaping it. Nor was there a way to make the message more palatable, so I just put it out there. "Ron and I are getting married."

"No, no, no," he said, before the words were all the way out, "and that's final."

"This is my choice, Daddy. I *am* getting married, and I'd like it to be with your blessing." Reading the expression in my father's eyes, I sometimes felt I was looking into a mirror, another proof of his paternity, I guess. Right then, anger had turned the green of his irises darker. "You just got rid of one 'boyfriend.'" His tone supplied the quote marks. "What's going on, young lady? What aren't you telling me?"

If that was the way he wanted to play this, I could give tit-for-tat. "What's 'going on' is simple. Marrying Chuck was not the right thing to do. Marrying Ron is."

Anger became concern. "What kind of life can he give you?"

Of all the things I might have found to worry about, the kind of life Ron Spencer would give me had not made the list. He had his parents' work ethic, no question there. But when it came to ambition, Ron's drive for a better life went way beyond the example he had been shown at home. I heard it in his voice, saw it in his face. No way would he be hindered, and no way would he compromise. Knowing this, and knowing that my father would never understand that level of passion, my anger became useless also. "Daddy, I know what I'm doing."

The harsh lighting showed every wrinkle my father had accumulated in his fifty-nine years. "You don't know anything. What about college? Two classes and you think you know it all. You can neither read nor write."

At nineteen, I wasn't accomplished in a whole lot, but reading and writing were points of pride with me, and my father knew it. The comment hit home, bringing up flashes of a girl with big dreams but not enough courage to pursue them. Yet I had no desire to retaliate with *his* list of failed dreams: nurse, physician, leader of men, inventor, auctioneer, poet, artist, tiller of the land—all lost to neglect or whim or ineptitude. His worst nightmare, I suppose, was that I would follow in his footsteps, failing to find a true purpose in life.

Letting the conversation end with his words, I went through the screen door and across the porch to my own little space, where I could hear the same sounds I'd heard in the kitchen and feel the same breeze through my open windows, but where the atmosphere was untainted by the disappointments my father had never resolved and now feared his daughter would suffer because of her own hasty choices.

Chapter 28

IN 1965, PEOPLE in my socio-economic bracket stuck with traditional roles. A woman who worked used her smaller paycheck to bolster a husband's income rather than his ego, which often suffered when she took a job. The ideal of husband as provider and wife as homemaker was portrayed in sitcoms and commercials, newspaper ads and glossies. My sister had never worked after she was married, so I decided to stay home too.

Ron and I toyed with the idea of living in the camper, somewhere other than my parents' yard, of course, for about three minutes. While the tiny space might work for the honeymoon, afterwards it would spell newlywed suicide, so we settled on an apartment in an old church building directly across from Ron's parents. The ceilings were twelve feet high, and the kitchen would have been much roomier if we could have turned the room on its side. But young love casts a rosy glow over grim reality. Ron's mother contributed the books of TV stamps she had been hoarding. With those, we chose table lamps and household goods. Along with borrowed furniture and items from my trailer, we were set.

Back then, anyone younger than twenty-one needed parental permission to marry. Ron's parents were no problem. They had run away to Kentucky at eighteen when Margery was four months pregnant, and they may have figured we were rushing the wedding date for the same reason. Their next door neighbor was said to keep a pile of throw rugs inside her front door so she could run outside and shake them if something exciting was going on. As soon as she heard Ron and I were getting married, she shook her rugs assiduously, hoping for a glimpse of a baby bump. She was in for a long wait, since gestation for our first child would have been at least twenty-one months by her reckoning.

Mother was also ready to sign, believing as she had when Barbara and Russell married, that I was getting away from the annoying company of my father as well as making a better choice of husband than she had. Her example, she hoped, had taught her daughters to choose more wisely. Casting aside the old wives' tale that girls marry their fathers, she counted on my being smarter than that. She took me shopping for a dress, a white street-length suit, appropriate for our simple wedding. My father, on the other hand, fumed and fussed and made unpleasant comments while preparations proceeded without him. He had refused to sign and, by God, he meant it. Mother told him straight up that Ron and I would complete the deal elsewhere if he didn't comply. She kept it up until he made the trek to the Court House and signed away his daughter and his last hope of controlling any of the women in his life.

Since Charles was to be out of town the weekend of the wedding, we sought out our second choice, an elderly

Presbyterian minister we had met while working at the store. Reverend Stebbins insisted on a counseling session and offered common sense advice. A few days after the wedding, he showed up at our apartment with a refund of five dollars, saying that the ten dollar bill Ron had given him was double what most couples paid. He wasn't fooling anybody. He had us pegged for exactly what we were, a pair of innocents with no money and no idea what we were getting into. What a sweet man.

The church took no time at all to decorate, and I mean that literally, no time at all. There were no candles, no ferns, and no white runner for the bride to walk on. The only flowers in my wedding were in the corsages the bridesmaid and I wore. The two corsages would have been identical had the lady at the flower shop failed to question me when I stopped to pick them up. "One of these is for the bride?" she asked, as if I'd pulled a blooper.

"Yes," I answered, wondering what law of wedding etiquette I had transgressed.

"Well, just a minute then." She hustled to the back with one of the corsages. When she returned, it was larger, fancier, and bridal-worthy.

"What do I owe you?" I asked, figuring the upgrade wouldn't come cheap.

"Not a thing, honey. And best wishes." Leaving with my flowers, I wondered what other *faux pas* I had committed in my planning.

Once Daddy had given his permission, I pushed for one last favor, that he give me away. I entered his new shop on Courthouse Square, where he was now his own boss, as he was about to head up to Mark Rest Center and give haircuts to patrons living there. He had become a familiar sight one evening every week, walking up Kennebec Hill at the end of the day, black barber case in hand. While he had never appreciated his skill as a barber, everybody said no one could give a straight razor shave quite like Rip. He down-played his sign painting ability too, discounting the talent required in hand-lettering. Yet all over town, R. J. Rippey's bold, precise hand gave silent testimony to others' appreciation of his work.

"It will be all I can do to attend." He arranged shears and clippers in his case, dropped the lid, and snapped the clasps, closing this case, too, and just as emphatically.

Unexpectedly, I felt my throat tightening. "I'm sorry, Daddy," I said, wishing we could enter this new phase on better terms.

"I know, Punkin," he said, a crack in his voice as he used the old nickname.

Disregarding the issues that separated us, I took the few steps to where he stood and rested my face against his shoulder. At times, he had been the best father in the world and at others a nearly intolerable tyrant. But even tyrants have feelings, and he was choking up too. "Just be happy, little girl." His arm came around me, and we stood for that long moment, mending the rift that had threatened to remain a pall on an otherwise hopeful event.

And our wedding *was* a hopeful event, with hope being one of the few things we had in abundance. As my bridesmaid, the girlfriend of Ron's best friend, and I waited in the rear of the church, the organist played selections I had been too ignorant to choose myself. On cue, Dixie gave me a nervous smile and made her way to the front. Watching through a crack, I saw Ron in his black suit beside his friend Danny and was struck by the thought that I was marrying a stranger, but I didn't for a minute consider backing out. Suddenly the opening bars of Mendelssohn's "Wedding March" sounded, and I was on, walking toward a smiling Ron and a somber Reverend Stebbins. As he led us through our vows, I concentrated on the words. "Until death," to me, meant exactly that. This was the one time I was going to make this commitment, of that I was sure.

It had been a cool, rainy day, and as Ron and I drove to my sister's house for a small reception, the drizzle continued, but we were in that unreal state of newly-wedded oblivion and barely noticed. Barbara served cake and punch, and we opened the gifts, all practical items, in keeping with our lifestyle; we needed no crystal vases or porcelain figurines. Even though there wouldn't be a honeymoon get-away, we had planned for one uninterrupted week-end, and we almost had it.

Late Friday night, Ron's mother knocked frantically on the apartment door. Charlene had gone to Bethesda Hospital in the Spencer's car and now Margery had no way to get there. Ron handed his mother the keys, noticing that his car was covered with wet streamers and "Just Married" messages glowing in the light of a streetlamp. His sister Donna, the culprit, giggled and waved from the Spencer's front porch while Margery chirped the tires and took off like a streak. Sitting the rest of the night near the maternity wing, Ron's car spoke of an imaginary couple who could have used another slogan that night: "In the nick of time."

———————

Before long, I had done what I could to the apartment, replacing nine foot funereal drapes with white panels I hemmed on Mother's sewing machine and camoflaging the worn couch with a throw, but the place remained what it was, an ancient brick church masquerading as an apartment building. Three months in, we used my travel trailer as down payment on a brand new twelve-by-fifty foot mobile home which came to rest on Halcyon Avenue in McConnelsville. Wise decision for newlyweds or foolish, we had made it, and I determined my new home would be the best-kept dwelling in town.

Even when he took a job at Taylor Woodcraft, Ron was thinking beyond that. Taylor Woodcraft was not where he wanted to spend his working life, nor was any facility in Morgan County. His dream employer was E. I. DuPont de Nemours, a plastics conglomerate with a production facility, the largest plastics producing plant in the world, near Parkersburg, West Virginia. In the meantime, living expenses tugged always at the boundaries of our budget, thanks to the new trailer and Ron's insistence on keeping a nice car, so Ron and his father started a chip wood business on the side. I saw my new husband off to work in the mornings, when he returned after work at Taylor's and hurriedly ate the dinner I had waiting, and again well after dark, when he came in filthy, exhausted, and starving from an evening in the woods.

After another feed and a soak in the tub, he slept like a baby until time to start the routine all over again.

I found plenty to keep myself occupied—cooking and baking, keeping the mobile home spotless. The trailer court had a wash house with a wringer washer and outside clotheslines where I hung sheets and watched them rise, flapping and white against the sky. Folding them into a basket, I held the smooth fabric to my face and breathed in the fragrance. Most days I visited Mother or Barbara at the other end of town or ran errands on foot. And there was church.

When the Main Street church hosted the concert choir from Kentucky Christian College, I helped prepare and serve the meal. As women hustled around the kitchen, the choir practiced upstairs, flooding the building with majestic sound. While we served, one of the girls asked me where I was going to college. Me? Why would she assume I was in college? Couldn't she tell I was one of the housewives?

I tried to brush off the discomfiture which hovered over me after the meal while I collected plates and dropped silverware into a pan of sudsy water. But beneath the protective layers of security and contentment I had wrapped myself in, something rubbed, sort of like the pea which the princess felt under her mattress. Before going upstairs to the concert, I headed to the restroom. The mirror reflected just what the student had seen, a girl about her age, bright and eager looking, easily mistaken for her peer.

Thoughts I seldom allowed to surface came to the fore. Instead of going ahead with classes at OUZ and eventually achieving a degree, I had chosen to marry into a family that was far removed from the professional world I had once hoped to inhabit. Regardless of the respect and affection I felt for Ron's parents, I could never get away from one major difference between us, a cultural gap which carries assumptions on both sides.

No matter how little the Rippey family had or how pathetic our housing, we always spoke properly. By contrast, in the Spencer house, language was poorly articulated and infused with the phraseology of Appalachia. It took serious finesse for me to use my embedded speech patterns without giving offense. Ron had recognized the difference, too, between his own speech and that of his family. He confided that as a youngster, he had received a dressing down for "trying to sound like other people." "Other people" were the educated and the affluent, two groups seen as a single entity that looked down on hard-working common folk. Reverse snobbery, just like its counterpart, exerts its own rules.

Facing that girl in the mirror, I couldn't deny I had made concessions. While I loved my life with Ron and the sense of belonging I felt with him, I feared that some of my choices would dog me for the rest of my days. I remembered Mrs. Gage's last words as clearly as though she were standing beside me: "I hope you find what you're looking for." I had a feeling the annoying pea would continue to irritate also. One thing was certain, though. Unlike the princess, I had made my bed, and now I had to lie in it.

Chapter 29

ARRIVING AT THE trailer on a breezy afternoon in May, 1966, Mother broke the news: "Barbara is pregnant." Her voice and manner were void of excitement, and I remembered my sister's emphatic statements that two kids were her limit. Mother sat down at the table, and tapped out a Kool. The flame from her lighter fought with the fresh air moving through the screens and lost. Impatiently, she cupped her hand and made another attempt.

I had been cleaning windows and hopped off the chair, setting Windex and paper towels on the table. Beyond the wash house, frisky white and orange kites fluttered themselves dry. And my iron waited, there on its board, to tame them back into kitchen curtains. Having delivered her news and smoked her cigarette all the way to the filter, Mother stubbed it out, got up from the table, and headed through the door. I followed her out, basket in hand to collect my curtains. "I'll check on her," I promised. Removing clothespins, my mind was filled with the numerous complications babies could cause.

Come the end of June, I discovered a complication

of my own. But even before the evidence was in, I knew. Afternoons, all I wanted to do was sleep, and sometimes I awoke barely in time to get Ron's dinner. Missing a period confirmed my suspicions. I told Mother but hesitated to say anything to my sister, who had resigned herself to a joyless pregnancy. Ron seemed okay with the news, but I could see the wheels turning, calculating the effect another mouth to feed would have on his goal of financial security.

Used to the insular environment in which I enjoyed free rein, I wondered how pregnancy and motherhood would affect my life. That concern and others as they came along were buffered by ignorance. Except for a short bout with morning sickness, good health continued through summer and fall. Then, with December, a heavy, inexplicable sadness settled in. Even the soft punches of growing arms and legs didn't cheer me. Dr. Daw, attending a new generation of mothers and as abrupt as ever, recommended a stiff upper lip.

When I met Ron at the door one evening, sobbing and unable to explain why, he called his mother, who showed up with a time-honored remedy for hysterics. First, she settled me on the couch with pillows and blankets. In the kitchen, she brought the tea kettle to boil and produced a bottle of whiskey from somewhere on her person. When the hot toddy was ready, she warned me to sip it slowly. Gradually a luxurious drowsiness overtook the sobs. Margery wasn't long on explanations or sympathy, but her words heartened me amidst the raging hormones of a first pregnancy. "You may have a lot of strange feelings," she said, tucking the bottle away. For the rest of my pregnancy, I returned to normal.

Three months after Barbara gave birth to Carol Denice, I went into labor while rolling out pie dough in my kitchen. I'd had my weekly check-up that morning. No change, baby in birth position. The first contractions were mild, circling from back to front, so I filled the crusts waiting on the counter, one raisin and one peach, then topped and crimped the edges. More contractions followed, not as easy to ignore this time, and then a rush of water. Shakily, I called Mother and Margery. The women arrived together, Margery's hair hastily shampooed following a brand new perm and beginning to stick up in peaks as it dried. Mother covered the pies in plastic wrap and stuck them in the fridge while Margery made short work of cleaning my kitchen. Even with childbirth pending, one doesn't leave pie crust stuck to the counter.

As we motored up Route 60, Margery's foot got heavier on the accelerator with my every grimace. Notifying Ron took time; it was Saturday so he and his father were deep in the woods. Deciding he was too filthy to arrive at the hospital, Ron grabbed a shower first. By the time he got there, I was way past uncomfortable, and as the evening progressed, it only got worse. The shot they gave to relax me did nothing for the pains, and as time neared for delivery, bad news came from Dr. Daw, who showed up in a red and black plaid lumberjack shirt.

"The anesthesiologist won't be here, so we'll do this the old-fashioned way," he said.

By the time they wheeled me into delivery, I didn't care

whether I was knocked out or not. With two final contractions, out slid my baby just as Dr. Daw announced, "We have a big boy."

I asked every mother's first question: "Is he all right?"

"He's perfect," Dr. Daw assured me, flopping a warm, wet mass onto my abdomen.

I strained my neck to see, and reached down to touch him. How amazing was this, a little human being had just emerged from my body. Once we were separated, someone put drops in his eyes, and I heard his robust objections and the attendant laughing at his show of spirit. He was wrapped and put into my arms, where he quieted, his face scrunched from the tight confines of his exit and the insult of the eye-dropper, tons of black hair still sticky from birth. His feet were his father's in miniature, each fitting into my palm with room left over.

We handed him off to Ron, who looked at his red, wrinkled son with more consternation than pride. Having never encountered a newborn minutes old, he had no idea how rough the journey can be on beauty. It was well after midnight when the grandmothers took turns holding the new arrival, and they found him impressive in all ways. Margery's hair had dried, new-perm frizzy and as wild as her grandson's. I would have laughed had it not hurt so much. Six pounds, seven ounces of humanity had just exited a one hundred pound mother, a sizable feat, indeed.

Our last day in the hospital, Dr. Daw marched in and informed me that if I wanted to take my baby home, I had to give him a name. Early in the pregnancy, Ron had made up his mind we were having a girl and chose the name Sandra

Lee. Whenever I suggested a boy's name, just in case, he found a reason to dislike it. Ditto, even after Boy Spencer arrived. So now an executive decision was in order. I took the birth record from Dr. Daw's hand and wrote my son's name: Ronald Lee Spencer, Jr. My husband's easy compliance made me wonder if his desire all along was to have his son named for him. Men, I was learning, were puzzling creatures.

With a new baby in the house, I continued to learn a lot of things, among them sleep deprivation. Gender roles put full responsibility for Ronnie's care on me, but Ron was attentive when available and appeared to grow prouder of his son every day. Small wonder, the ugly duckling had become an exceedingly handsome swan. Among his admirers, my father ranked near the top and showed up at the trailer every day to check on his grandson's progress. If Ronnie was sleeping, Daddy was content to stand beside his crib and watch his chest rise and fall in perfect rhythm. For a man so set against his daughter's marriage, he certainly approved the product. It was Grandpa, of course, who showed up with the first toy, a red plastic wagon, just large enough to place Ronnie, swaddled in his blankets, in its bed.

Another admirer was Ron's maternal grandmother, Bertie Gheen, who had delivered nine children of her own at irregular intervals, beginning with Margery in 1926 and ending with David in 1950, a twenty-four-year span of pregnancy, childbirth, suckling, and all the rest. Numerous grandchildren and three "greats" had preceded this newest one. Still she never tired of babies. She took Ronnie off my hands as soon as we arrived and held him sleeping in her lap where she could watch the tiny red mouth suck an imagined nipple and the arms flail in startle reflex when the screen door slammed.

Three of Ron's uncles remained at home at the time, two younger than he. On Sunday afternoons no one ever knew how many kids and grandkids might drop by or how many Chevrolets and Fords would line up in the creek bottom below the house. Weather permitting, country music poured from car radios, and trouble-shooting and banter supplied conversation on the grassy bank. It was hard to imagine the tiny house holding all those kids, and one lone woman in charge, but Bertie had done it, was, in fact, still doing it. Her children learned courtesy and kindness through her example, amid threats that their father, Denzel, the enforcer, would handle serious offenders when he got home. On this afternoon, she welcomed one more member into a family that could never grow too large.

Chapter 30

LACK OF SLEEP and a doubled workload were minor problems compared to the financial hits we took following Ronnie's birth. Ron's health insurance didn't cover all the hospital and doctor fees, and, of course, babies always need something. Even with the second job, Ron brought in barely enough to cover the bills. Anything unexpected put us into the red. Small tiffs between two exhausted people stretched into longer and more intense arguments. We had no one to blame but ourselves for getting in over our heads, but that didn't matter when we clashed. Pretending to be seasoned adults, we were really just a pair of scared kids. So to ease the financial strain, we down-graded the car to cut out the monthly payment and agreed to sell the trailer and rent a house in Stockport.

We weren't the only ones having problems that summer. Shortly after birth, Barbara's little one, Carol, developed a pulmonary infection, and Barbara developed a phobia about exposing the baby to drafts and germs. Carol recovered, but Barbara didn't. She remained nervous and overprotective, hysterical at the slightest indication that Carol might be catching another infection. Someone recommended a field therapist who made in-home visits, offering counseling and relaying information to a psychiatrist in Zanesville who in turn prescribed medication based on the reported symptoms. The dicey set-up resulted in my sister's taking pills and capsules which left her alternately spacy and agitated.

The therapist, whom everyone called Michael, admitted that he sometimes popped one of the new meds, amphetamines, when he had trouble getting started for the day. Barbara swore she felt better and, given my fractured state of mind, insisted I get in touch with Michael too. I complied, and while Michael and I talked, he admired little Ronnie, rolling around on his blanket spread at our feet, gurgling and cooing and purposefully reaching for toys.

"He's very bright," Michael commented, as one who understood the connection between motor skill development and cognitive ability. No wonder, I thought. His mother used to be smart. Now her world seemed splintered into a million pieces. I took the pills for a while and didn't mind the increased energy, but I didn't like the sharpened awareness. Thinking too much had always been a problem for me.

We made the move to Stockport later that summer and during the fall and early winter recovered from the most desperate of our financial crises. With cold weather came moldy spots on the walls of the rented house, spots that disappeared when I scrubbed them, only to return. The baby's room proved musty and cold, so we moved his crib into the living room. By then Ronnie was a master crawler and explorer who could pull himself to standing and reach for everything he shouldn't. If I settled him into his playpen with toys and blocks, he shook the sides and objected in loud squalls. Freed, he took off at warp speed toward forbidden territory—the gas heater in the living room, the water which crept mysteriously into the kitchen and pooled on the floor. When I worked in the kitchen, Ronnie had to be confined to his highchair beside me, and he didn't enjoy that either.

A year earlier, Grandpa Hosom had died quietly in his sleep. Cataracts and deafness had reduced the size of his world, and dementia had heightened his suspicions. You never knew when you entered the room whether he would regard you as friend or foe. Left alone, Grandma died during our winter in Stockport. One Sunday morning, our neighbor knocked on the kitchen door to relay the news my mother had given him. While I had taken Grandpa's death stoically, at word of Grandma's passing, I dissolved into tears, mourning the woman who had saved my life at birth, and my sister's too, and who had chorded tunes on the piano during summer afternoons. She had always rushed to Mother's defense no matter how sorely her daughter disappointed her. Grieving her death brought back memories of Grandpa also, our chicken noodle soup feasts, walks to Philo to see the Doodlebug, and crisp autumns at Carter's farm suffused with the perfume of apples. And I mourned him as well.

Conditions in the house and fear for the baby caused us to rethink our move. We went trailer hunting again and found a reasonable choice. Daddy offered money for a down payment, and Ron and I were in no position to refuse. Personally, I had another reason to bid Stockport a glad farewell. The town and the school where I had excelled and dreamed big dreams were blatant reminders of the divergent course my life had taken and the chances I'd blithely tossed aside. I loved Ron and cherished my baby boy. Shouldn't that be enough? Guilt for harboring longings about a wider world than the one I had settled for drove me to a desperate act not long before we left Stockport. In the backyard of the rented house was an incinerator where page by page I burned the unfinished novel I had worked on throughout my years at Windsor High. Now, I thought, as the last sheet of notebook paper turned to gray ash, there is nothing left to tie me to the past.

We were back on Halcyon Avenue in our new trailer for eight months, just long enough for me to settle into the routines I loved, close enough to visit Mother and Barbara, surrounded by the safe and familiar. Ron, on the other hand, was pawing and snorting, his desire for a better job eating at him relentlessly. Finally the letter came. E.I. DuPont de Nemours was hiring. Would he call to set up an interview? Ron was officially hired in August and we faced another move. This time, it was a matter of securing our possessions in the trailer and having it towed to Belpre, directly across the Ohio River from Parkersburg and Washington Works, Ron's new place of employment. I tried to match his enthusiasm about venturing into a more prosperous lifestyle, but in actuality, uncertainty and dread had accompanied this possibility since its inception. Forty miles from home might as well have been a thousand.

The new trailer park was huge by comparison, filled with young couples and children. How grim it seemed here to be surrounded by strangers, and how long the hours while Ron worked. He was on a swing-shift; days were doable and midnights passable, but afternoons, when he left at three and returned at midnight, were unbearable. A creature of habit and reliable schedules, I found this way of life as foreign as the intimidating new grocery stores and the unfamiliar streets on which I resolutely wheeled Ronnie in his stroller, giving assimilation my best shot.

Once again, my overloaded psyche yielded against the strain, radiating fissures in the form of all the fearful thoughts that had ever plagued me. Before I knew it, I was facing another crisis of faith, if not as sudden and shocking as the first, certainly as disheartening because I thought I had put the issue behind me. And there was no one to soothe my angst. The church we attended in Parkersburg was a featureless red brick building filled with strangers. Sunday after Sunday, week after week, my despair deepened. Not realizing the extent of my troubles, Ron urged me to adjust. How could I ever explain?

More than once, I became so terrified of my thoughts that I rushed up the street, clutching the baby to my side, and called Ron on a payphone. A time or two he came home, but he couldn't afford to jeopardize his new job. By late October, I had worked myself into such a state that Ron threw essentials into a bag and drove wife and child to McConnelsville. Mother settled me on the living room couch and welcomed her grandson into her arms, and Ron returned to Belpre.

Mother and Barbara talked me into seeing the psychiatrist

in Zanesville who had authorized drugs for patients under Michael's care. An old house converted into offices, the clinic had walls as thin as paper. In nearby rooms, I could hear a baby crying, a toilet flushing, and typewriter keys rat-a-tat-tatting. The doctor asked me two questions, worded as one, "Do you love your Mommy and your Daddy?" Not waiting for an answer, he slid a prescription pad into the middle of his desk and wrote orders for three medications. Too ignorant to mistrust such haphazard medical care, I filled the scripts and swallowed the pills with unpronounceable names.

Lethargy, at first, was a relief, and dry mouth endurable, but I knew I was in trouble when I woke up the third morning unable to speak. Mother called Ron, who flew to McConnelsville in record time, scooped me up, and proceeded up Route 60, emergency flashers on. A patrol officer pulled us over, but after one look at me huddled in the backseat, facial muscles frozen and grotesque, he escorted us to the hospital. The emergency room staff assumed I was a deliberate overdose, and there was no way I could explain, nor could Ron, since he hadn't waited for Mother's play by play of events. Even though I couldn't speak, I saw and heard everything—the cold block walls and cabinets of bizarre instruments, the nurses' skeptical expressions as their questions remained unanswered.

I spent three weeks in the psychiatric unit while medications, amphetamines and tranquilizers, were adjusted and readjusted, their ideal balance a chemical-induced equilibrium. The result of the process was a mishmash of symptoms and mental exhaustion. But as long as I could feel less and think less, I was grateful. A regimented schedule took all the guesswork away and eliminated decision-making. The group counseling sessions felt contrived, and all I gained there was the realization that others were suffering also.

My roommate, Marlene, was there because she had walked in on her husband having sex with his secretary. Her husband said it wasn't what it looked like. When Marlene threw the kind of fit that required physical restraint, guess where she ended up. On tranquilizers, Marlene had become dopy enough to question her own perceptions. Her husband didn't inspire confidence in me, though, despite the flowers and Whitman Samplers.

Another woman, Peg, kept a *Physicians' Desk Reference* on her nightstand, and she knew every mind-altering drug by name and side-effects. Between sessions and before lights-out, she logged miles up and down the hallway on long, thin legs, hands behind her back, head and shoulders thrust forward as if to outrun an adversary. She gulped her meals with equal dispatch and filled us in on the poisons flooding our bodies, but she never revealed the source of her paranoia.

Others in our motley crew included a girl of sixteen, Becky, who had tried to slash her wrists. She was forced to use plastic utensils in the interest of safety; nevertheless, she came to breakfast one morning, wrists bandaged from an attempt using a straight pin. Becky saw herself as fat, ugly, and stupid. Who would want to live like that?

A couple of women were mid-fifties and must have succumbed to The Change. If Grandma Hosom had still been around, she could have prescribed Lydia Pinkham and fixed them right up. I was struck by the high percentage of females over males in the unit. Perhaps we were proof of conventional wisdom: Women can't cut it when the going gets tough.

During group sessions I heard all manner of self-induced horrors which had driven the others here, and I politely cheered their determination to master them. Success was achieved and release imminent once they convinced the group leader they were ready to resume their lives, brain chemistry altered by insidious orange capsules and slick blue pills. I understood the process, just as I understood why I was here. And pills or no pills, it was up to me to get out.

I remembered a story my father had told about his time at McClain, the mental hospital in Massachusetts where he had worked as an orderly. One of the patients had made repeated suicide attempts, all to no avail. My father told him how to succeed: Convince the doctors he was cured. Once he was outside their purview, he could do as he pleased. Daddy never knew whether the man took his advice or not, but the story demonstrated what I would have to do to get out of here, and soon.

My duties at home were waiting, and my absence was a burden to everyone. Every visit, Ron asked when I'd be getting out, reminding me that his sister Donna and Mother were trading off Ronnie's care. Mother came once and sat uneasily on a plastic chair, cigarette smoke hovering over her head like a halo. Clearly, she recognized the landscape all too well and wished her daughter free of it. During the third week, I knew it was time to make the required declaration, unadulterated fiction, of course, since I wasn't about to vent my real demons to a group of unstable strangers. Verbally, I shouldered my obligations as wife and mother, feeling like a fraud, so I could shoulder them in actuality and feel like a bigger fraud. Thank God for the pills. They dulled the sharp, cutting edges of my doubts and my reality too.

Discharged from the unit, I returned home as robo-wife, robo-mommy. A few weeks after my return, on a whim, I took a job at Montgomery Ward for the Christmas rush, and Mother came to Belpre to baby-sit, relieved to see me confident enough to take such a step. Of the girls I worked with at Wards, one starved herself and another insisted she was accident prone when she came to work with bruises where bruises usually aren't. Even in my cloud of wonder drugs, I knew their lives were far worse than mine.

I came home after work one evening and tossed my purse on the television set. Early the next morning something woke me and sent me to check on Ronnie, and I found him on the floor in front of the TV, my purse open, pill bottles and capsules and tablets scattered all around. I pried his mouth open and shoved my finger down his throat. By then, Mother had awakened from her spot on the couch and Ron was up too. We threw on clothes and rushed Ronnie to Camden-Clark Memorial Hospital. An emetic was administered and Ronnie was kept under close watch for a day. That's it, I decided, I *will* lick this craziness that brought the hideous pills into my house. No way would I endanger my child again. During the rest of the winter and spring, I eased away from the meds, stayed sane, gave my little boy the care he deserved, and I survived. Just as my mother had found strength in her primary role, so did her daughter.

Chapter 31

AS USUALLY HAPPENS, better times came on the heels of bad. By his second birthday, March 18, 1969, Ronnie had become a miniature man with silky hair the color of new pennies and a pair of dimples in his cheeks. His disposition was sweet and his energy boundless. In the trailer directly behind ours, lived a couple with two boys a little older than Ronnie. Although their mother, Naoka, had never been in a mental ward, she had her blue days and needed a friend as much as I did. As I dared to look beyond the walls constructed of fear and doubt and self-flagellation for unidentifiable offenses, I felt less and less like a displaced person and more like myself.

With Ron at DuPont, we cleared any outstanding debts within a year or so and found room in our budget for the next logical step, purchasing a house. Looking at homes in and around Belpre gave me a different perspective on the community. Outside the crowded trailer court were attractive houses with hedges and shade trees and room for swing sets and monkey bars. And although just a year before I would never have believed it, I began thinking another baby might be nice. Ron was afraid I was pushing my luck, considering the emotional ups and downs I had been through since our move to Belpre. But once a woman makes up her mind it's time to have a baby, everybody else might just as well stand back.

Except for a couple of blips, my first pregnancy had been a breeze—not so the second. As soon as I suspicioned I was pregnant, the problems began with recurrent bleeding episodes. My neighbor and friend Naoka was a God-send, pampering me and taking Ronnie next door to play with her boys whenever another spell of mild but worrisome bleeding would begin. She had miscarried before her boys came along, and she filled me in on what to expect, just in case. I informed her, and myself, that *this* baby was staying inside until the appointed time to exit. My bold stance didn't eliminate concerns that a less than perfect pregnancy might be a sign the baby was in trouble, but I turned that worry over to God. I had enough to deal with even after the bleedings stopped: day-long episodes of morning sickness, water retention, and a baby who rode so low I wished I had a wheel-barrow to prop up my belly. And this one was twice the kicker his brother had been and an acrobat too.

We had settled into a house along the Ohio River at Porterfield six months before Stephen Mark was to make his appearance in October, and during the final weeks, I tried to keep his brother corralled since he could out-distance his front-loaded mama in no time. Even so, he gave me the scare of my life one afternoon by climbing the aluminum post which held the television antenna. He had been out of my sight for maybe five minutes. With Ron at work, I could do nothing except sweet-talk him down while fighting off panic. It's a wonder I didn't deliver right there in the driveway. But the baby in residence this time was in no hurry to leave his personal gymnasium and kept me waiting for ten long days past his due date.

Finally, after hours of steady backache, I decided I might be in labor and away we went to Saint Joseph's Hospital in Parkersburg. That afternoon, I was wheeled into delivery at three o'clock, and Ron was told I would soon be out, baby in arms. But a uterus that was slow to contract post-delivery delayed our reappearance, and Ron was ready to tear the place down, as "soon" became four o'clock, then four-thirty. This time I was totally groggy when I reappeared because I'd been knocked out for the grand finale. Vaguely, I remember Ron bending over the railing of my bed and kissing me. "Thank you for my two boys," he said, the simple words expressing a world of meaning.

And when Ronnie learned that the baby in Mommy's belly had turned out to be a brother, his comment and tone of voice seemed rather discerning for a three-year-old: "Now my daddy has *two* boys." His meaning was clear; this interloper would take some getting used to.

All during the pregnancy, I had wondered how I could love another baby, boy or girl, the way I loved Ronnie. And yet, from the moment he was laid in my arms, Stephen Mark claimed his full quota. Our first evening at home, I was lying on the couch with Stephen tucked into the crook of my arm. He appeared as focused on my face as I was on his, and I experienced the mutual recognition my father had spoken of when he first laid eyes on me. And thinking of Grandma

Gheen and her brood of nine, I knew I shouldn't have worried about having enough love for both of my boys; something as important as love doesn't come with limits.

Being a mother would ever remain a work in progress. With two little boys, I never knew what a day might bring. What scheme would Ronnie dream up to hurt himself? Would Stephen have another episode of earache? It was a rare day that something didn't demand immediate attention, totally disrupting any tentative schedule I had made. Yet I juggled the boys' care, the budget, and household chores and still maintained relative psychological health. Having been raised by a mother who read to me and told me stories at bedtime, I determined to pass the experience on. Sitting on Ronnie's bed, Stephen kicking and cooing or peacefully asleep in his crib, I read one or more stories with dramatic flair. Charlie Brown was a favorite, and Ronnie and I applauded his victories and empathized with his failures. By the finish of prayers and hugs and kisses, Ronnie was heavy-lidded and Stephen already in baby dreamland. Sometimes I lingered to watch them sleeping, especially if I had been short-tempered that day or felt more than usually inadequate. Round little bodies snuggled under blankets made me wish mightily for a do-over. One thing for sure, Donna Reed or June Cleaver I was not. Motherhood for me was all about trial and error and trying again tomorrow.

My emotional stability narrowly escaped another crash

during our second year at Porterfield. And if I hadn't remembered how susceptible I was to obsessive thinking, things could have turned ugly. A minister transferred to our church bringing with him strong political opinions. His sermons jolted the congregation out of complacency with warnings that communist conspiracies were at work in our government and freedom as we knew it was in jeopardy. Saturday evenings, as I polished shoes and laid out our Sunday best, I dreaded the next morning. Hours alone with a baby, a small child, and rote tasks left me open to contemplating a one-world, socialist government with jack-booted KGB enforcers. Tucking my boys into bed at night, for a time, I not only questioned my performance as a mother, I also feared for their future. What sort of world had I brought them into?

Then I remembered my history of distorted thinking: clinging to Mother as planes went over or sirens sounded, fearing I would choke to death on solid food, pass out at school, be struck down by The Glare, or abandoned by God through a loss of faith. What a tangled mess my mind had been so much of my life. No wonder I had trouble sorting out the real from the imagined. Was I doing it again by making too much of this talk? Common sense told me I had a choice: Continue to follow this present course and kiss my sanity good-bye, or jump off the crazy train while I still could.

Forcing the unwanted thoughts from my head took every ounce of stubbornness I could muster. Doggedly, I persisted. Eventually, I delighted again in the way Stephen picked up my words and inflections and imitated his brother in all things. And I could watch Ronnie chasing a foundling kitten, legs pumping and hair shining copper in the sunlight, without dark paranoia spoiling the moment. Bull-headedness had gotten me into plenty of trouble in my life, but this time, supported as it was by the grace of God, it had saved me. This time it had saved all three of us.

———— ⋙⟪⊚⟫⋘ ————

Our lives continued to change for the better as time progressed in the Porterfield house. During our four years there, Ron made several improvements to the place; the most useful was turning the built-in front porch into an attractive space for relaxing and the boys' inside activities. Then he turned the downstairs bedroom into a study, where I spent what free time I had reading, having inherited a selection of books from the next door neighbor, another young mother, Terri. Terri had three kids: a boy roughly Ronnie's age, a girl Stephen's, and a toddler who kept up with the others until her legs gave out and she plunked down. I was shocked the afternoon Terri showed up at the kitchen door, a string of kids, hers and mine, behind her, carrying books. "You're giving away your books?"

"I've read what I want." Terri made light of her gift and directed the kids to stack the books on the dining room table. Two more trips and the munchkin crew had completed delivery. Sorting the books, I recognized authors I'd already read, mostly during high school. Others I had never heard of but would grow to love from this exposure. I had won the sweepstakes!

During our summers in Porterfield, Terri and I made

time to sit outside and chat while our kids played in the adjoining yards. She and her husband had rented the farm house next to ours which she kept spotless, not because she was a cleaning freak like I was, but because her husband expected it. He also expected her to keep her legs hidden under long skirts. Desperate in summer heat, she sometimes put on a pair of shorts when we lounged outside, but she made sure she was back inside or properly attired before he, or Ron, showed up. Jack would have gone berserk if another man had seen his wife's legs.

While Ron and I adhered to traditional male-female roles, Jack's ideas of male dominance were over-the-top. His word and desires ruled. The kids were her responsibility, from diapers to discipline, and a misbehaving child was a black mark on her character. I heard the heaviness in her voice even as she tried to make light of her situation. To an extent, I could identify with her because I normally deferred to Ron's preferences and managed the house and the kids on my own. And, truth be told, Ron and I had our upsets. Whenever we disagreed, I ended up apologizing. As for our neighbors, I wondered if Terri's marriage was worse than my mother's. Jack was crude and physical in a way that my father could never have been. Although Terri and I could chat on any number of topics, I feared that she harbored secrets too painful for sharing. Instinct urged me to question, but respect for her privacy kept me silent.

Reading Terri's books had more than entertainment value; submerged once more in the world of stories, I decided to give writing a try. When I told Ron about wanting to write again, he hustled me over to Sears, Roebuck and Co. and insisted I pick out any typewriter I wanted. His willingness to set me up in style came as a shock. For so long, I had seen myself as housewife and mother, buzzing through my work, shelving any reminder that there might be more to life than this role I had taken on. I assumed Ron saw me that way too, but his acknowledgement of my writing as important negated those assumptions.

And as grateful as I was to have a brand new electric type-writer with self-correcting tape, the best to be had in 1973, I was even more thankful to have married someone who saw me as a being separate from the role which occupied so much of my time and energy. Before the emotional upheavals, the long financial drag, and the inevitable disagreements which come from living with someone temperamentally differ-ent, Ron and I had been two kids trying to figure out where we fit in a great big world. I had chosen Ron because I saw steadfastness and persistence, and he had chosen me because I would not only take ownership of any task I encountered, I would also add to it a spark of life and imagination. Knowing this creative side was part of the whole package, Ron, the dependable, was only too willing to foster it.

We were still in the house at Porterfield when Grandma Rippey passed. She had maintained good health and a clear mind until her last couple of years and died in January 1973 before turning nine-one in June. She had enjoyed a long life for a woman of her generation. Daddy took her death well, mirroring Grandma's practical side by accepting the inevitable. Mother and I would always differ in our view of Grandma Rippey, and I respected Mother's feelings. To me, though, Grandma remained the snake-killer, the guardian of gentility, and the one-quarter of my genetic code which gave me a love of knowledge and rock-solid determination. I had no trouble identifying with the woman from Wolf Creek who had wanted a better life, but who had dealt practically and doggedly with whatever came her way.

After the Jehovah's Witness service in McConnelsville and burial in a blistery cold Stockport Cemetery, the whole extended family gathered back at Aunt Joyce's for food and talk. My cousin Darlene and her husband Leslie had returned to the Ohio Valley from Illinois. A stone mason and bricklayer, Leslie started his own business in Morgan County. I was next to her in the food line, and once we were seated, she gave me a condescending smile. "You're still wearing cat-eyes? I wore them too, when they were in style."

She glanced toward our Northern Ohio cousins, Uncle Carl's daughters, who appeared oblivious to her remark as they reconnected with family members here on the border of Appalachia. I had taken special pains that morning to look my best, and nothing had shouted "No!" upon inspection, not even my somewhat out of fashion eyewear. Balancing a paper plate of baked ham and funeral casseroles on my lap, I suddenly felt like the poor, ignorant cousin, whose wardrobe *faux pas* everyone must tsk-tsk over once she's out of earshot.

The stair-step sisters who had ignored Darlene's remark—Colleen, Twyla, and Jeannine—were more than a decade ahead of me in age, and I had seen them only a few

times. Over-hearing their conversations, I was as impressed
by the precision of their speech as I was with their ease moving from group to group and engaging others. Instinctively,
they knew how to speak and dress and present themselves,
abilities that grew from self-confidence. That was one of
the things I had so admired in Mrs. Gage, and in Grandma
Rippey. In that moment, right there in Aunt Joyce's living
room, I determined I would have it too, even if I wasn't sure
just how to go about getting it. Self-confidence was, after all,
on my short list of must-haves. Ron Spencer had contributed splendidly to my first, a sense of security. But the third,
personal achievement, was light-years away, unreachable as a
distant galaxy.

Ron had left the gathering to pick up our boys from his
mother's house where they had stayed during the services.
When he returned carrying Stephen in his arms, Ronnie
close at his side, the women in the room let out admiring
"Oohs." They were adorable, all three of them: Ron, tall and
handsome in suit and topcoat, and my boys, bundled up for
winter, cheeks pink from the cold. There couldn't have been
a more revealing moment for me, seeing my family as others did and my life as supremely blessed, regardless of its
limitations.

But the first thing I had to do was visit the optometrist.
It *was* time to ditch the cat-eyes.

Chapter 32

THE CALL FROM my sister that morning in January, 1977, came as no surprise. The last time I'd stopped at Mother's, I'd been on her case about the persistent, wracking cough. "It comes and goes," she insisted, nervous blue eyes begging me to drop the subject. Not long before calling me, Barbara had discovered our mother seated at the kitchen table, cigarette smoldering in the ashtray, struggling to get her breath. The squad from next door had wasted no time getting Mother to Bethesda Hospital, lights flashing, Barbara at her side. Now I was about to make a trip to Zanesville on sloppy roads, the sky overcast in solid gray and threatening another round of snow.

We were no longer in Porterfield, having purchased a brand new house not far from Belpre. Here, a huge, sloping yard, a meandering creek, and acres of neighboring woodlands provided Ronnie and Steve plenty of space to roam. From a spot against the end wall of the living room, I could view the entire living-kitchen-dining area and the hallway to bedrooms and baths, and sometimes I sat there, absorbing the mystique of newness. A stairway led to the split-entry, all the rage in the seventies, and from the landing to a basement garage and a family room, which Ron had finished himself.

From the substandard housing of my youth all the way to the American Dream—who would have guessed? What Ron and I had managed was typical of the time; all around us young couples with kids were upgrading, adding on, and reaching out. What made our climb different was the level at which we had started; in that respect, we were on the cutting edge.

One thing had not changed: I still existed in a protective, anesthetizing bubble, reinforced by the preoccupation of raising my boys and managing a household. Cravings, like shadows, flitted across the outer surface of the bubble sometimes, their features indistinct. Other times, disquieting reminders made direct hits. Sitting in conference with one of the boys' teachers, I was often haunted by the realization that it could have been *me* on the other side of the desk. Or even coming across a stack of Windsor yearbooks shoved into the back of a closet brought back memories of the girl who believed herself destined for bigger and better things. Forced to face facts in those moments, I acknowledged that the choices which had given me an otherwise full and rewarding life had failed to satisfy a specific, personal need. Such a need, if it could never be met, was better kept buried under a mountain of busyness.

My boys did all they could to keep me busy. In March, Ronnie would turn ten. Chief commando in the woods, he led his band of three (the neighbor boys and his brother) through imaginary battlefields, reinventing history as he pleased. At six, Steve had already revealed artistic and musical talent and could mimic anyone he chose, including Grandpa Rippey, who spent a few days at our house now and then, absorbing enough of his grandsons' antics to hold him until next time.

———— ((◊)) ————

The Bethesda Hospital Emergency Room was exactly as I remembered it, and unwanted flashes of being wheeled in, mute, defenseless, and assumed a danger to myself, made entering of my own accord a reason to be thankful, even in this unhappy moment. Mother was behind a light aqua curtain, reclining on a cot. Twin leads snaked into her nostrils, and an IV bag dripped saline into her forearm. The stark lighting leached the bright blue from Mother's irises. Her forehead, when I kissed her, felt overly warm in the dry, industrial heat. After a moment, Barbara and I joined the doctor at the nurses' station.

"Your mother has pneumonia," the young doctor told us. "In a patient with emphysema and congestive heart failure, pneumonia is a serious complication." Even spoken gently, his words were alarming. We had known this moment was coming, but it was easier to think about as a future event than as one in the here and now.

While Mother was transferred to a room, Barbara and I went to the cafeteria, although neither of us felt like eating. We pondered unasked questions as we shared kid news and sipped bitter coffee, avoiding for as long as possible the necessary conversation. "Once she's dismissed, then what?" I asked, cutting to the chase as I reached for a packet of sugar to ameliorate the bitterness of my coffee.

"She'll go home, I suppose," my sister answered.

To whose care, though? My parents' attempt to reconcile a dozen years ago had long since petered out. Even if Daddy were to step up, she wouldn't want his help. Barbara and I tossed around possibilities and finally settled on a shared arrangement. After two weeks in Bethesda, Mother was wheeled out to Barbara's station wagon and transported to my sister's house for starters, where Russell had transformed a back porch into bedroom and bath for his mother's use when she stayed there.

The old trade-off method, a while with Barbara, a while with me, worked for a year's worth of rotations. During Barbara's shifts, my sister's timidity over all things confrontational permitted Mother to lie abed as she pleased. Rusty was all grown up and married, Teresa in high school, and Carol the same age as Ronnie. Their comings and goings created a mix of people and activities. Mother's semi-isolation in the room off the kitchen seemed to suit everybody. Barbara catered her meals, helped her bathe when she didn't object too strenuously, and otherwise left it up to Mother how she would spend her hours. Russell, seeing Mother's care as Barbara's prerogative, complied.

When Mother was with us, things were different. I couldn't let go of the notion that life, whatever its limitations, deserved the effort to make it better. While she still had the physical strength, I tried to involve her in family activities and insisted on a higher level of personal hygiene. When she would go, I took her to church with us, and I even gave her a trial run at living back on Union Street on her own, which she thought she could handle. That was an utter failure, so back she went to Barbara's, and I felt like a tyrant.

Eventually, she balked at cooperation. "I'd rather stay in my room," became the predictable response, eerily close, I realized later when I studied American literature, to Bartleby the scrivener's "I prefer not to," the fallback line of Herman Melville's most puzzling character. Mother, like Bartleby, chose to absent herself from the world, a view I found unacceptable. Often, Mother gave no answer at all, but just lay there, face to the wall, pretending sleep, too exhausted or psychologically crippled to find value in discourse. This disengaged woman was identical to the one I had watched those other painful times. When I questioned her doctor about treatment for depression, he hedged with a wait-and-see approach. But then, it wasn't *his* mother walling herself off from human contact.

So there we were, my sister and I, dividing Mother's care, watching as her health worsened and her depression deepened. There were especially low moments, such as the morning I found her on the floor of the bedroom where she had fallen during the night and had lain in silence and her own urine rather than disturb the rest of us. "Never again, Mother," I pleaded, once Ron had her up and back into bed, where I bathed her and changed her gown. "It's okay to wake us. Please, wake us up!"

And there were the cigarettes, which Ron truly hated having in the house and around the boys. Having grown up watching my mother smoke in every conceivable circumstance, I knew better than anyone how they had contributed to her condition. And, for the same reason, I understood her addiction. Ron and I compromised and restricted her smoking to the kitchen bar area, next to the patio doors which I could open as the chilly spring weather blessedly warmed. Since she couldn't bring herself to quit smoking entirely, I tried to comply with the doctor's orders that she at least limit the number. Policing the smokes, I watched as she sucked every last morsel of nicotine from each poisonous stub and attempted to wave away the offending fumes with her hands.

Russell's mother had first claim to the extra space at Barbara's, and her visits dictated when Mother shifted venues. Transferring her back and forth at the whim of others denied her visits any semblance of dignity, so toward the end, she spent her time with us. By then, I was frazzled emotionally, exhausted physically, and at my wits' end as she weakened before my eyes. The boys did not recognize in this silent woman, who moved like a shadow between bedroom and kitchen, the gentle constancy they had known as Grandma. They fought their own feelings of guilt over a natural, childish resentment that home was no longer the place where they had free rein and where their mother's attention was theirs alone.

Eventually, Mother needed more help than any of us could give. And the lowest of low moments occurred early in the spring of 1978, shortly after Barbara and I made arrangements with the nursing home. Mother had sought me out that morning, with just the two of us in the house, and lay across my bed, exhausted from the unassisted journey across the hall. The visible pulse in her throat was reminiscent of those times in my childhood when I would find her reclining on the couch waiting out another palpitation. And she had grown so thin, the pale flesh on her arms hanging in striations of tiny wrinkles. That's the morning she begged me to let her stay. She wouldn't be any trouble, she swore she wouldn't. She'd even give up her cigarettes if I'd keep her here with me.

I hope to God I never have another moment as bad as that one. Choking on tears, I told her I had used the last of my resources. I simply hadn't the strength for the round-the-clock care she needed. And if she fell again, and Ron wasn't home, how would we manage? Then, my words fell silent. It had all been said when Barbara and I broached the nursing home option, and besides, it wasn't what that morning was about. In this house, life went on in familiar ways, forestalling the inevitable. The nursing home, on the other hand, marked the end of the line. Ill as she was, Mother, not quite seventy, wasn't ready for that. Even though I could not change what had to be, I could respect how she felt. Lying together on the heirloom bedspread, the bond forged on that other morning when I had arrived in a rush, impatient to begin my life, was our comfort. And Mother's death, when it did come, did not wrench quite so profoundly. We had already passed the worst of it.

Chapter 33

READJUSTMENT, AS I knew well enough, was never easy. Getting to the next step after Mother's death took some doing. After her funeral on a lovely afternoon in June, we gathered around gravestones in Fairview Cemetery, many of the sunken spots marking resting places of Mother's relatives, including James Perry Hosom, her paternal grandfather, whose stories she had loved to tell. Somewhere inside, Mother had retained a hero-fantasy, and a dashing young soldier making death-defying runs into enemy territory appealed to her romanticism. She had a ready supply of tales from her childhood, in which her father, also, showed a side both heroic and tender. "Ka-wah, the Chicken" is one such story, told here with my personal embellishments.

Back then poor kids on a farm seldom had pets, maybe cats to keep mice out of the barn, feral entities who fought, hissing, over scraps and resisted attempts at friendship. Few dogs showed up in her stories, either. Unless it had a purpose, herding or protecting, a dog wasn't much use on a farm. One type of animal, though, was perennially useful, the chicken. There was always a flock around the farm, hens cackling over eggs just laid, roosters strutting and crowing in their latest conquests. Mother, Uncle Homer, and to a lesser extent Aunt Edie had tried to make friends with chickens. Roosters, testosterone–filled and nasty, would rather spur a child than play nicely. Most hens preferred to scratch in the dooryard for morsels between feedings.

Not so, however, a stunted pullet named Ka-wah, who had never laid an egg in her life, perhaps because she didn't realize she *was* a chicken. Shunned and mistreated by her robust peers, Ka-wah trailed the kids in their endeavors, giving out with the strange call which had inspired her name. Ka-wah permitted herself to be wrapped in ragged towels, a Salvador Dali baby-doll, or trundled about in a wheelbarrow. Fact was, whenever you saw one or more of the Hosom kids, you saw Ka-wah.

The current flock had grown especially large, Mother said, and the hens were aging, losing productivity. At breakfast, Grandpa Hosom announced his solution; he would crate up the old hens and haul them away to the butcher. As Mother and Uncle Homer left for school that morning they knew their avian population was about to decrease, but they weren't concerned. Who cared about chickens? Chickens didn't make good pets. Their friend Ka-wah was an excellent pet. Therefore, Ka-wah could not be a chicken. If Ka-wah had identity issues, an observer might conclude, the kids with their cock-eyed syllogism were the culprits.

The school day ended, and Mother and Uncle Homer walked the dusty road home where they joined their little sister and their father at the farm wagon on which wooden crates, filled with ruffled, squawking chickens, were secured by lengths of rope. "Can we go?" they begged, ready for a trip anywhere if it would get them out of chores and away from their mother's scrutiny for part of an evening. Grandpa pulled the last rope tight, knotted it, and spit a long stream of tobacco juice into the tall grass beside the barn. Glancing toward the house, to be certain Grandma was otherwise occupied, Grandpa secured the hitch, mounted the driver's seat, and settled Aunt Edie, contentedly sucking her thumb, beside him. Eagerly, the older two climbed in beside the chickens.

Once the journey was underway, the squawking from the crates quieted, as if chicken brains could anticipate an unhappy ending, entirely out of their control, and therefore useless to protest. Breaking the silence, a single, unmistakable voice sounded from among the imprisoned: "Ka-wah!" Perhaps the familiar chatter of the children had given the speaker courage and hope. Perhaps the speaker had just been pecked by her pen-mate. Regardless, the voice blurted again, louder, and in earnest, "Ka-wah!"

In shock and awe all three children set up a desperate echo: "Ka-wah! Ka-wah! Ka-wah!" Determined to find their pet, Mother and Uncle Homer jammed hands between slats and tugged on ropes. How had Ka-wah been mistaken for a chicken? What had their father been thinking? "Daddy!" they shouted. "You can't take Ka-wah!"

Grandpa had no more said, "Giddy-up!" than he had to shout, "Whoa!" The confused horse looked back in exasperation. By then, the kids had located Ka-wah among the forest of Rhode Island Reds' plumage and were doing their best to free her from the crate. Grandpa's favorite expletive,

"Hells bells!" came out more forcefully than was generally allowed around the children, but Grandma was safely inside the house, tending the baby James. Grandpa set the wagon brake before he lost children and cargo over the side. Violent flapping and raucous cries issued from the crates as ropes were loosened and Ka-wah was extricated and delivered into loving hands.

Mother's story ends there and well so for the children's version. Revisiting the story as a grown-up, I could imagine the rest just fine. Grandpa Hosom would not receive a hero's welcome when, tired and hungry, he returned later that evening with empty crates and a couple of extra dollars in his pocket. He would bear Grandma's list of complaints with his customary silence. His children would be busy with lessons and chores, Ka-wah's release old news already. But during that one brief moment, when a round autumn moon ghosted low in a sky as blue as his daughter's eyes, my grandfather had watched his children pelting toward the house, the rescued Ka-wah safely in their clutches. That sight alone was a true hero's reward.

And on his solitary journey to deliver the remaining poultry, he had time to ponder that and other weighty matters, which he did throughout his lifetime, his jaw ruminating a good chew of Mail Pouch. The story of Ka-wah was never told as a cautionary tale, but I like to imagine the remaining chickens, bouncing along in the bed of the wagon, with weighty matters of their own to consider. The misfit whom they had spurned and abused had escaped the cruel fate soon to be theirs. No frantic hands would tear at wooden slats to save *them*. If chickens can appreciate irony, and what a loss if they cannot, for however many hours remaining to them, these aging hens had something worthy of contemplation.

———⬤———

Remembering the best of Mother, her stories and her staunch and fearless support even when it was ill-placed, brought sadness shooting up out of a place I didn't know existed. And for most of that summer, I couldn't even listen to music without tearing up. My sister, my father, Ron, and the boys were all adjusting to her death, but I couldn't get past the feeling that I had let her down when she needed me most. Even knowing that blaming myself would have been anathema to her didn't help. I finally had to shelve the dilemma in the hope that someday it would find resolution.

In the meantime, I kept myself busy, turning full attention to kids and housework and mending fences with my father. Daddy had taken Mother's death hard too, and in those last days of her life and the days following, I got a glimpse of that emotion they both had sworn they never felt for each other. With her, his last touches were gentle, his last words soft, and the tears he shed when she died, real. Again, I had to ask myself: Who *are* these complicated people and how did they ever manage to produce a child?

But I had to love them both, and through it all, I truly did.

Chapter 34

NOTHING HAD COME of my writing during the days in Porterfield other than a much-needed escape from a world of sameness. The short snatches of time I devoted to writing were insufficient, for one thing. For another, anything I attempted sounded predictable, trite, and boring, even to me. The sheltered and limiting life I led was at fault, I decided; the well I drew from was too shallow. With time on my hands after Mother's passing, I brought the typewriter out to the dining room table and began again, this time with purpose. I had identified a model for the kind of story I felt qualified to write.

The Lookout, a weekly magazine I picked up every Sunday at church, was put out by Standard Publishing Company in Cincinnati. A regular feature was a piece of short fiction, a quick, enjoyable read, often written from the distaff. On the surface the stories appeared simple, yet these pithy little tales taught a moral or religious precept without beating the reader over the head with it. My first attempt, "The Good Life," was shipped out to the editor with eager anticipation. Soon, housewives all over the country would be sitting down with their Monday morning coffee and reading my words. When my self-addressed, stamped envelope returned, a strip of paper was attached to my manuscript: "Your submission does not meet our publishing needs at this time." Well, so much for that.

Months continued to pass. The boys were coming into their own. Ronnie took an avid interest in history and all things military, and Steve's creativity showed up in school art displays as well as piano recitals. My schedule was full enough without worrying about some stupid story. I found plenty to keep me reading those days too. Book clubs with glossy-jacketed offerings. *Readers' Digest* condensed books. Collections of short stories from the library. And magazines. *Redbook* and *Ladies' Home Journal* published fiction so polished, so sophisticated the writers were obviously well-schooled in an existence I could barely fathom. Everywhere I turned were reminders that people were writing and selling. And their secrets were buried somewhere in those columned paragraphs; if I dug hard enough, I just might find them.

Rereading the rejected submission, I could see numerous flaws. I reworked it and sent it again. When it came back the second time, the editor had attached a note, which began, "I imagine your story is autobiographical." At the time, I could see little similarity between my life and the life I had constructed for my protagonist, Allie. She was the mother of five boys living on a shoestring with a long-suffering husband who filled in for her while she attended a women's retreat. The speaker at the conference was witty, well-traveled, stylishly dressed and eager to share her message. The "good life," she told her audience, came from making the best of one's situation. During the sessions, a growing cynicism invaded Allie's mind; the "good life," if there were such a thing, had passed her by long ago.

Allie was *so* not me. My drive for something nameless was not the same as Allie's feeling that her life had dead-ended. Ah, the bubble again. But at least I knew what the story's acceptance would require: Allie must accept the status quo and find fulfillment in children, cramped housing, and Frank. She must label the desire for more, after sufficient soul-searching, plain old self-pity. I had it, the tone and the message, and it sold.

Over the next year and for a decade following, I mass-produced variations on "Allie's story" with protagonists of myriad names and circumstances. What they all had in common was a desire for something just out of reach. In virtually all of their stories, the protagonist found satisfaction in something she already had or in some change she could make in herself. My stories really hit the spot with *The Lookout* as well as with *Home Life*, a higher dollar publication put out by the Sunday School Board of the Southern Baptist Convention. My heroines boldly faced unplanned pregnancies, uprooting moves, problems with overweight, fears of encroaching middle-age, and insecurities too numerous to mention. They found, without exception and within the 1500 to 1800 word limit, the answer: Look *inside* for resolution.

It's easier now to admit that I *was* Allie and Rachel and Phyllis and Lou and Carrie, all of my characters who sought something more. The solution for my protagonists felt too easy, too quick. But who was I to complain? My stories were selling, and my readership, those I knew about at least, always had kind words for me. One aspect of my heroines' struggles was certainly true of mine: The answer *was* inside. Accepting life as it is, however, and giving it a rosy spin, was not for me. From somewhere within, I had to find the courage to reach out and explore greater possibilities. And my feeble little stories, with all their flaws, opened the way for me to do just that.

⸺⸢⟨◉⟩⸥⸺

Ron would gladly have paid for my first creative writing course at Parkersburg Community College, but it was a point of pride with me that the revenue from my stories cover the cost. As the boys returned to school in the fall of 1979, I re-entered the classroom after a sixteen-year hiatus and with much trepidation, driven by the certainty that if I were ever to publish beyond the level I had achieved, it would take some serious catching up. Class was held on Monday evenings, and I remember wondering how my long absence from all things academic would play out. But I had a purpose. I would "learn how to write" and then go after the bigger markets, the slicks. To open a *Redbook* while I stood in line at the grocery store and see my byline would be Nirvana.

I lucked out with the instructor, Nancy Pelletier Pansing, a generation ahead of me age-wise and light-years ahead in sophistication and savvy. She reminded me of Mrs. Gage in her ability to engage students through a sincere interest in them and yet retain high standards for acceptable work. Nancy began with elements of the short story, assigning reading and writing exercises weekly. Tuesday mornings, I would begin writing, so I could have the rest of the week to hone the manuscript. Without exception, her remarks were generous and kind, but she wasn't afraid to point out anything that didn't ring true. This arena demanded intellectual digging I hadn't done since high school. But what fun! What daring, outrageous fun it was to learn again!

Having wondered in the beginning if I'd pass the course, I received an A and Nancy's offer to serve as my advisor if I continued to study at PCC. I had learned so much in so short a time that I felt I could share with her my earlier ambition to teach English. To that, she nodded in her shrewd way. "You can get an associate degree here that will transfer," she said. And, in fact, she arranged for a tuition scholarship. All I had to do was buy my books and show up again in January. I had never felt so generously included. Imagine me, in that rarified element, academia.

As for writing, my culminating piece for the course was a short story, "Limits," a first attempt to address my mother's struggles with depression, using a fictional format for the sake of distance. At Nancy's urging, I submitted that story and a couple of other pieces to *Gambit*, a literary journal compiled of PCC student writing, and all three were published. I was beginning to experience something I had believed was out of reach. But it had been there all along, just like Allie's "good life."

Adjusting to life outside the bubble didn't happen overnight. The offer of a two-year scholarship came with the stipulation that I maintain a B-plus average and carry at least nine hours each semester. Choosing my classes brought to the fore a nagging question. Just how badly did I want to teach? Was the attraction based on an intrinsic need or simply a desire to emulate Mrs. Gage? It had been writing, after all, which had driven me to PCC. Fortunately, I could postpone that decision, so I tested out of Comp 1 and signed up for Comp 2, Psych 101, and another creative writing class, this one with a different instructor, Jane Somerville.

On the home front, times, they were a-changing. Ron's long-awaited promotion to supervisor became reality, so he had a lot on his plate and little tolerance for distractions. As for my taking classes, as long as the boys were covered, it was fine with him. And when hadn't the boys been covered? I knew my boys and what they needed. Ronnie was a pragmatic, analytical thinker, and by the time he was twelve he carried on adult conversations. He managed his own homework schedule and needed my help only for the occasional proofreading. Steve, on the other hand, was a holistic thinker and required supervision and redirection. Corralling his attention for homework was like catching jumping beans with a teaspoon. So the nightly sessions at the breakfast bar weren't going the end anytime soon.

That year, I wanted Christmas behind me more than ever. The core of sadness over losing Mother had not yet dissolved, and writing her story had dredged up uncomfortable memories. Christmas was always difficult for me anyway, bringing with it images of a scrawny tree atop the sewing machine cabinet, its single strand of multi-color lights casting a tiny magic circle in which a little girl could conjure the kind of Christmas other families had, filled with wonderful smells and elaborate gifting. And the realization that Mother had done her best and gone without to provide the tokens.

Daddy spent Christmas with us and enjoyed the festivities he had shown little value for when I was a child. From crispy skinned ham and homemade cookies to an abundance of flashing tree lights and a mountain of colorfully wrapped packages, I put all the heart I had into it. Once he'd eaten his fill, opened his gifts, and spent time with his two exceptional grandsons, Daddy was back to his solitary life.

Holidays over, I tucked away ornaments and gift boxes, mental to-do lists filling my brain. January 1980 was upon me, and with it, college.

Chapter 35

PARKERSBURG COMMUNITY COLLEGE was a
haven for the nontraditional student, and in 1980 the halls
and classrooms were full of women my age taking advantage
of the second chance, but none of them were more grateful to be there than I was. It was a relief to discover that I
was still a natural student even in classes where writing was
not the main focus. Composition and psychology were day
classes, both on Tuesday and Thursday, and creative writing
was again on Monday evening, so it wasn't a hard schedule
for a beginner.

I felt I'd fallen down the rabbit hole, however, that first
Monday night when an artsy blonde wearing a flowing scarf
and accompanied by a female protégé dressed in black swept
into the classroom. Three elderly students would need rides
to and from class, Jane Somerville announced with theatrical
flair. "Volunteers?"

When no other hands appeared, mine lifted. Thereafter
on Monday evenings, I made a stop at a senior high-rise
and picked up my octogenarian classmates and later returned
them safely to their door. Their bones, if not their spirits,

were brittle, and when four inches of snow fell during class one evening, I herded my three charges into my car and crept across snowy roads, windshield wipers thumping, and breathed easily only after I had led each one into the lobby of the high-rise.

Unlike Nancy, Jane disdained "selling" one's work. It was so much more meaningful to be published in a college-sponsored literary journal—the *right* literary journal, of course, and *Gambit* was marginal. That's not to say I didn't learn in Jane's class. Avoiding the comment "Nice," which was her way of saying a piece was lame, became my ultimate goal. One of my best pieces came in response to her character sketch assignment.

"I have something to share with you," she announced one evening as class began. She proceeded to read "A Matter of Time," the piece I had turned in the week before. The real kudos came when she suggested I send it to *The Atlantic Monthly.* When I later showed her the rejection letter, which gave as justification the story's lack of plot, she was not pleased. The fiction editor's rigid division of genres showed a lack of imagination. However, to receive an actual letter from *The Atlantic* instead of a form rejection slip was an honor in itself.

In "A Matter of Time," Miss Mellie was a melding of Grandma Rippey and an elderly teacher who had made regular trips to Central Market while I worked there, wicker basket on one arm and the exact amount of her purchases mentally calculated by the time she reached the register. The piece found immortality in the next edition of *Gambit.* I sent that volume to Mrs. Gage, along with a letter of appreciation, long overdue.

I attended a writer's conference hosted by Standard Publishing Company during my third semester. The conference experience helped chart my course by giving me a glimpse inside the machine of professional writing. As much as ever, I wanted to write, but teaching was something I *had* to do; otherwise, I would look back with regret. Teaching offered a means to pay forward what had been given to me, beginning with Mrs. Gage, who had demonstrated, during those pivotal and impressionable years, professionalism laced with humanity.

━━━◦《◉》◦━━━

Before I graduated from PCC with an associate degree in English two years later, I had learned about juggling. Keeping all those balls in the air was not for the faint of heart. It might have been the progressive eighties in other parts of the world, but in Belpre, Ohio, gender roles for my generation and socio-economic level hadn't changed much. My workload at home did not diminish to a noticeable degree, although the boys did become more self-reliant. They could no longer shout "Mom!" and expect an automatic fix. When Ron had given his okay for me to take classes, the stipulation was understood: College was an add-on, not a replacement for duties already mine. The rules of the game were not viewed as unfair in our world; it's the way things had always been.

Whether or not our efforts were appreciated, to an

overwhelming extent it was the women of my generation, swarming to community college and the workplace, double-stepping to maintain home and hearth as we did so, who brought about a fairer playing field for our daughters. We didn't appear on the nightly news brandishing banners. We were far too busy teaching by example that women, as well as men, can reach the impossible. Meanwhile, we taught our sons that manhood is uncompromised by washing a load of laundry or cleaning up the detritus of a family meal. My husband, raised by a working class mother who never questioned gender boundaries, learned these lessons in small steps; his sons, raised by a mother driven to uncover what lay beyond, learned by leaps and bounds. And later, as men, my sons could face domestic chores as tasks shared by a household rather than the "woman's work" of earlier generations.

Compared to other women attempting college, though, I had the advantage of a husband who encouraged my efforts. Another student at PCC, Lydia, provided a glimpse into the other side of the looking glass. Nancy Pansing caught me between classes one day during my second year to ask a favor. There was this woman who was also taking classes, not sure how she could manage things with two little boys and a husband in Army Reserves. Maybe I could encourage her, make some suggestions? Nancy gave her my number, and Lydia agreed to meet in the cafeteria during a break. She had described herself as tall, dark-haired, and wearing jeans. She had failed to mention that she was also startlingly beautiful, or would have been if she had appeared a little less timid. We laughed over our lunch choices, identical cartons of low-fat milk and high-fat packaged crackers. As Lydia spoke about her goal of becoming an elementary teacher, her face grew animated.

Lydia's story was only too typical. She had been in college when she and Mark married. Along came the kids eleven months apart, Mark joined the Army, and Lydia and Co. followed from base to base. A reservist, Mark was frustrated with the local job market, and the time and money Lydia spent on her classes had become an issue. Mark, she told me without saying the words, was neither supportive nor easygoing, and I agonized for this lovely woman whose future lay in the hands of a husband who either didn't know or didn't care what a remarkable woman he had married. Although Lydia and I met a couple of times after that, her dilemma was no closer to resolution. Telling her to ditch Mark wasn't in my repertoire at the time.

Not long after my last meeting with Lydia, Nancy told me they were moving to North Carolina where Mark's family lived. I could imagine Lydia packing up for another move, her dream of a classroom smelling of mimeographed papers and chalk dust evaporating before her eyes. And for some reason, a memory of my friend Terri came back, sitting with me in the shady expanse between our houses, sipping iced tea from sweating glasses and losing track of time. At the sound of a pickup, she's on her feet, and those long, white legs are tearing across the grass. If she can just run fast enough, she can forestall the dreaded outcome.

With both women, I sensed the tightening of reins—pulling them in, holding them back, redirecting their purposes. We all had our reins back then, whether they were imposed by others or invited through ignorance. None of us had galloped as we pleased across open fields or reveled in a freedom that defied our gender's history. But we had made it one step closer to goal. The luckiest and most persistent of us would eventually complete the journey, but not without a look over the shoulder and a memory of restraints taken on before we knew we could run like the wind.

Chapter 36

A WEAK JANUARY sun didn't do much to alleviate the cold, but it brightened the leafless trees and allowed a glimpse of pale blue sky beyond their stark branches. Students hustled back and forth across the brick street separating Ellis Hall from the coffee shop hang-out where they grabbed a hot drink on their way to the next class. So many students, scurrying every which way, bundled against the cold and carrying on conversations or walking with heads bent, focused on the task ahead. It felt surreal to be here, at long last, on the Ohio University campus. I sat at a small café table, a warm cup in gloved hands, absorbing my good fortune, before heading to McCracken Hall for a methods class.

Since graduating PCC in May, 1982, I had finished recovering from a hysterectomy that had blindsided me just as I was completing my last semester there. The problem proved more of an inconvenience than a serious medical issue, but it had thrown me a curve just the same. The free summer had been just what I needed to gear up for the hectic months I anticipated. Then another delay, due to poor planning, had caused me to lose what would have been my first quarter on campus.

During my two years at PCC, I had planned to attend Marietta College. For one thing, Marietta was closer than Athens. More relevant, though, I had harbored a preference for Marietta's stately green campus ever since I had visited there as an eighth grader on a rare field trip from Stockport. Leaping off the yellow bus, I had gazed at the impressive array of red brick buildings open to only the most fortunate people, whose passage was purchased by superior brain power and somebody's deep pockets, my father had told me that morning. A science classroom displayed fetus specimens floating in formaldehyde baths, umbilical cords curled against them like sleeping snakes. Classrooms were theaters where students raptly absorbed knowledge just as an audience would hang on the words of the actors. I was enthralled by the campus library and its floor-to-ceiling books. In separate buildings, dorm cubicles awaited the smart and lucky inhabitants. The whole place seemed like a wonderland and the chance that I would ever attend there remote.

Each spring thereafter, when I took the scholarship test in English at the Marietta High School atop a steep hill just above the college campus, I admired the expanse of green and the brick edifices all over again, as well as the atmosphere of the entire town: houses with turrets and mullioned windows and carriage houses in the rear, and the quaint shops and aged storefronts on Putnam and Front Streets. As reward for representing Windsor High in the state sponsored tests, once we had finished, sixteen students, four for each level from freshman through senior, could walk down the wide brick street to a restaurant just below street level. Then we boarded the bus again for the return to Stockport.

Early memories of Marietta College might have blurred over the years, but the desire to be part of such a prestigious company had not, and graduating from PCC with high honors gave me the necessary academic clout. The other part of the equation was money. And when late in the summer I began to calculate the actual cost, I could not justify putting added strain on the family budget just so I could realize a dream. Always generous when it came to finances, Ron said the choice was mine; we would work it out. Still, I decided a quick run to Athens was in order. There I discovered another glitch. Classes had already begun for fall quarter, and I hadn't considered the difference in starting dates. I could apply, and did, but it looked like I would have to sit out a quarter, upsetting my plan to graduate in June, 1984.

A woman in the admissions office sent me to Jessie Essex, in the College of Education, who suggested an alternative. I could study for three literature courses independently and take a three-hour exam for each one before the end of the quarter. I could also take an educational psychology class by correspondence. In January, with twelve quarter hours under my belt, I'd be set to enroll as a full-time student. Her expression let me know this wasn't going to be a piece of cake, but she sealed the deal when she eyed me across her desk and announced in her been-there-done-that way, "You look like an English teacher."

My first real contact with Ohio University, Mrs. Essex held the door wide open for me, much as Nancy Pansing had two and a half years earlier at PCC. One more fortunate encounter had just moved me another step closer to my destination.

————))(())((————

In some ways it was good to have the extended time at home, without the need to run off to class every other morning. In other ways, it was more difficult, walking away from windows that begged washing and walls in need of repainting, to closet myself with the romantic poets or Shakespearean dramas and sonnets. No matter how much time a woman who sees her primary role as homemaker allots to spend on housework, I later read in Betty Friedan's *The Feminine Mystique*, she will manage to fill it. And to that point, my real job had remained housewife; college was extra-curricular. The temptation to put my house into pristine order hovered, but I couldn't give in.

Some demands, though, could not be ignored. As a freshman, Ronnie played second string football and held the 145 weight spot for the varsity wrestling team, so I spent a lot of time hitting the books while I waited for practices to end and during day-long wrestling tournaments, propped against the wall at the top of the bleachers, filtering out the noise and confusion of the gym as I crammed my head with the finer points of English literature. I will always associate John Keats' "Ode to a Grecian Urn" with a ref's hand slapping the mat to declare a pin. And Steve, not to be outdone, played pee wee football and began Suzuki piano lessons in Athens, adding more miles to my day as well as a touch of culture to round out the grid-iron and wrestling events.

I allotted myself a month for each of the three independent courses and worked psych readings and midterms into the cracks. At the beginning of October, I drove to Athens early one Saturday morning and sat for the first of the literature exams. No notes, no texts. The monitor handed out several sheets of unlined paper and four writing prompts. I focused my thoughts on the first and began, retrieving quotes and references from memory. All around the room, pencils scratched, bodies shuffled. Eventually, people began turning in exams and leaving. Hoping I had done justice to all of the prompts, I turned my papers in just as time ran out. In a trance somewhere between euphoria and the bleak certainty that nothing I had written rose to the level expected, I barely noticed the pristine blue of the sky or the luxurious foliage of the campus trees beginning to show autumn colors, a few leaves drifting to sidewalks buckled and cracked from time and tree roots.

A week later the torture was over. "You appear to have read extensively and retained what you read," was handwritten on the official-looking form. "Grade for course: A." I barely had time to celebrate because I was already into cramming for the next one. The exams which followed were equally well received. Because the Ed Psych textbook didn't hold a candle to Norton anthologies, I gave that course short shrift. They must have graded on a serious curve because I managed to pull an A there too. When we broke for the holidays, I could hardly wait for January. Ohio University, here I come, better late than never.

By that cold January morning in 1983 when I gave myself time to take in my new surroundings, I had already discovered that faces and expectations at OU were night-and-day different from PCC. I was the sole non-traditional student in virtually every class, and my schedule was tight; every quarter included classroom observation as well as an evening class that kept me on campus until ten. Hikes across town to the Athens Middle School and long walks to remote parking were routine.

Some of the students appeared nonchalant about the whole college thing and got by with minimal effort. Not surprising, since Ohio University was known as a party school and infamous for public intoxication arrests on Halloween. A lot of those casual learners were in the College of Education, and I wondered what kind of teachers they would make. Other students, generally girls, seemed overwhelmed by the workload. And that baffled me too. Following classes, they had the luxury of dorm space or Alden Library where they could spend the entire evening if they chose, uninterrupted by the need to prepare dinner, oversee homework, clean-up, pick-up, and counsel sons on anything from girl troubles to the best form for an essay.

With my schedule, I couldn't waste time worrying about getting everything done or understanding what was expected; all I could do was plow ahead with the occasional glance to the rear to see if anything vital had dropped. The title of Virginia Woolf's book about the difficulties of being a woman writer, *A Room of One's Own*, never tantalized me more than during my time at OU. Oh, for that quiet, private space in which to work uninterrupted. And there was always the fear lurking in the back of my mind that had nothing to do with how hard I labored or how well I did. It came from some dark, unresolved issue about self-worth. Sooner or later, somebody would figure out I was a fraud, a relatively unschooled bumpkin who had fooled a lot of people into thinking she was college material.

Despite the rosy glow with which I greeted the campus in January, 1983, I encountered some serious hitches during the eighteen months I was there. For one thing, there was the wild ride from Olivet Ridge one night after we had stopped for a routine visit on our way home from Ron's parents' house. We had no more than breached the doorway when Daddy demanded we take him to the hospital. He said he had been in unbearable pain all day, so we loaded him in and headed for Parkersburg. I later regretted putting him in the backseat with the boys because Grandpa did not suffer in silence.

Hours later, when I stopped by Steve's room to tell him good-night, he was still upset. "I thought Grandpa was dying," he confessed. Following surgery to clear his ureter of blockage, my father recovered well under Aunt Joyce's care. He kept his collection of kidney stones in a small glass jar as a reminder of his narrow escape from death. His flair for exaggeration never failed him.

Daddy had another medical issue shortly after that, a hip replacement. He'd suffered from hip pain for some time, thanks to all those years behind a barber chair. Again, he came through the surgery and recovery with flying colors. When the doctor told him he could resume his normal activities, he headed for the farm and began hauling saplings up from the meadow to cut for firewood. His method of transport was to hitch himself to the young trees with a hand-made harness and drag them up the long hill. Few people would consider this "normal activity" for a man well along in his seventies, and it proved foolhardy, even for him. He loosened the implant and had to have the work redone. But that's a story for another time.

Chapter 37

DURING THE FALL of 1983, I made a disturbing discovery myself one morning in the shower, what felt like a lump in my left breast. But checking more closely, I could feel nothing. Nevertheless, I made an appointment and shoved the whole thing to the back of my mind. My physician ordered a mammography and nothing showed up. Since I'd had a benign lump removed a couple of years earlier and had a long history of fibrous cystic disease, he suggested I consider having the breast tissue removed and replaced by implants—both procedures during one surgery. Here was another wrinkle I could have done without. Not only was the whole thing a great big interruption in my regimented life, deciding what to do brought on a nagging worry that darkened my normal exuberance.

One of my instructors, whose class in women's literature was hands down my favorite that quarter, noticed my change in demeanor and asked me what was wrong, so I just blurted it all out after class that late October day, grateful to have a sympathetic ear. She, too, was enduring the discomfort and annoyance of fibrous cystic breasts and knew of a doctor in

Columbus who treated the disorder homeopathically. Her suggestion that I consult with him before undergoing surgery made sense.

I'd had more than my share of doctor's offices thus far in my life, albeit mostly for routine complaints. The exception had been the frightening lead-up to the hysterectomy eighteen months earlier, which had nearly overshadowed the triumph of receiving my first degree. Fortunately, the suspicious results of an ultrasound proved false, but by then the deed was done. My PCC instructors had been wholly supportive, administering my finals early and cheering me on as I walked across the stage in robe and mortarboard, not entirely steady on my feet. At that point, I figured it would be a long, long time before I had to face another such ordeal. So dealing with a second medical dilemma with graduation from OU only a few months away seemed like *déjà vu* of the worst kind.

⸺⸻❖⸻⸺

The medical office was at Ohio State University Hospital, situated in a run-down part of the city. The ugly landscape and a steady rain ushering in the depressing month of November did nothing to lift my spirits. Ron let me off at the door so I could avoid the deluge and after parking the car joined me in search of the suite. In the waiting room were rows of connected, plastic chairs with no armrests and a dense questionnaire requesting a detailed account of my dietary and living habits. The space was crowded with edgy females, comparing notes, zoned out, or leafing through coverless magazines. An afternoon soap played above a sliding window that opened when communication was necessary. After an hour's wait, I was led into a cubbyhole examining room and questioned by a nurse.

Eventually the doctor showed up with three male interns in tow. Had I been less intimidated, I would have sent the extras packing, but I acquiesced to their presence and tolerated the perfunctory exam. The interns seemed amused by the questionnaire I'd filled out, especially the "ringer" questions, designed to trip up the less than forthcoming patient, and stood to one side, their purpose in the room one I could not fathom. When I told the doctor I was considering surgery, he appeared chagrinned and informed me my fibrous cystic condition was minimal and since nothing had shown up in the x-rays, he would prescribe a dietary regimen that would take care of my problem. The four white coats disappeared, and a female nurse emerged from the shadows, primed to explain the details of the wellness program. By that point, I was in what Grandma Hosom would have called "a state." Ignoring the nurse, I tossed the inadequate gown and yanked on my own essentials, grabbed my purse, and stalked back to the waiting room where Ron sat in a stupor, the only reasonable way to endure such an atmosphere.

"I'm leaving," I said, grabbing my coat and heading for the door.

Not fully awake, Ron followed. "Don't we need to stop at the window?"

"If they want me, they can find me." I marched toward a junction in the hallway, made a wrong turn, and burst into tears. Ron's superior sense of direction got us headed the right way, and by the time we found the car, my hysterics had calmed to the extent that I could tell him what had happened.

In retrospect, the experience may not have been as degrading as it seemed at the time. Nevertheless, I made up my mind I'd choose the scalpel over treatment by this guy any day. Surgery was scheduled right after Thanksgiving, and I was far from the life of the party that year. My mind preoccupied with finishing up the quarter and debating the wisdom of subjecting myself again to the knife, I rushed through Christmas shopping and gift wrapping and left the tree and the rest of it to Ron and the boys.

And, as it turned out, the choice to have surgery may have been life-saving. When the lab results came back, everything was benign with one exception; a miniscule spot of tissue from the left breast was declared "undetermined." A second lab sent an identical report. The plastic surgeon who had performed the procedure many times, assured me the offending tissue was gone and even if anything suspicious had been lurking in the tiny specimen, it was at what he called "the birth stage." Problem solved. Patient cured. No further treatment required.

Anyone else would have offered up a "Thank you, God" and moved on. I, however, could not dismiss the possibility, however remote, that a malignancy might still exist. I lay in bed one evening, watching *It's a Wonderful Life* and bawling my eyes out. Since I couldn't tell my boys I feared I might not be around to see them grow up, I said I was crying over the movie. Conveniently, George Bailey had just been declared "the richest man in town" by his war hero brother, and strains of *Aude Lang Syne* flooded the room. Ronnie didn't buy my story and called his father, who came right home.

Regaining mental and emotional equilibrium was a slow process. Rigorous questioning about the surgery and diagnosis earned me Most Difficult Patient status, but I finally flushed the doubts from my mind. Recovery proved painful and prolonged, partly because of my second-guessing the diagnosis. The six-week winter break barely gave me time to get back on my feet. Come January, I didn't have my groove back, but I hit the sloppy roads and slick streets of Athens head on. The shining reward was a mere two quarters away, and no way was I backing off. Jumping back into the saddle was probably the best way to handle what could have become an obsessive and debilitating worry for someone of my temperament.

One thing I didn't do, though, was pay for the office visit at Ohio State University Hospital. After I had ignored a couple of statements, the business office called, and I unloaded on the unfortunate billing clerk. Never had I been treated more shabbily and never had a potentially serious condition been dismissed so nonchalantly. And no, I would not be sending payment. The billing clerk, probably wondering how she had stumbled into a nest of hornets, apologized and assured me the statement was cancelled.

⟫⟪◉⟫⟪

Come the end of March, 1984, I was in for another new

experience, student teaching at Belpre High School, in my son Ronnie's English class. I'd spent a lot of time observing and pitching in during classroom observations, but this time, the teacher would ease out and I would take over planning, teaching, grading, and what I dreaded most, discipline. And challenges awaited, especially among sophomore boys not sure how to handle the untried rush of testosterone. In private, my son told me which students might be trouble. In class, he was a model student, keeping a low profile and showing that he had learned something about respect. But then, teachers had been bragging about his good manners and integrity for years. Finally, last hurdle vaulted, I was ready to graduate.

The icing on the cake was learning at the last minute that I was graduating summa cum laude and had been named outstanding graduating senior in secondary education. What with the upheaval of the last few months, and self-doubt ever ready to pounce, it would have been easy to lessen the effort, but the habit of giving it my all was too engrained. One of my professors, breaking the news to me, shook his head at my surprise. "Your self-deprecation is almost laughable, Lois. There wasn't even a close second." It *was* validating to be recognized and good to see my father proud. But this wasn't all about me; my two boys now saw college as an expected next step and high achievement as doable. And that made the victory sweeter still.

Chapter 38

SPEAKING OF SWEET victories, walking into my classroom at Fort Frye Junior Senior High School on a humid
day in August, 1984, has to be one of the sweetest. This room,
like Mrs. Gage's, had a wall of windows which looked out on
a huge, lush maple tree that I anticipated turning yellow as
autumn arrived. A much-scarred wooden teacher's desk and
wheeled swivel chair, thirty metal-framed student desks, and
one file cabinet was it, except for an assortment of battered
literature texts and a row of brand new grammar-composi-
tion books.

During that first year, I learned more about teaching
than I had in the previous four combined, and a lot of the
credit goes to fellow teacher, Jim Creighton. Jim, also from
Stockport, held the deserved reputation of master English
teacher. And there I was, the novice next door, observing
the ease with which he maneuvered eighth graders, always
knowing what was needed, even before they asked, be it
lunch money, a new journal, or a chance to brag about a calf
born the night before or a blue ribbon won at the county fair.
Luckily for me, Jim took on new teachers as special projects

too. While bringing me up to speed on practical matters, he tossed out tidbits of profundity in the form of quotes, books I might like, human interest data. Rarely, have I run into anyone as broadly knowledgeable as Jim. That first year, he must have witnessed blunders that made him shudder, but unless I asked for his advice, he afforded me complete autonomy. You'd never know from his demeanor that I was anything less than a seasoned professional.

And then there were the students, six classes of seventh graders in a junior high fed by four separate elementary schools and housed with the high school. The population included a lot of farm kids, and most of the "townies" came from blue-collar homes. Discipline in this environment, except for the one study hall I monitored, was less an issue than among those sophomores at Belpre. A week into my position, I couldn't imagine myself anywhere else or teaching any other age group. So many people have done the old eye-roll when they learned I taught junior high, and some, I imagine, have doubted my sanity. But I have found, in those scattered pre-adolescents, struggling to figure out how the world works, some of the finest human beings and keenest minds.

All of my time on the job was not spent on literature and composition, spelling and vocabulary. In many ways, instruction was the easy part. Not long into teaching, I learned that one out of four under-aged girls is sexually abused at some time. This statistic took me back to my Duncan Falls days and the brief association I had with Charlotte's friends, street smart adolescents whose furtive looks and nervous bodies told a dark story that I was too young to recognize at the time. Since then, I had heard all the horror tales of molestation and realized that in some cultures, including those close to home, it was open season on girls of a certain age. How could I watch those budding young women trooping into English class, giggling and goofing off or quiet and pensive, and imagine such a damaging reality once they left the safety of my classroom? Kids are great secret keepers, and relatively few abused girls seek help openly. Now and then, though, one will put out a cry for help, sometimes unaware. A girl I'll call Angel, a student I had during my early years of teaching, used a journal entry as her outcry.

Angel loved writing in her journal and getting my comments in the margins. While she didn't have the best home life or the nicest clothes and lived in the remote reaches of the District, she showed up every morning squeaky clean and ready to go, honey-blond hair shielding her face as she bent over her work. Once she left seventh grade, she asked to continue sharing her journal with me, so the black and white notebook appeared on the corner of my desk once or twice a week. All through eighth grade and as ninth began, her entries continued to be about friends and classes and her annoying little sister, pretty lame stuff.

Then I found the entry that began: "I don't know why people make such a big deal about age. Take Danny and me." Reading through a stack of student notebooks on a sultry September afternoon had lulled me into a state of limited consciousness, but Angel's words brought me fully awake.

Danny? Who was Danny? I flipped back through her entries and saw no mention of anybody named Danny.

Finishing the page filled with girlish scrawl, I learned way more than I cared to know about Danny, seven years older than Angel, and how he and Angel spent their time together. I got up from my desk and went into the hallway to the drinking fountain. The floor was littered with papers, pen caps, broken pencils. From the gym a few doors down, I could hear the cross country coach calling out encouragement. A couple of other teachers waved absent-mindedly as they escaped into the luscious afternoon.

As much as I'd have liked to follow them, duty drove me back to Angel's journal. Surely, I'd read more into the entry than was really there. Rereading, I was impressed by how much she had improved as a writer since seventh grade. She could tell it like it was, details of sneaking out at night to meet Danny, Danny wanting her to "do it," hinting of running away together.

But why, Angel? I wondered. Why unload all this intimate stuff on me? Have I given you the impression I would approve? Angel was one of those kids I felt might be guided toward a higher academic goal despite her background. Maybe, I told myself, shoving take-home necessities into my satchel, she was feeding me a line, testing the boundaries. But that didn't matter. Fact or fantasy, Angel's expose` made my responsibility clear. Angel was fifteen. If Danny, whoever he was, was seven years older, statutory rape was imminent, if not a done deal.

Before I left the building, after debating whether I should alert her parents first, I made the call to Children's Services.

Driving through Beverly, I observed kids ramping off curbs and porch steps on their skateboards, taking chances that kids their age, like it or not, are going to take. By comparison, the chances Angel was taking made these seem tame. And I imagined Angel, at that very moment, bouncing home on the school bus, daydreaming about her twenty-two year old lover-boy and feeling like Cinderella revisited, oblivious of the fact that her favorite teacher had just ratted her out.

Angel's innocent recounting of Danny's shenanigans opened an ugly can of worms. During the investigation which followed, a history of incest came leaking out, making me doubly grateful I had not called her parents. And, like I said, Angel wasn't stupid. She stopped speaking to me and glared when we passed in the hallway. A few weeks later, she changed schools. Eventually, Angel graduated and went on to college and began a career. I was thrilled to learn that she had realized her potential, but I doubted she would ever find it in her heart to forgive the one who had wrecked her dream escape with Danny.

Years later, a letter showed up in my school mailbox, in which Angel explained how she had hated me for dragging everything into the open. By then, she understood that I'd had no choice but to follow the dictates, not only of the law, but of my conscience. And she recognized that her own revelation had indeed been a cry for help. The last time I saw Angel was on the street in Marietta, pushing a little boy in a stroller, and she said her life was good.

Two years into teaching I decided to begin a master's degree. Ronnie was starting at Ohio State, leaving a big empty spot at the dinner table. A little extra money would come in handy, but the driving force was not financial. In order to do justice to the profession and meet my self-directed goals, I needed a stronger core of knowledge than four years had given. The graduate class which I thought would be pure enjoyment, creative writing, served instead as a rude awakening.

By then, I thought I knew a bit about writing, having published stories regularly for a decade and written articles for the SOCTE (Southeastern Ohio Council of Teachers of English) Journal. Professors and instructors since PCC had been pleased with my work. No wonder my head was slightly inflated when it came to writing. And then, during fall quarter of 1987, I entered the Tuesday evening class I had anticipated along with students of the highest caliber, members of the elite honors program.

The first story I shared was based on an incident which my husband, son, and father-in-law had encountered driving back from a stock car race late one night. An accident had just occurred ahead of them. Naturally, Ron stopped to help. The instigator stumbled around, drunk and incoherent. The windshield of a Trans Am bulged out like a sightless eyeball, fissures running every which way in the safety glass. Facing the side window was the driver, dead on impact, eyes wide open and seeming to stare at the three guys who were approaching to see if someone needed help. According to

Ronnie's account, his father had slammed his fist into the hood in helpless rage but stayed on scene to help the survivors and to deal with the drunk who had caused the tragedy until the authorities arrived. His grandfather had turned away from the carnage, keeping to himself whatever emotion the scene evoked.

Told from the boy's perspective, the story, I felt, was compelling, and I shared it in class. To my chagrin, those snotty little under-grads tore it apart. I had tires "skidding to a stop." Thank goodness, one of them observed, the tires had not "skidded to a *halt*." Other comments were equally severe. Off my stride, I struggled to write pieces I felt I could share in this forum. Before that class, I hadn't received a B since OUZ days when my attention had abruptly shifted from math and American history to a guy named Ron Spencer. I swore *this* B would be my last. Looking back, I can see that the experience was a long overdue lesson in humility. No longer would I take my flair with words as a birthright.

Chapter 39

IN ADDITION TO having my tail feathers clipped in creative writing class, other events were making the fall of 1987 one impossible to forget. For the first time in the school's history, Fort Frye teachers went on strike to protest the failure of the administration to negotiate in good faith. For months the contract committee had battered against what felt like an impenetrable wall. Late in September, the Fort Frye Teachers' Association declared a work stoppage. Despite its being my fourth year of teaching, I was still altruistic enough to believe professionals should remain above the fray. Some of my cohorts were walking the picket-line, others were breaking the line to return to classroom, and others, like me, were trying to stay out of the mud-slinging. Eventually, I took donuts and coffee to teachers gathered around burn-barrels and helped prepare meals at the VFW meeting hall, along with others who didn't feel they were picket-line material. All we could do was wait it out while Ohio Education Association lawyers battled Fort Frye Local School District lawyers.

While all this was going on, I received a letter from my sister. A couple of years before, Barbara, Russell, and the two girls had exchanged the corner house on Liberty Avenue for an A-frame cabin near Burr Oak Lake, where they could live surrounded by squirrels and birds instead of traffic and noisy neighbors. My first thought as I slid my thumb under the flap was this: Why didn't she call? Except for Christmas and birthday cards we never corresponded. Barbara had written two sentences on the sheet of paper. She had been diagnosed with cancer of the esophagus, and it was inoperable. I don't remember walking back into the house from the mailbox or putting the rest of the mail on the piano at the top of the steps. I had heard of people feeling numb with shock; that morning, I knew what it meant.

The year before, Barbara had called to say that she and Russell were on their way to Ohio State University Hospital. I was shocked that day too, but I had known she had a heart murmur, the result of rheumatic fever as a child. The valve had weakened and had to be replaced. This was no low risk surgery in 1986, but she did well and recovered in her house in the woods. The kids were grown, Russell's job with the Park Service was low-stress, and life had smoothed out. They had bought a motorhome and were making plans to see the West. The cancer diagnosis would have seemed anti-climactic after the heart surgery had it not been so unspeakable.

Still clutching Barbara's letter, I headed straight for the phone and forced my sister to do what she had been trying to avoid, talk about it. Her doctor was holding out a slim hope that the tumor might be operable, but surgical risks were high, due to her artificial heart valve. A few days later, I arrived at Bethesda Hospital in Zanesville as Barbara waited for transport to surgery, her odds of surviving the ordeal about thirty percent. Russell stood beside her bed, his rough, workman's hand clasping hers, just as I'd seen so many evenings at the dinner table while they chatted about the day. I kept my visit brief, so they could have their privacy when the gurney arrived.

Barbara had struggled with self-esteem issues her entire life and no wonder. So many times she had referred to herself as a "mistake." My come-back was always, "That makes two of us." But we understood that being an "oops" in a marriage was one thing and another entirely to be the product of a married man's dalliance. Russell North had been the one stable presence in her life and had given her as much reassurance as anyone could.

And there he was, holding on until the last minute. An hour later, Barbara was in recovery. The tumor, wrapped around the aorta, would have been impossible to remove. A heavy chemo load, given to shrink the tumor and prolong her life, made Barbara's last year a mixture of physical distress and emotional adjustment to the inevitable. She was fifty-two when she died the following December. She still had the abundant auburn hair, absent visible gray and seemingly unmolested by the chemo. My sister was just a tiny thing, lying in the big, oak casket which Russell had selected to honor the woodland existence she had finally, and briefly, enjoyed among squirrels and birds; the acorns etched into the wood were reminders of hopeful days.

Finally, the long dispute over contract negotiations ended that fall of 1987. After the vote to return to work, high school teachers formed a double line and walked down Fifth Street and entered the building. It was definitely coat weather and the sky was a heavy gray that portended no good. The attempt to stand up against unfair labor practices was in shambles, and we were returning to jobs that even in the best of times garner few accolades. I can't say why my colleagues had chosen the profession or why they remained in it. I was there that morning because I believed teaching was my calling, and I was sorry that we'd reached an impasse with those who had trusted us to teach the children of Fort Frye.

Our return had not been announced, so we created quite a stir as we entered the building. Mouths dropped among subs, office workers, custodians, and teachers who had remained on the job or returned early. When I entered Room 82, the kids looked on in silence. As I hung up my coat and appproached my desk, a young man I had never seen before said, "Well, I guess you're back." He quickly gathered his things and made his exit.

Despite the hard feelings that persisted among staff members who had disagreed about the work stoppage, we got back to the business of teaching. On my part, it was an especially difficult year. I had eight full periods of teaching, graduate classes, and a sister who was dying. I had also begun a junior high drama club that year, and I was spelling bee coordinator. It fell to me also to plan all career education activities for seventh graders and execute an annual field trip. Despite the eventful happenings of the 1987-1988 school year, anything on my day-to-day calendar during that time is no more than a blur.

The week before our brief Easter break, the politically savvy eyed the calendar. Thursday was the deadline for teacher evaluations as well as for notifications of non-renewal of teachers' contracts with the District. Given the grudge-fest generated by the strike, FFTA expected action. State law prohibited non-renewal without just cause once a teacher had completed four years with a district or city; until that, a teacher whose contract was up for renewal could be dismissed for no reason at all, and with no legal recourse.

I remained oblivious to the politics, busy trying to keep my head above water. Besides, having been renewed twice already, I was expecting my two-year contract to be no problem. The principal, who usually put things off until the last minute, completed a cursory classroom observation Thursday morning. His checkmarks were all in the "Excellent" and "Good" columns, so I had no reason to worry. With the holiday pending, I was showing the last segment of *Shane*, the classic western and one of our class novels, that afternoon. Seated in the back, I could keep one eye on the students and the other on the stack of *Shane* exams I was attempting to grade. Then there was a knock on the door.

The vice-principal said he'd come to watch my class while I went to the principal's office. My stomach reacted first, clenching into a fist. Calm down, I told myself as I headed down the hallway. If my job were in jeopardy, the principal would have mentioned it. The building was quiet and classroom doors shut; I wasn't the only teacher preserving the peace with low-impact activities that afternoon. I went through the outer office and tapped on the principal's door. The superintendent as well as the principal sat there, waiting.

"I have a letter for you," the superintendent said without preamble as he handed me a sheet of paper bearing his official letterhead. The letter informed me of his intention to recommend my nonrenewal. One line in particular jumped off the page: "Your attitude and performance do not meet the standards of the Fort Frye Local School District."

At that point, I whirled toward the principal. "How can you give me a good-to-excellent evaluation and an hour later tell me my performance doesn't 'meet the standards'?"

"The letter is from the superintendent," he said, eyes remaining on his littered desk top.

I turned to the other man, who sat, arms folded. He had no trouble meeting my stare with the smug assurance of absolute power. "As a professional courtesy, you owe me an explanation," I informed him, careful to keep my tone in line.

"No, I don't," was all he said.

Really nasty things had been known to come out of my mouth if I got riled enough, and right then, riled was an understatement. Besides, further insistence was pointless. I shook my head at both men and walked out. In the hallway stood a chief participant in the strike, who had rallied the hesitant ones, like me, to take a stand. When she saw the paper in my hand and the expression on my face, she put a fist into the nearest locker door.

She had been stationed nearby since noon, she said, watching a procession of teachers, all up for contract, enter and leave the office, some in tears, all looking shell-shocked. The superintendent was making a clean sweep. If you had participated in the strike, were between contracts, and not protected by the four-year provision, you got the ax. While we stood there, the superintendent exited the office, signifying the end of the carnage. Five others had received letters that day, one of them an elementary teacher who was out on maternity leave.

I don't remember driving home that afternoon, but I must have arrived without running anyone over. As soon as he heard, Ron was ready to hire a lawyer. Home on spring break from OSU, Ronnie was of the opinion somebody ought to beat up the superintendent. Or at least show up at his door and flex some muscle. His brother was ready to join him. I can't say I wasn't tempted to turn them loose. Family loyalty, though, could only go so far in assuaging the hammering frustration, which had, at its core, the old fear that no matter how hard I worked, or how much I achieved, I was never going to measure up.

Even with OEA attorneys arriving on the scene, I wasn't sure I wanted to throw my fate into a pile with everybody else's. My son did some digging at OSU and found an adjunct professor who also practiced law downtown. Her name was Jacquelyn and she had a slightly rumpled appearance and eyes that could drill through steel. The best part was she had started out as an English teacher. We shook hands, and I trusted her instantly.

When I handed her the infamous letter and all the written documentation I had kept of every contact, interaction, and overheard tidbit having any possible bearing on my case, she smiled broadly. She *wanted* the board to non-renew me. It would be a sweet case, regardless of the four-year provision. There were a number of things we could sue over, starting with age and sex discrimination. And that was only *if* the court refused to acknowledge the grievous vendetta for what it was. Jacquelyn had once walked in my shoes, no doubt about it.

The worst part of the whole fiasco was breaking the news to my father. Daddy had begun to feel his age, so he opted to live at Morgan Manor, independent senior housing in McConnelsville, where men were in the slimmest minority. A charming eighty year old male was a hot commodity there, so his social life was lively. Sitting on his couch in the living-dining area, I gave him the short version. He shrugged, indicating an implicit trust in his daughter's ability to land on her feet. His pride in my becoming a "schoolmarm" wasn't to be shaken by some nonsense. As I kissed the cheek beginning to show the tiny blue veins that had been in Grandpa Rippey's, I realized he could have had no other response. No one believed in me more than Raymond Rippey.

———※《◎》※———

One by one, the intervening weeks ticked off pending the vote by the Board of Education which would determine not only my fate, but that of my five colleagues. My students were amazingly sweet while we all waited, and some slipped me notes of encouragement. The most original came as a faux newspaper article written on notebook paper and bearing the headline: "Fort Frye Fires Best Teacher!" However hard I tried to stay positive, though, every day I awoke to the possibility of nonrenewal and every night I went to sleep with it. A meeting with the superintendent was scheduled for each teacher before the evening of the vote, and that number had dropped to four when two of the six resigned. The superintendent wanted our assurance that, if granted new contracts, we would put the past behind us and perform acceptably in the future. That sounded like one more chance to rub our noses in it, but I went along with the charade. I knew the superintendent's game, and he knew I was jumping through one last, obligatory hoop.

Finally, the night of the fateful board meeting arrived. The gymnasium at Lowell Elementary, the roomiest venue in the District, was packed. Everybody sat on bleachers or cold metal folding chairs while routine business was dealt with. At last, the matter of teaching contracts came before the board. Teacher by teacher, the superintendent made his recommendation, and teacher by teacher, the board voted. I received a two-year contract just as I would have had the strike and its aftermath never happened. Two others received the contracts they had been expecting as well. The gymnasium overflowed with cheering and hugging and relief while the superintendent sat behind the table as silent as the Buddha, arms crossed and face absent of expression. One young man, labeled a firebrand, was singled out as the lone example, and that was another needless tragedy. The battle over his contract would plod through the court system for years.

Nothing had been gained by the strike, nothing by retribution. No one had benefitted except the lawyers, who walked away with full pockets. Productivity during 1987-1988 had been as low as the morale. What students lost that year while their teachers were distracted seems a heavy price for proving a point, on either side.

Chapter 40

WITH SUMMER THAT year came my last two classes, one in which I wrote my seminar paper and the other in gifted education to complete my forty-five quarter hours. Drained emotionally, I was tempted to put things on hold, but there was a certain satisfaction in receiving a hike on the salary scale following such a debacle. Fortunately, I had already begun my research for my seminar paper, so I managed to whip out a sixty-three page document in four weeks.

And then, late in the summer, Aunt Joyce called to ask if I could meet her and Daddy at the farm as he wanted to have the place surveyed and divided between the joint owners. Ownership of the farm had fallen to the four heirs after Grandma's death. Out of misplaced generosity, my father had bought out his brothers' two shares and given them to Aunt Joyce. He had turned his share over to me at the same time, wanting to free himself of loose ends.

So there we were, Aunt Joyce and Daddy and I, back on the old home place as the late August evening grew damp and the cicadas sounded, the endings of their robust pulsing receding as lightly as a sigh. Harvest bugs, at once reassuring and melancholy, were always a sure sign of summer's end. I noticed a heaviness in my father's step as we circled the house through neglected grass and made an effort to consider how best to divide the twenty-five acres. My options were pretty slim, given the scant amount of frontage: a land-locked piece of hillside and creek bottom or a twenty foot wide strip along the western boundary. From his manner, it was obvious that my father had not instigated this meeting. Aunt Joyce wanted the entire farm for herself. The other two quarters had been my father's gift to her. So why not the fourth?

I suppose the decent thing would have been to sign over my small stake and make everybody happy. And if I hadn't remembered the pig, I might have been tempted. Just beyond the barn and down-wind of the house, the remains of the hog lot stood in knee-deep weeds and served as a reminder of Joyce's least appealing side, pure self-interest. I could still see our little company on that bleak Sunday morning, circling the remains of the unfortunate hog, belly distended from its final feast. I could still hear Joyce's sniffling and the quick intake of my mother's breath at the revelation that the casualty of her sister-in-law's stupidity was my father's hog and therefore his loss. Our compensation, a macabre pig's head, which I picked clean to the white skull, had never left my mind either.

Perched on an old wagon bed in the side yard, we talked things over, and for the first time in her dealings with family, Aunt Joyce got a disappointment. I told her I'd rather keep the fourth interest as it stood. Aunt Joyce wasn't happy and subsequently neither was Daddy. What made me dig my heels in even more than remembering the pig was the way she had tried to maneuver me to do her bidding through my father. Rather than unload on her and make the situation worse, I let my decision speak for itself. She knew me well enough not to argue.

This rift in our relations was an inauspicious beginning to a sad, sad autumn, which not only included my sister's impending death, but my father's diagnosis of cancer. I'd noticed that Daddy ate little when we were together, insisting it didn't take much to fill him up. Since his mother had eaten like a bird as she grew older, I wasn't too concerned. But when Daddy began complaining about difficulty swallowing, the symptom that had signaled my sister's esophageal malignancy, the warning bells sounded. Sure enough, tests revealed the same diagnosis in my father. How bizarre, I thought between waves of disbelief that I was soon to lose two more family members. The fact that my sister and the step-father she had once hated were dying of the same disease hinted at a dark, cosmic irony. But that wasn't where I wanted my mind to go.

With Daddy as with Barbara, an attempt was made to remove the tumor. At eighty-one, he wasn't the best candidate for extensive surgery, but even partial removal of the mass might buy him time and allow him to swallow. He went into surgery that December morning expecting to come out with a shortened esophagus and a shrunken stomach, but he showed up in recovery a short time later with a feeding tube inserted into his small intestine. The surgeon shook his head when he saw me, and I put aside the tiny hope I had allowed myself. Daddy accepted the diagnosis gracefully and opted to spend his last months at Mark Rest Center since it was close to Aunt Joyce's.

Teaching full time, I could not be on constant call, so I offered to take a leave of absence. Daddy wouldn't hear of it. He would be fine, he assured me, and I had important work to do. In that respect, at least, my mind was at rest. But, as I already knew from losing Mother, anticipating the death of a parent is hard. And driving the extra-long circuit several times a week which Daddy's illness made necessary gave me plenty of time to think, to remember our complicated relationship, the times we had disappointed each other, the times we had clashed. But that first bonding, formed when he rushed home to discover a tiny replica of himself embodied in a blue-eyed baby girl, had endured. It takes a lot more grief than he had given me for a girl to disown her daddy. No way could I relinquish the foremost fact of all: He was my father and I loved him.

But those were lonely drives, and they gave me plenty of time to think. A bridge was out on Route 60, so I traveled from Fort Frye to McConnelsville by way of Hackney Ridge, the one-time home of my Hosom grandparents as well as Barbara's birthplace. Returning from the nursing home, I crossed from Route 60 to Stockport where I caught the last leg of my journey, passing the lower end of Olivet Ridge and the property on which my mother was born and my father had lived briefly as a child. I completed my travels following Wolf Creek, a section of the tributary where Grandma Rippey had dreamed of becoming a teacher and from which she had set out for Sturgis with Grandpa. My recent origins could be encircled in an hour's drive. And I hadn't yet wandered far afield, regardless of how remote Belpre had seemed at first. But I had traveled a distance in other ways.

Until the last, Daddy liked to walk down the hall when I visited him, holding the IV pole from which hung his nutrition bag, a constant reminder that mealtime was a thing of the past. He could still sip a little water, and he never complained or asked for pain medication. One evening toward the end of February, the windows of his room were already black by the time I was ready to leave, save for the flash of passing headlights and the windows across the street behind which other lives went on as though they would last forever. When I kissed him good-bye with the promise I'd see him in a couple of days, he hung onto my hand.

"I know I wasn't a very good daddy, Punkin."

The urgency in his voice told me how important it was that he say this. There were so many ways I could have responded and plenty of truisms to fall back on, but none were adequate. I put my cheek against the hair that had once been shiny black and scented with tonic and whispered, "I love you, Daddy, and you love me. Nothing else matters now." I felt him nod and knew my simple words were enough. When I left, his expression was peaceful, that of a penitent having received absolution. I waited in the parking lot until my vision cleared. Then I drove down Kennebec to the square and took the river road to Stockport and the country route home.

On March 17, Ronnie made the drive from OSU to McConnelsville to check on Grandpa, planning to continue home and celebrate his twenty-second birthday. That afternoon, Aunt Joyce had called me at school with the news that Daddy was unresponsive. No matter how well you prepare, I had learned when Mother died, you're never ready.

I left school early and went to the nursing home. Ronnie was standing beside his grandfather's bed, watching the sleep that wasn't sleep, Grandpa's chest rising and falling with gentle breaths. I shed my coat and went to the opposite side of the bed.

With one of Grandpa's hands in Ronnie's and the other in mine, we recounted times when Grandpa had visited our house. The way he loved to finish off left-overs, no matter what they were. How he wiped his plate with his bread and cooled his coffee in a saucer, blowing across the top to make tiny waves. When he snored, the boys swore they could feel the walls vibrate, and peals of giggles inevitably sounded from their room. In the afternoon, Grandpa loved to retire with a Perry Mason mystery, stretch out on the bed, and pretend to read. A few minutes later one of the boys would sneak a peek, and, sure enough, Grandpa would be sound asleep, book open on his chest, ankles crossed and feet, still in shoes, resting on a towel. The topper that always sent the boys barreling into the kitchen to report were the gloves. Summer or winter, when he took a nap, Grandpa wore gloves. The boys had a lot of laughs at his expense, but they relished his foibles as proof that he was unique among grandfathers.

The nurse told me he could go on like this for hours, maybe even a day or two, so I sent my son on home. I was planning to spend the night at Spencer's, just in case, and Aunt Joyce would check on him later. It was probably best that it happened the way it did. In the early hours of March 18, Ronnie's birthday, Aunt Joyce called to tell me my father had died. It was a good death; one minute he was breathing, and the next he wasn't. I threw on clothes and drove downtown with the sky still dark. Even with so gruesome an illness, Daddy had remained well-fleshed and alert and remarkably pain free.

———◦((◦))◦———

Following Daddy's funeral, I focused on finishing the school year. While only one teacher was non-renewed, several of us felt the ax in other ways. For four years I had taught seventh grade English, and except for the fiasco the previous spring, I had never questioned that the job was mine. However, for the following year, I was assigned small, overflow classes in reading skills, a move both dismissive and wasteful. Returning to school in August to face an all-new schedule, I found gifts strewn about my room—bins for student journals, supplies of various kinds, posters—even a framed picture of Albert Einstein with one of my favorite quotes: "Imagination is more important than knowledge." Taped to my desk was a huge note: "All right now. Show those bastards!"

It was Jim's hope that I would rise from the ashes of my experience and put the superintendent and Co. in their places. I wish I could tell the story that way. Or at least blame my less-than-stellar efforts that year on my sister's death in December, which had come right on the heels of my father's diagnosis, making the following months a scramble of comings and goings and unhappy days. But if I am to be honest, I have to admit that for the first years following the strike, I wasn't sure how I felt about teaching. I'd spent the greater part of a decade preparing to do something I'd lost out on once. And my reward? I could still feel the wind from the guillotine's near miss. Was I going to stick my neck out again by pouring heart and soul into my work at Fort Frye?

Feeling at odds with the whole notion of public school teaching, I spent evenings and summer quarters at Washington State Community College instructing technical writing and creative writing students, thinking that if a full-time position opened, I would apply. I toyed with the idea of going to law school and investing my efforts in the battle against inequities. At odd moments, I wondered where my fire had gone, why teaching seemed more like a job and less like a calling.

The most telling observation and the one which eventually woke me up came from Jim Creighton after school one day as the last straggling students made their way out of the building. Locker doors were silenced, the squeak of sneakers on floors finished for the day, and I was stuffing student papers into my briefcase, wishing there were some way to avoid grading them.

Jim stuck his head into my room and, without preamble, said, "If those bastards hadn't messed with you, you'd be a master teacher by now." Comment made, Jim went back into his classroom.

I stood there, hands stilled, digesting his words and the damning implications. My mentor and friend, who had nurtured me through those early years and stood by me during the aftermath of the strike, had weighed me in the balances and found me wanting. In his estimation, I had let the bastards win.

I finished packing the homework, grabbed my jacket and purse, and left my classroom. Tempted to confront Jim, but lacking the courage, I went out into the early spring afternoon where daffodils vied for attention among the dry stalks and winter debris. I tried to shrug off the remark, telling myself I wasn't doing a bad job. I did what was expected, what most teachers were doing post-strike. So I wasn't a Jim Creighton or a Dorothy Gage. The fate of the world did not hang upon it. Still, Jim's words wouldn't leave me alone.

By the time I admitted the remark had to be addressed, summer was drawing to a close, August was reaching its pinnacle, and teachers were showing up in classrooms, restoring order after summer clean-outs, covering bulletin boards, and anticipating a phalanx of new students. It wasn't anyone's fault but my own that I hadn't developed into a master teacher. I'd had the opportunity to learn from the best, and I had learned. What I had been unduly accused of following the strike, attitude and performance below the level I was capable of, had, through my own bitterness, become a fair indictment. That realization had been grinding away at me ever since Jim's comment.

Well, enough was enough. Forget who had won or lost and whether or not I would ever measure up. Forget, too, how much time and effort I had invested in becoming a teacher. What faced me on that hot August morning in a humid, non-air-conditioned classroom was a decision, maybe the most important of my career. In that moment, I forced myself to answer the critical question: When I looked back on that morning twenty years later, which of the two options open before me would have given me more satisfaction and peace—continuing as I was, a half-hearted might-have-been, or transforming myself into the teacher God had intended me to be?

Instead of putting up the tired old posters from the year before, I ditched them in the giant bin the custodians had put out for our use. I would find something more challenging for my bulletin boards and walls. Leafing through my files, I found tests that had long since served their purpose, writing prompts that lacked imagination, essential skills worksheets—bland, lifeless, and unengaging. Folder after folder followed the posters into the trash.

Even though I knew I was sentencing myself to a year of long hours and hard work, dumping the past and starting fresh felt really, really good.

Epilogue

THE GYMNASIUM IS lit by what look like the same suspended, caged lights which survived innumerable basketball games. The same bleachers line the walls; the same ancient class photos, one of them my father's, are displayed the entire length. Folding tables, folding chairs, some or all replacements, create the welcoming effect exactly as it was years ago. From the tiny kitchen come the smells of regional comfort foods—ham, scalloped potatoes, cakes from boxed mixes—a carbohydrate and cholesterol feast. It's just one more annual gathering of Windsor High School Alumni. But this year, two things are different. An honest-to-goodness sound system pumps out Beach Boys' and Beetles' hits, thanks to my son Steve. And this time my class is sitting at the table of honor, celebrating fifty years as Windsor High School graduates.

The table fills and classmates catch up and share stories and pictures of grandchildren, and I realize again how truly blessed I am. Ron and I are still together, and both sons have productive and fulfilling lives. Ron, Jr. is a Colonel in the U.S. Air Force JAG, his chest covered in medals attesting to his varied accomplishments and honors. Steve is a video producer for SuddenLink Media and an entrepreneur on the side, operating both his own DJ service and a photography business. Ron and his wife Lisa have given us our two grandchildren, Eli and Elise, young adults forging their way in the world. Steve's wife Jen brought Jacob and Alexandria to their marriage, and Jacob and his girlfriend Kelli have opened the next generation with an adorable little boy, Isaac.

I certainly have no complaints about where I am in life or how I arrived here. Once I got my mojo back after the strike and its aftermath, I helped revamp and broaden the junior high language arts curriculum. Taking on additional roles, including National Honor Society Co-advisor, and Power of the Pen Writing Coach, recharged my confidence. As for writing, *Ohio Teachers Write* and *Iris: A Journal About Women* showcased early versions of some of the writings in this narrative. And yes, I finally made it to the stately campus of Marietta College where I earned a Master of Arts in Liberal Learning, focused entirely on creative writing. As an Appalachian Writing Project Fellow through Ohio University, I continued to sharpen my writing and teaching skills into retirement. Now, I teach English and creative writing as an adjunct instructor at Ohio Valley University in Vienna, West Virginia. I'll probably never see myself as the master teacher Dorothy Gage or Jim Creighton was, but teaching has answered an intrinsic need that no other career could have. Teaching has been, and continues to be, my calling.

From my spot at the table, I take a moment to reminisce. It was in this building that I learned to square dance to the fiddles and guitars of Grandma Rippey's nephews. Here, I produced my first written script and became a charter member of the Windsor High School National Honor Society. Here, an anxious crowd waited for my friend Allen to show up, little knowing they would never see him again. Sock hops, assemblies, daily lunches, forgotten minutia and high drama, it all happened here. Even the pivotal event of my high school years, the honor's banquet during which I was to receive a scholarship to Ohio University, proceeded in this place, while I was foolishly absent, having given in to less considered choices. But had I not made what appeared at the time to be grievous errors in judgment, my life would have taken a much different turn, and I cannot imagine that it would have turned out better.

CPSIA information can be obtained
at www.ICGtesting.com
Printed in the USA
LVOW11s0031031017
550976LV00001B/4/P